# Canopy of Titans

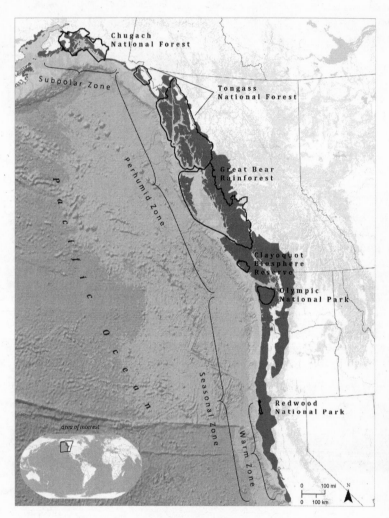

A map of the temperate rainforest. Courtesy Jessica Leonard/Geos Institute.

# Canopy of Titans

The Life and Times of the Great North
American Temperate Rainforest

## PAUL KOBERSTEIN
## JESSICA APPLEGATE

O/R

OR Books
New York · London

All rights information: rights@orbooks.com

Visit our website at www.orbooks.com

The authors wish to acknowledge with deep gratitude the important contribution of Terri Hansen (Winnebago Tribe of Nebraska), who is the author of Chapter 12, "A Resilient Community."

The authors also thank the following organizations which published articles that were later incorporated in revised form into this book:
*Mongabay*:
"Where the Forest Has No Name," May 24, 2019, https://news.mongabay.com/2019/05/where-the-forest-has-no-name/.
*Sierra Magazine*:
"Forest Liquidators," December 19, 2018, https://www.sierraclub.org/sierra/forest-liquidators.
*Earth Island Journal*:
"Trump Doubles Down on His Assault on Alaska's Old-Growth Forests," October 7, 2019, https://www.earthisland.org/journal/index.php/articles/entry/trump-doubles-down-on-his-assault-on-alaskas-old-growth-forests/.
"Carbon Conundrum," December 2020, https://www.earthisland.org/journal/index.php/articles/entry/trump-doubles-down-on-his-assault-on-alaskas-old-growth-forests/.
"Native Alaskan Company Involved in Controversial Carbon Offsets Project to Quit Logging," January 21, 2021, https://www.earthisland.org/journal/index.php/articles/entry/native-alaskan-company-involved-in-controversial-carbon-offsets-project-to-quit-logging/.

Library of Congress Cataloging-in-Publication Data: A catalog record for this book is available from the Library of Congress.

Typeset by Lapiz Digital.

First printing 2023

Printed on 100% recycled paper.

paperback ISBN 978-1-68219-345-7 • ebook ISBN 978-1-68219-346-4

We dedicate *Canopy of Titans* to the children of this and future generations, especially in the authors' immediate families —Paul's children Joel, Teri, and Marla, and grandchildren Ada, Elliot, and Margot, and Jessica's children Julian and Sophie, and nieces and nephews Ana Victoria, Evelyn, Esiason, Brendan, and Kyle, and cousin Adelaide. We also dedicate *Canopy of Titans* to the scientists who have been persecuted for debunking corporate propaganda and greenwashing—most notably Beverly Law and Alexandra Morton.

# Contents

Prologue: Amazon of the North                                              ix

**Part 1: Forests and Climate**                                              1
Chapter 1: Where the Forest has no Name                                      3
Chapter 2: Too Good to be True                                              25
Chapter 3: Guardians of the Climate                                         35
Chapter 4: The Playbook                                                     53

**Part 2: Oregon**                                                          67
Chapter 5: The Siuslaw Liquidation                                          69
Chapter 6: "Looters of the Public Domain"                                   83
Chapter 7: From Agent Orange to Atrazine                                    95

**Part 3: The Keystone Species**                                           113
Chapter 8: The Invasion                                                    115
Chapter 9: Mayhem on the Nehalem                                           131
Chapter 10: The Blue Carbon Zone                                           143

**Part 4: This Is Their Forest**                                           171
Chapter 11: Stolen Ancestral Homelands                                     173
Chapter 12: A Resilient Community                                          197
Chapter 13: Husduwach Nuyem Jees (Land of Milky Blue Waters)               209
Chapter 14: Up on Fairy Creek                                              221

**Part 5: Alaska**                                                         235
Chapter 15: Trump's Great Alaska Forest Liquidation Sale                   237
Chapter 16: Coming Back for the Rest                                       249
Chapter 17: Greenwashing the Climate Apocalypse                            263

**Part 6: Aftermath**                                    **279**
Chapter 18: The Run-up to Glasgow                         281
Chapter 19: The Procrastination Summit                    291
Epilogue: The Solution Grows on Trees                     299

Acknowledgements                                          301
Endnotes                                                  305
Further Reading                                           337
About the Authors                                         339

# Prologue

# Amazon of the North

*...the care of the earth is our most ancient and most worthy and, after all, our most pleasing responsibility. To cherish what remains of it, and to foster its renewal, is our only legitimate hope.*

—*Wendell Berry*

In the summer of 2020, while writing *Canopy of Titans*, an unprecedented ring of deadly firestorms engulfed the giant conifer rainforest surrounding our hometown of Portland, Oregon, packing blood-red skies with a thick grit. Our lungs filled with smoke. We ached with every labored breath.

Some of the most severe wildfires ever in the American West torched the parched landscape with great fury, but we weren't alone in the crosshairs. Forests burned everywhere: the Americas, Europe, Africa, Asia, and Australia. The most intense fires burned through the giant eucalyptus forests of southern Australia. Australians called the season their "black summer," the smoke so thick it triggered home fire alarms in Sydney. Smoke also smothered Africa from the Sahel to South Africa. And in South America, more than 80,000 fires blazed through the Amazon rainforest, many ignited by humans clearing land for agriculture.

Forests were supposed to be our last line of defense against climate chaos, but instead have morphed into an existential threat. Fires, insect infestations, and deforestation have transformed forests worldwide into big polluters, alongside coal and other carbon-belching industries.[1]

Over the last decade, people died by the thousands in heat waves, fires, hurricanes, floods, and famine – all supercharged by the chaotic climate.[2,3] But the rampaging climate is just getting started down its fiery path of destruction. Severe weather events rarely seen in normal times are now seasonal menaces. Seasonal menaces are now the new normal. We decided to write *Canopy of Titans* to see what can be done to get back to the *old normal*, or if it's even possible.

We are concerned about wildfires, but do not intend to disparage them. Forests evolved with fire. Fire is a necessary element in a healthy, fully functioning ecosystem. Fires enable ecosystems to regenerate. After a fire, the forest will regrow. But wildfires can bring horrific consequences to the human communities that encroach too deeply into the forest. Wildfires burn homes and towns, causing death and destruction all along their path.

Climate change is drying out the fast-burning organic material that collects on the forest floor, and has been linked to a doubling in the number of large fires between 1984 and 2015 in the western United States.[4] Unless communities move out of the way, fires will become increasingly more dangerous as the climate continues to change.

Doomsayers tell us human civilization is already toast. The worst consequences of climate change may be avoidable, but we see no sign humanity will take the necessary actions. Optimists, on the other hand, insist there is still time to act. Resolving the climate crisis will be a test of our will, ingenuity, and ability to cooperate.

From the start, we knew the solution must include no more burning fossil fuels. Decisive steps have been taken in this direction. Internal-combustion engines and coal plants are on the way out. Renewables, electric cars, and batteries are in. Much more must be done to shut off the oil spigot, but ending the oil age won't end the crisis. There are some three hundred gigatons of excess carbon in the atmosphere, mostly emitted by burning fossil fuels since the beginning of the Industrial Revolution in the eighteenth century. It's a vast amount.[5,6] We won't be safe until we capture this legacy carbon and find a secure place to store it.

But how? Where? People are spouting all kinds of ideas, some loony, some self-serving, some promising. Corporations are betting on unproven technologies known as carbon capture and storage (CCS), methods that would trap carbon pollution before it enters the atmosphere, or remove it from the air and store it underground. The technology so far has failed to deliver the promised results. Globally, only twenty-six CCS plants are in operation today, removing a paltry 0.1 percent of annual carbon emissions.[7]

In our search for a more effective way to deal with the excess carbon, we reviewed hundreds of academic papers and interviewed dozens of scientists. We concluded the most promising and proven carbon capture technology is the tree. Only forests – ecosystems of trees, roots, soils, and woody biomass – can remove carbon from the air and store it at the necessary scale.

But not just any forest will do. Some people say we should be planting trees, but as a climate solution, the benefits of tree planting have been exaggerated. The tree you plant today won't store much carbon for several decades. We don't have much time to wait.

On the other hand, existing forests can help right now. Old, mature, and maturing forests are already sequestering massive amounts of carbon and, if protected, can continue storing it for centuries. Protecting these forests must be part of any climate mitigation strategy, along with shutting down carbon emissions.

If we can't protect all forests from logging and deforestation, which ones should we save? Which ones can we safely cut down? International climate politicians have long favored protecting tropical rainforests such as those in the Amazon basin, Africa's Congo basin, and Southeast Asia.

But acre-for-acre, tropical rainforests are not particularly carbon-rich. Our research told us the world's most carbon-dense forests are located on the Pacific Coast of North America,[8] right here in our backyard. It is the largest temperate rainforest in the world and home to the world's tallest trees. The Amazon of the North.

If you need to catch up on the climate crisis, here's what you need to know. We are in a climate emergency, threatening the lives of everyone stepping onto this planet far into the future. The greenhouse gas carbon dioxide ($CO_2$) is the main problem, though other pollutants like methane also pose risks to the climate. There's too much $CO_2$ in the air, and our continual burning of fossil fuels is pumping out more. But if we take strong and decisive action to reduce $CO_2$ emissions, there is hope.

In 2015, 195 nations signed the Paris climate agreement, pledging to reduce global warming to 1.5° C above pre-industrial levels. This is the "bright red line" scientists warned us not to cross if we hope to avoid environmental devastation, as journalist David Wallace-Wells explains in his book *The*

*Uninhabitable Earth: Life After Warming.*[9] As of late 2021, the planet warmed by 1.1° Celsius since the 18th century, with only 0.4° C to spare before it reaches the bright red line, and yet is already experiencing severe, unprecedented weather disasters. And things are getting worse. There's easily more than enough $CO_2$ in the air to push temperatures far over the red line within a decade or two, even with the most stringent emission-reduction measures. And more $CO_2$ is being dumped into the air every day. When people tell you more global warming is already "baked in," this is what they mean.

You don't have to read the latest scientific literature to see what life on a hotter Earth could be like. Just look out your window. Or, for the gory details, pick up Wallace-Wells' book, which reads like a Stephen King horror thriller. But for a somewhat more nuanced view, you might want to read *The New Climate War* by Michael Mann, the celebrated climate scientist.[10]

Mann puts the date we cross the red line at 2035. "It's simply a matter at this point of how bad we are willing to let it get," he writes. But as Wallace-Wells tells it, "It is worse, much worse, than you think." Wallace-Wells predicts we will cross the line in 2025, just two years from now. But that's just the start. The Intergovernmental Panel on Climate Change (IPCC) says we are on track to reach 2.7°C by 2100, when all hell will break loose and we will be living in a *Mad Max* world.[11]

We know how to solve this crisis: keep carbon in the ground and remove the excess carbon that's already in the air. That's where trees come in.

We asked William Moomaw, the co-author of five IPCC reports and a Nobel Laureate, Which should we do first? "It's not either/or," he told us in an interview. "It's both/and."

# PART 1

## FORESTS AND CLIMATE

*I wish that I could photosynthesize. To make food out of light and water, to make medicines and give them away for free. To do the work of the world and for the world, while standing silently in the sun.*

—*Robin Wall Kimmerer*

# Chapter 1

# Where the Forest has no Name

Fifty miles north of San Francisco's Golden Gate bridge, you enter the world's largest temperate rainforest, an inspiring cathedral of ancient redwood, Douglas-fir, and Sitka spruce, the tallest trees on Earth. If you travel the full length of the rainforest, you will end up 2,500 miles away, on the far western side of the Gulf of Alaska.[1]

Don't look for any signs marking an entrance to the rainforest. There aren't any. What's more, the rainforest has no official name, according to the National Geographic Names Information System database. So, what should we call it? We asked James Meacham, a professor of geology at the University of Oregon and an author of the *Atlas of Oregon*.[2]

"Great question," he told us. "I don't have a definitive answer for you."

There is no shortage of suggestions, however. At various times, people have called the temperate rainforest Salmon Nation, the Rainforests of Home, Northeast Pacific coastal temperate rainforest, Pacific coastal temperate rainforest, Pacific Rain Forest, Cascadian Raincoast Forest, or the Northwest Coast Cultural Area. None of the names have stuck.

Indigenous nations living in the rainforest for millennia had names for many of the places within the temperate rainforest, but no name for it as a whole. *The Oregonian* newspaper often refers to the rainforest as "Northwest Forests," a plain vanilla handle you could attach to just about any old stand of trees in the region.[3] The distinguished environmental newspaper *High Country News* has used something almost as generic: "The ecosystem that runs from Northern California to the Tongass National Forest in Alaska."[4] That's like identifying the Amazon, the world's greatest tropical rainforest, simply as an "ecosystem running from the Andes to the Atlantic," and leaving it at that.

All these names are technically accurate, but where's the inspiration? The name we use in this book is "Pacific coastal temperate rainforest." Outside a small cadre of scientists, no one calls it that. We admit: this name is boring too. We just aren't sold on any of the alternatives.

Settlers arriving in the temperate rainforest during the 19th century attached names to everything, including seven national parks: Redwood, Crater Lake, Mount Rainier, Olympic, North Cascades, Glacier Bay, and Kenai Fjords. Canadians also attached memorable names to their special places: Tweedsmuir, Strathcona, Pacific Rim, Clayoquot Sound, and the Great Bear Rainforest. Even individual trees were named: Hyperion, Stratospheric Giant, Del Norte Titan, Illuvatar, Kootchy Creek Giant, Cougar Flat Sentinel, Carmanah Giant, Nooksack Giant, Big Lonely Doug, Doerner Fir, and Goat Marsh Giant. Most of these trees are over 300 feet tall, the height of the Statue of Liberty, or taller. Hyperion, the tallest tree in the world, exceeds 380 feet. The tallest tree in history, so far as we know, may have been Nooksack Giant, a 465-foot-tall Douglas-fir in Washington's Whatcom County that was logged in 1897.[6] In the arboreal race for the sky, the runner-up might have been another Douglas-fir, the Lynn Valley Tree, a 415-foot monster in Vancouver, B.C., that was cut down in 1902.[7]

Before Europeans began colonizing the West in the nineteenth century, the Pacific coastal temperate rainforest was fully stocked with carbon in the form of gigantic trees, large accumulations of dead wood, and rich, loamy soils, interspersed with some burnt areas. Today, most of the old growth, generally defined as a forest older than 175–250 years, is gone.

Some of the giant trees of the past were taller than the giants of today, but there's no record of them, other than Nooksack Giant and the Lynn Valley Tree. As you journey deeper into the temperate rainforest, you will see large ugly, empty wastelands enveloping the hillsides where monstrous trees once stood. These are clear-cuts. Clear-cut logging rips almost every tree in sight off the land, all at once. Compared with less intensive forms of logging, like selective harvests, clear-cutting saves the logging companies time, effort, and money. Corporate accountants approve, even if the tree-hugging public does not.

Clear-cutting drains the forest of most of its carbon. After a forest is clear-cut, a little less than half of the carbon—leaves, branches, stumps, and roots—remains in the forest. The rest of the carbon remains embedded in the harvested logs, and eventually will become stored in manufactured wood products like lumber, plywood, and toilet paper. As these products decay slowly over time, their carbon will also return to the air. While it's alive, the tree continues to sequester carbon. Wood products are dead and sequester nothing more. After each clear-cut, that part of the forest transforms immediately from carbon sink to carbon polluter. Even if quickly replanted, the clear-cut forest won't be sequestering any significant amount of carbon again for many years. As Suzanne Simard, a University of British Columbia professor of ecology, points out, clear-cutting destroys much more than just trees. Simard, author of the insightful book *Finding the Mother Tree: Discovering the Wisdom of the Forest*,[8] explains that each clear-cut drives out a hundred species from the area, reduces the forest's ability to retain water, and removes the top few feet of soil and humus. Typically, a forest stores at least half its carbon in the soil. Repeated clear-cutting can release up to 90 percent this carbon back into the air, she says.[9]

Not long after clear-cutting the trees, loggers often set fire to the slash—the dead leftover branches, leaves, needles, and unmerchantable downed logs. These slash fires emit carbon while killing soil microbes, plant roots, and seeds. Then, the loggers summon a helicopter to shower the ground with herbicides, spelling death to the forest's remaining understory, and replant the now-bare ground with rows of saplings. Again and again every forty years, they repeat the destructive cycle of clear-cutting, spraying, burning, and replanting. This is how industrial forestry destroys natural forests, and as we document in this book, wrecks the climate as well.

Until thirty years ago, ecologists paid little attention to the rainforests that border the continents in the temperate latitudes. Instead, they focused on protecting the exotic, but vastly different, rainforests in the tropics, the planet's hot zone between the Tropic of Cancer and the Tropic of Capricorn, with the Equator drawn down the middle. Temperate rainforests exist in the cooler zones outside the tropics, in both the northern and southern hemispheres. Temperate rainforests are home to a large number of species, but tropical rainforests harbor ten times more.

On the rare occasions ecologists mentioned temperate rainforests in their scientific papers, they usually referred to them as "high latitude rainforests." That changed in 1991 when Paul Alaback, an ecologist at a Forest Service research station in Juneau, took a closer look. He noticed that forests in Southeast Alaska were a lot like forests in British Columbia and Washington, and even bore a striking resemblance to rainforests in the Patagonia region of southern Chile.

Alaback realized he had discovered a special, often overlooked type of ecosystem: the temperate rainforest. In a paper published in a Chilean journal,[10] Alaback was the first to define temperate rainforests. They are close to an ocean, cool in summer, very wet year-round, and far from the tropics.

Almost all temperate rainforests exist in just seven regions of the world: the northern Pacific Coast of North America; eastern British Columbia; eastern Canada; Japan; Patagonia; northern Europe; and Australasia (southern Australia, Tasmania, and New Zealand), according to Oregon ecologist Dominick DellaSala.[11] In his 2011 book *Temperate and Boreal Rainforests of the World*, DellaSala calculates that about eighty million hectares of temperate rainforest still remain on Earth.[12] The Pacific coastal temperate rainforest makes up a little more than one-third of that total, and by far is the largest.[13]

In 1995, Ecotrust, a non-governmental organization based in Portland, published *The Rain Forests of Home: An Atlas of People and Place*, the first detailed maps of the rainforest.[14] Two years later, Ecotrust produced a companion book, *The Rain Forests of Home: Profile of a North American Bioregion*, an anthology of essays about this "new" temperate rainforest. Spencer Beebe, Ecotrust's founder, told us *Rainforests of Home* and the companion atlas were inspired by a visit to Alaback's research station in Juneau, where he spotted a map of the rainforest on a wall. Alaback divided the temperate rainforest into two narrow belts: a western belt tracking the coastline from California to Alaska, extending some fifty miles inland; and another belt one hundred miles further inland tracking the crest of the Cascade Mountains. The two belts merge north of Vancouver, B.C. Alaback further divided the rainforest into four subzones south to north: warm, seasonal, perhumid and subtropical. Ten million people live in the gentle lowlands separating the two belts in Vancouver, Seattle, Tacoma, Portland, Eugene, and Medford.

The anthology begins with a stunning description of the vast, forested landscape:

> Stretching from the redwoods of California to the vast stands of spruce and hemlock on Kodiak Island, Alaska, the coastal temperate rain forests of North America are characterized by an unparalleled interaction between land and sea. The marine, estuarine, and terrestrial components combine to create some of the most diverse and productive ecosystems in the temperate zone.[15]

The book said only half of the world's original coastal temperate rainforests still remain. By comparison, Norwegian ecologists estimate only one-third of the world's tropical rainforests in existence in 2001 still stand.[16]

Ecotrust took special note of the Pacific coastal temperate rainforest's vast potential to store carbon. It asserted that temperate rainforests play a crucial role in mitigating human-caused climate change, and no forest is more valuable to the climate than this one.[17] They based this statement on a paper written in 1990 by Mark Harmon of Oregon State University and other ecologists. They reported that logging in the rainforest "has been a significant source of carbon in the atmosphere." Harmon's team determined that logging twelve million acres of ancient rainforests in Oregon, Washington, and Northern California over the previous century sent up more than one gigaton of carbon into the atmosphere, an enormous amount. The old forests were subsequently replanted with tree farms. Harmon calculated it will take at least 200 years for the tree farms to recapture the lost carbon.[18]

In his groundbreaking paper, Alaback compared the Pacific coastal rainforest to the Valdivian Temperate Rainforest, the world's second largest temperate rainforest. Valdivia is located in Patagonia, at the far southern end of Chile and Argentina. Consisting mostly of broadleaf trees, Valdivia's flora and fauna have little in common with the Pacific coastal rainforest. The tallest tree in Valdivia is the 184-foot coihue tree, an evergreen less than half the height of the coniferous giants in the Pacific coastal rainforest. The understories of each rainforest—the vegetative layer between canopy and ground—are also different. The ground in Valdivia is covered mostly with bamboo, while in the Pacific coastal rainforest, the understory consists of deciduous woody shrubs and a thick mat of mosses, lichens, and ferns.

At the subpolar extremes of each rainforest, low elevation icefields border the sea. Each rainforest is lined with a maze of fjords, inlets, and bays, crossed by big rivers flush with raging waters. The rivers in the Pacific coastal rainforest are populated with the world's most abundant wild salmon runs.

But Valdivia has no salmon, other than those raised artificially in fish farms.

Strikingly similar geologic histories shaped the natural histories of each rainforest. Each is situated on the Ring of Fire, the seismic belt encircling the Pacific Ocean where 90 percent of Earth's earthquakes occur. Movements of tectonic plates offshore of both temperate rainforests have triggered the most cataclysmic earthquakes the world has ever seen, the biggest of the big ones. On May 22, 1960, a rupture in the plates off the Valdivian rainforest generated a 9.5-magnitude earthquake, the largest in recorded history, followed promptly by an eighty-foot tsunami. The earthquake permanently altered the shoreline, rendering all marine navigational charts of the affected area obsolete.

A massive volcano erupted two days after the main shock. Since 1900, numerous magnitude 8 or larger earthquakes have rocked Valdivia with unnerving regularity.

The Pacific coastal rainforest is similarly vulnerable to cataclysmic earthquakes. The "Cascadia Subduction Zone," a fault line some one hundred miles off the coast from California to Washington, triggered a 9.0 quake in 1700, wiping out tidal forests and lowering the coastal elevation by several feet. Stumpy remnants, "ghost forests," can still be seen at low tide on Neskowin Beach on Oregon's north coast. No one seriously thinks the danger has passed. The next Big One could strike at any moment.

Not every scientist agrees where the boundaries of the Pacific coastal temperate rainforest should be placed. Specifically, they don't agree whether California's redwood forest truly belongs in a rainforest. There's even some dispute about whether Oregon's towering Douglas-fir forests also belong.

But the Ecotrust map includes both the redwood and Douglas-fir zones, placing the southern boundary at the Russian River, near Santa Rosa about fifty miles north of San Francisco. DellaSala moves the boundary a couple hundred miles further south to Big Sur at the far southern extremity of the redwood forest. To qualify as a temperate rainforest, DellaSala says, a forest must receive at least forty-seven inches of rain per year, and Big Sur would not meet that definition, were it not for fog. Fog banks sweep in over the redwoods from the ocean almost daily, and can add 34 percent to the precipitation total.

David McCloskey, a retired geography professor and CEO of the Cascadia Institute, a group focused on bioregional issues, draws the line much further north, in the Olympic Mountains of Northwest Washington. The redwoods, McCloskey says, don't receive enough rain to be a rainforest. "It's absurd to say these trees are part of any kind of rainforest," he told us. "I believe it's not absurd at all," DellaSala responds. "Fog is the key here."

As you travel north from the Golden Gate Bridge, you soon reach the Russian River, where Ecotrust's map locates the temperate rainforest's southern border. Here, you enter a landscape dominated by the coastal redwood, the tallest tree on Earth. Expect to be engulfed in fog for the next four hundred miles, but watch out for wildfires. Fires have devastated communities in Napa Valley's wine country just east of Santa Rosa. Wildfires are bad for the wine business, which can be damaged just by the smoke, but the redwood thrives in the presence of fire.

Redwoods can survive even the hottest flames. Their great height and thick bark, devoid of flammable resins, protect them during a blaze. After the fire goes out, burls at the base sprout new growth and become the ancient redwoods of a distant tomorrow. Redwoods weren't geoengineered with stability in mind. Their root systems go down only about ten feet. Nevertheless, communities of redwoods are surprisingly stable. The roots of each individual redwood tree will inter- twine with the roots of its neighbors.

Redwood trees don't just loom over the ecosystem. They subsume every part of it, even the dead parts. Downed whole redwood logs, limbs, and branches fall into streambeds, creating spawning and rearing habitats for salmon and trout. Cavities carved by fire in redwood trunks, known locally as "goosepens," shelter four species of bats. The newly discov- ered Humboldt's flying squirrel[19] cruises through the crowns. Surprisingly, some species—tree voles, flying squirrels, worms, and salamanders—spend their entire lives up in the canopy. The marbled murrelet,[20] a tiny seabird listed as endangered by the state of California, nests just below the canopy in the upper branches, after spending its days bobbing for fish in the ocean. Three species of lichens known to ecologists as Alectoria, Bryoria, and Usnea drape themselves from the branches of the oldest redwood trees. Most people call them witch's hair, red beard, and old man's beard. In the crowns, organisms known as epiphytes – ferns, lichens, mosses, huckleberries, and even other trees – create a universe all their own.

High demand for the reddish, decay-resistant redwood almost led to its extinction. Logging removed about 96 percent of the redwood forest that existed before 1850. Once occupying two thousand square miles in Northern California and extreme southwestern Oregon, today, only 4 percent, or eighty square miles, of old-growth redwood forest still remains.[21] Loggers liquidated redwood forests in lowland valleys near the coast but passed over a few small patches further inland. Most of these patches are now permanently protected as state parks or Redwood National Park. Their continued existence bears testament to the work of the Save the Redwoods League, which has been buying redwood forest land and creating parks since 1918. Many of the redwood stands logged before 1950 have already been cut down a second time, and some are headed for their third harvest rotation. Logging the redwood forest has nearly wiped out an enormous carbon sink.

In his book *Half-Earth: Our Planet's Fight for Life*, the acclaimed naturalist E. O. Wilson put the redwood forest at the top of his list of Earth's "best places," based on its rich biodiversity, uniqueness, and need for protection.[22] In Wilson's view, the redwood forest is one of the places we should care most about:

> Mature redwood forests have created a new and mostly unexplored layer of life, within which exist species rare or absent elsewhere. Scientists and adventurers can camp there, enthralled by the archetype of the giant tree that rises to a mythic world in the sky.

Venturing deeper into the redwoods, you will see gigantic trees bunched in well-marked locations just a few miles off the highway. For example, Montgomery Woods State Natural Reserve, located in a valley near Ukiah in Mendocino County, contains at least eighteen trees topping 350 feet – rare heights for a redwood this far south. Montgomery Flat, a swamp at the valley bottom, provides enough water for redwoods to reach towering heights in the otherwise dry landscape. As recently as 2000, a 368-foot-tall redwood named Mendocino was thought to be the tallest tree on Earth. Since then, ten taller redwood trees have been discovered further north in California.

The 1,300-acre Montgomery Woods ecosystem sits at the southern end of the range of the northern spotted owl,[23] an endangered species. The old-growth forest provides the nesting, roosting, and foraging habitat spotted owls need. In the 1970s, scientists discovered that as the ancient trees vanished, the spotted owl's population fell along with them. In recent years, an invasive species known as the barred owl has moved into areas occupied by the northern spotted owl, often outcompeting it for food.

In 2008, a low-intensity wildfire burned through the forest understory in Montgomery Woods, but the vegetation readily grew back. Biologists say the quick recovery of burnt redwood forests attests to the restorative power of fire, a necessary part of a forest's life cycle.

As you proceed further north toward Humboldt Redwoods State Park, you encounter a narrow swath of even taller trees. Five of the ten tallest trees on Earth rise up on the silty flood-plain, or alluvial flat, above Bull Creek, a tributary of the South Fork of the Eel River. In this so-called "Grove of the Giants," a redwood named Stratosphere Giant stands 371 feet tall, the world's fourth-tallest tree.[24]

Headwaters Grove, a well-known stand of redwoods in the nearby foothills, is estimated to be two thousand years old. It would have been logged in the 1990s but for the dogged determination of forest activists loosely aligned with the environmental group Earth First! Headwaters was saved after activists organized several "Redwood Summer" demonstrations at a Pacific Lumber sawmill in nearby Scotia during the 1990s.

Their goal was to protect the entire 7,000-acre grove, nearly half of which is old growth. Charles Hurwitz, the Pacific Lumber owner, triggered their outrage when he tried to liquidate the ancient trees to pay off junk bond debt incurred in 1986 to finance his purchase of the company. In 1995, cops dressed in riot gear arrested 250 people for illegal trespass at the Scotia mill as police helicopters growled overhead.

Headwaters Grove was ultimately saved in 1999 after a young activist named Julia Butterfly Hill spent two years atop Luna, a thousand-year-old redwood in nearby Mattole Watershed. Perched on a platform set on Luna's branches, Hill prevented Pacific Lumber from cutting it down. Her protest bought valuable time while the state of California mulled over its purchase, eventually paying $380 million for the grove. In 2007, Pacific Lumber filed for bankruptcy.

The world's three tallest trees grow in Redwoods National Park north of Eureka, including the tallest, the aforementioned Hyperion, measuring 380 feet, 9 inches and still growing. At least thirty other trees in the national park top 360 feet. Trees grow taller in the national park because it gets twice the rainfall as elsewhere in the redwood region. Unfortunately, about 85 percent of the national park was logged before its creation in 1968. The national park covers almost 140,000 acres and is co-managed with the state along with several nearby non-contiguous state parks: Del Norte Coast Redwood, Jedediah Smith Redwoods, and Prairie Creek Redwoods.

Only seven tree species in the world grow taller than 300 feet, and the northern section of the redwood forest is home to three of them: Douglas-fir,[25] Sitka spruce,[26] and the coastal redwood. At one site in Prairie Creek Redwoods State Park, a towering specimen of each species—a redwood, a Douglas-fir, and a Sitka spruce—grow side-by-side, each exceeding 300 feet, the only place in the world where such a diverse assemblage of tall trees occurs, according to Robert Van Pelt, a professor at the University of Washington and author of *Forest Giants of the Pacific Coast*.[27] The planet's only other 300-foot trees are the giant sequoia,[28] in the Sierra Nevada; the yellow meranti,[29] in Malaysia, the world's tallest tropical tree; and two Australian eucalypts, blue gum[30] and mountain ash.[31]

Near Crescent City, just before you hit the Oregon border, you will reach Jedediah Smith State Park and its fifteen square miles of intact, old-growth redwoods. The park is home to Del Norte Titan, the most massive redwood tree on Earth. A relatively modest 307 feet tall, this giant tree contains more than 36,000 cubic feet of wood, or enough to make more than 1,400 telephone poles. As we will see in Chapter 3, no forest in the world stores more carbon per acre than the densely-packed redwood stands in Jedediah Smith State Park.[32]

As you leave California and the warm zone, you enter Oregon and the seasonal zone, which extends for the next 900 miles through Oregon, Washington, and Vancouver Island in British Columbia.

As in the warm zone, summers in the seasonal zone are also mediterranean, warm, and dry; winters are short and rarely severe. Rainfall often tops eighty inches a year. After crossing the border, you will still encounter redwoods for another 13.5 miles, but Douglas-fir is now the dominant species, mixed largely with western hemlock.[33] These two species are the two most abundant and widely distributed conifers in western North America. Unlike the hemlock, the Douglas-fir does not like heavy shade. Eventually, the shade-tolerant hemlock will take over the forest.

Another one hundred miles further north in eastern Coos County, you will encounter the tallest Douglas-fir on Earth. Some people call this tree Doerner Fir, others call it Brummitt Fir. It measures 329 feet in height. Along the way, you will also encounter a number of other conifer: Sitka spruce, Port-Orford-cedar,[34] western redcedar,[35] noble fir,[36] Pacific silver fir,[37] mountain hemlock,[38] Alaska yellow cedar,[39] incense-cedar,[40] Oregon myrtle,[41] and Pacific yew.[42] The first European settler to "discover" the Douglas-fir was a Scottish botanist, Archibald Menzies, as reflected in its scientific name, *Pseudotsuga menziesii*. The genus name, *Pseudotsuga*, means "false hemlock."

But the tree gets its common name from the Scottish botanist David Douglas, the first to cultivate the tree. Douglas-fir is not actually a "true" fir. Botanists insert the hyphen in the name to underscore its vague status. Nor is the Douglas-fir a pine or spruce. The National Wildlife Federation classifies it as simply an "evergreen." The foliage on the Douglas-fir, like all evergreens, remains on the branches year-round. Its cones dangle beneath the branch, pointing downward. The cones of a true fir, such as the noble fir, are on top of the branch and point straight up. The Douglas-fir reproduces only from seed; new saplings don't sprout from its base like a redwood.

The four native conifers found in the temperate rainforest referred to as cedars are also deceptively named. The western redcedar, Alaska yellow cedar, incense-cedar, and Port-Orford-cedar—a species found only in southwest Oregon—each belong to the cypress family, or *cupressaceae*. They are not true cedars. Of all conifers, the western redcedar is among the longest-lived, often surpassing 1,000 years. True cedars, or *cedrus*, belong to the pine family, or *pinaceae*. These are found in the Mediterranean region and the western Himalayas.

The moist and mild climate in the seasonal zone offers year-long growing conditions enabling trees to reach an enormous size. Ocean breezes cool the landscape in summer and warm it in winter. As you travel north, each succeeding zone will be cooler and wetter.

Douglas-firs grow like crazy in this wet climate free from extreme cold or heat. They are the most commercially valuable tree in the temperate rainforest, if not the world. Its tightly grained heartwood, the wood at the tree's core, yields beautiful veneers and long structural beams. The rainforest in Oregon and Washington contains about one-fourth of the entire standing timber supply of the United States, consisting mostly of Douglas-fir. Jerry Franklin, the renowned forest ecologist at the University of Washington, says abundant rainfall and genetic makeup are behind the Douglas-firs' amazing growth. People might tell you that at one time an unbroken sea of green, lush Douglas-firs stretched along the entire coast. Don't believe them. This is a myth. At any one time, only half the landscape was ever actually covered by trees 250 years old or older. Wildfire and windstorms took the rest. Throughout the rainforest's history, in areas blackened by fire, young trees of various ages, sizes and species emerged from seeds, creating a multi-age, multi-species natural forest.

Almost all of Oregon's coastal mountain forests have burned at one time or another, but each time grew back rapidly, according to George Bundy Wasson Jr., an anthropologist and elder in the Coquille Tribe.[43] In an essay published in 1994, Wasson wrote that Indigenous people often practiced "cultural burning," the setting of controlled fires to benefit wildlife and to sustain their culture, economy and way of life:

> Burning along the Oregon coast was such a regular and obvious practice that early sailors often referred to the area as Fire Land. Smoke shrouded the coastal mountains and fires could be seen burning the entire length of the coast. This regular burning, which prevented the growth of brush and cleared out the understory of the old-growth forests, also produced extensive grassy prairies on the ridges and southwestern slopes of the coastal mountains. On these ridges, people dug their deep pits, staggered in series along a ridge-line where the immense elk herds could be driven and some would inevitably fall in.

Today, the demands of society require all fires to be extinguished as quickly as possible. Throughout the seasonal zone, you will find countless clear-cuts criss-crossed with miles and miles of logging roads. In the early years of industrial logging in the rainforest, loggers first cut down all the trees in the flat lowlands near the coast. When those trees were gone, the loggers turned to the trees in the upland valleys, foothills, and mountains. To bring out the timber, they built thousands of miles of logging roads. Before roads, they floated the logs down a river, often with a boost from floods triggered by makeshift "splash dams."

Douglas-firs rarely grow close to shore. The tidelands are the domain of the Sitka spruce, the largest of the thirty-five spruce species. Sitka spruce is light and sturdy, perfect for pianos, other musical instruments, and warplanes. During the first and second world wars, nearly the entire fleet of Allied warplanes was made from Sitka spruce logged by the Army's Spruce Production Division on the Oregon coast.

The Sitka Spruce grows fast and dies young, according to research by Russell Kramer, a University of Washington ecologist.[44] By the time a Sitka spruce reaches 500 years of age, Kramer says it will be three times more massive than a coastal redwood of the same age. The spruce tree rarely lives beyond 800 years. The redwood can live for 2,000 years or more, enough time to far surpass the spruce. And of course the longer a tree lives, the longer it sequesters carbon that otherwise would go back into the atmosphere.

To find large expanses of unfragmented lowland old-growth forests that are still standing, you have to go all the way to the Quinault, Queets, Hoh, and Bogachiel watersheds in Olympic National Park in the far northwest corner of Washington. In a grove near Quinault Lake in Olympic National Park, you can find five of the world's ten tallest known Douglas-firs.

Further north in the temperate rainforest, British Columbia is also home to notable big trees, such as four behemoths near Port Renfrew on the southwest corner of Vancouver Island: Carmanah Giant, a 315-foot-tall Sitka spruce; Big Lonely Doug, a 230-foot Douglas-fir standing alone in a massive clear-cut; the 242-foot-tall Red Creek Fir, the largest Douglas-fir by volume in the world; and the 205-foot-tall San Juan Spruce, the largest spruce in Canada and the second largest in the world. At one time, these trees were much taller, but lost their crowns in high winds.

As you travel north from Vancouver Island along British Columbia's central and north coast, you enter the perhumid zone, and the Great Bear Rainforest, an expanse of intact river valleys stretching seven hundred of miles all the way to the Alaskan southern border, where it abuts the Tongass National Forest. Originally named the "Great Bear Wilderness" by Peter McAllister, co-founder of the Raincoast Conservation Society, the Great Bear is a fully functioning ecosystem that supports gigantic grizzly bears, the white-furred spirit bear, and countless other species. In the early 1990s, when the Great Bear was targeted for logging by the timber industry, McAllister initiated a campaign to save it, culminating in 2016 when the provincial government gave it permanent protection.[45] Here, you can expect damper and milder summers and colder winters. In winter, snow comes and goes, and temperatures rarely exceed 7° C (44° F), impeding tree growth. In addition to the western redcedar, the dominant trees are Alaska yellow cedar, Pacific silver fir, mountain hemlock, and Sitka spruce.

The prehumid zone continues in with the enormous 16.7-million-acre Tongass National Forest in the Southeast Alaska Panhandle and stretches another one thousand miles around the Gulf of Alaska to the Kenai Peninsula. In the Tongass, the mountainous coastline is dominated by fjords and the 5,000-island Alexander Archipelago. Many of the islands are unnamed. Southeast Alaska also features the spectacular Misty Fjords National Monument and Glacier Bay National Park.

Here, mountain hemlock and Sitka spruce grow up to 200 feet—miniature trees compared with trees to the south but tall enough to dominate any landscape in the world. Here the old-growth forest understory is lush with ferns, berries, mosses and many other types of plants. Summers are cool, winter snow is persistent, and temperatures are chilly. The wettest places in the entire temperate rainforest are located on Baranof Island near Sitka, which can get 300 inches of rain per year, and in Southeast Alaska's coastal mountains, which can get 800 inches of snow.

A vast inland marine sea straddling the United States/Canada border separates the northern and southern halves of the Pacific coastal temperate rainforest. The sea consists of three connected large bodies of water: Puget Sound, the Strait of Juan de Fuca, and the Strait of Georgia. Few people viewed it as a single marine ecosystem until the 1980s when Bert Webber, a retired professor at Western Washington University in Bellingham, proposed calling it the "Salish Sea," after the Indigenous people who lived throughout the area for millennia. "In order to better understand the inland marine sea, we needed to be able to accurately and consistently reference it, and to do that, it needed a name," Webber wrote. In 2008, the Salish Indian Tribes in Washington and First Nations in British Columbia gathered in Tulalip, Washington to discuss whether to adopt the new name. After three days of deliberations, they gave their consent. "The designation of the name Salish Sea is a historic acknowledgement of our peoples' connection to our lands and waterways since time immemorial," said Squamish Nation Chief Gibby Jacob. In 2010, the geographic naming boards in both the United States and Canada officially designated the waters as "The Salish Sea."

Today, few people see the sprawling Pacific coastal temperate rainforest as a single ecosystem, though many hail its spectacular individual parts. *The Great Bear Rainforest: Canada's Forgotten Coast*, a book co-authored by Ian McAllister, the aforementioned Peter McAllister's son, called

British Columbia's Great Bear Rainforest one of "the planet's last large expanses of coastal temperate rainforest."[46] The Washington *Post* called the Tongass National Forest in Alaska "one of the world's largest intact temperate rainforests."[47] Though technically correct, both failed to see these magnificent forests as part of something much larger. They missed the forest for the trees.

Protecting and restoring the Pacific coastal temperate rainforest is an essential part of any solution to the climate emergency. And yet, it remains on the sidelines while climate scientists focus almost solely on protecting tropical rainforests. Giving the Pacific coastal temperate rainforest an inspiring name could significantly elevate its profile, a necessary first step toward granting it the international recognition it deserves as one of the world's most vital carbon sinks, alongside the Amazon.

# Chapter 2

# Too Good to be True

In 2007, Richard Branson, the British entrepreneur, offered a $25-million prize for anyone inventing a device capable of removing lots of carbon dioxide from the atmosphere. Andy Kerr, the noted Oregon environmentalist and author, drew a picture of a tree and sent it in. But he didn't win, foiled by contest rules specifying the winner must be the inventor of such a device.

Kerr didn't invent the tree, but he had a point. Through the process of photosynthesis, trees inhale carbon dioxide ($CO_2$), one of the greenhouse gasses behind the rise in global temperatures. $CO_2$ is one part carbon and two parts oxygen. Trees are about one-half carbon. They retain the carbon to make glucose, and recycle the oxygen back into the air. Living and dead trees, along with forest soils, hold the equivalent of 80 percent of all the carbon currently in the atmosphere.[1]

If there's one thing the planet has in abundance, it's trees. A study in 2015 by Yale University ecologist Thomas Crowther counted three trillion trees on Earth, 422 for each person.[2] Without trees, life would be difficult, if not impossible. Trees are a source of food, medicine, fuel, shelter, and recreation for billions of people. In the Pacific coastal temperate rainforest, trees freshen the air with signature scents of fir, pine, spruce, and cedar. They stabilize soils, retain moisture, and filter pollution from the air and water. They cast a cooling shade over streams that are home to millions of salmon. Salmon return the favor by bringing nutrients from the ocean in an ecological feedback loop.

The tree's most important task, however, may be removing carbon from the atmosphere, but it's not something a single tree does alone. The clusters of trees we call forests perform this service on a massive scale, free of charge, without complaint. They are carbon-capturing machines.

Scientists estimate human activities emit about eleven giga-tons of carbon every year, almost all from burning fossil fuels. About half the carbon stays in the atmosphere, heating the planet. The rest is sequestered in the ocean, or in terrestrial ecosystems like forests, wetlands, peatlands, estuaries, and grasslands. Ecosystems sequestering large amounts of carbon are known as "carbon sinks."

Currently, forests store about a quarter of all carbon emis-sions, but could store far more. There are two ways to increase the amount of carbon stored in forests: planting new trees, and improving the way forests are managed. Ultimately, forests could provide two-thirds of the cost-effective mitigation needed to hold warming to below 2°C, according to "Natural Climate Solutions," a 2017 paper published in the *Proceedings of the National Academy of Sciences*.[3]

In order to stabilize the climate, we would need to plant a crazy number of trees—perhaps as many as one trillion – according to a July 2019 paper on trees by a team of scientists at Timothy Crowther's lab at ETH Zurich, the Swiss Federal Institute of Technology.[4]

But the idea of planting a trillion trees raises some difficult questions. Where should they be planted? Where will they get water? Will they take land away from food crops and crowd out cities and urban areas? And, most importantly, how much good would planting a trillion trees actually do for the climate? Crowther's data-driven model calculates that 900 million hectares (2.2 billion acres) not already used for agriculture or cities could be planted with trees. Doing so, the study says, could sequester 205 gigatons of carbon (out of the 300 gigatons of excess carbon now in the atmosphere), making tree planting the "most effective climate change solution to date." That might be enough to end the climate emergency, but only if we also shut down all carbon emissions. But no one should expect the trillion-tree strategy to produce the desired result anytime soon. Crowther projects it would take fifty to one hundred years for all one trillion freshly planted trees to absorb all 205 gigatons. But his critics say it would take a lot longer.

The news media nevertheless hyperventilated over Crowther's claims. "Tree planting 'has mind-blowing potential' to tackle the climate crisis," a headline in *The Guardian* proclaimed.[5] "What's low-tech, sustainable, and possibly the most effective thing we can do to fight climate change? Planting trees. A trillion of them," was how CNN put it.[6] "Got An Overheating Planet? Plant 1 Trillion Trees. Problem Solved," the website *CleanTechnica* trumpeted.[7] *National Geographic* had a similar take: "An area the size of the United States could be restored as forests with the potential of erasing nearly 100 years of carbon emissions."[8]

It's hard not to get excited about solving an existential crisis with such a simple solution. And yet, despite the headlines, Crowther's paper received strong pushback from climate scientists. Some were astounded by conclusions they considered preposterous.

"That sounds like a dream!" exclaimed Stefan Rahmstorf, a climate scientist at the University of Potsdam in Germany, in a blog post.[9] "And it was immediately welcomed by those who still dream of climate mitigation that doesn't hurt anyone. Unfortunately, it's also too good to be true."

A letter to *Science* from Pierre Friedlingstein of the University of Exeter pounced on the authors' misunderstanding of climate science.[10]

> Without radical reductions in fossil carbon emissions, forest restoration can only offset a share of future emissions and has limited potential. The only long-term and sustainable way to stabilize the climate at any temperature target is to reduce anthropogenic $CO_2$ emissions to zero.

"Yes, heroic reforestation can help," Myles Allen of the University of Oxford told *Science Media Center*, "but it is time to stop suggesting there is a 'nature-based solution' to ongoing fossil fuel use. There isn't. Sorry."[11]

Yes, nature-based solutions are valuable, but are no substitute for fossil fuel reductions. We need them both. However, there are many types of nature-based solutions, and tree planting is not even the most promising, a point Crowther now concedes.

Several months after *Science* published the Crowther study, he corrected the manuscript. The original version said tree-planting "is our most effective climate change solution to date." The amended version now says tree-planting is only "one of the most effective carbon drawdown solutions to date." The editors at *Science* offered their own correction:

> They did not mean that tree restoration (a synonym for tree-planting) is more important than reducing greenhouse gas emissions or should replace it, nor did they mean

that restoring woodlands and forests is more important than conserving the natural ecosystems that currently exist. The authors acknowledge that climate change is an extremely complex problem with no simple fix and that it will require a full combination of approaches.[12]

Some climate scientists, however, credit Crowther for steering public attention toward forests as a solution to the climate crisis. In a letter to *Science*, Alan Grainger of the University of Leeds wrote that if Crowther gave impetus to using forests to mitigate climate change, "then the results of this early research can finally be used for the purpose for which they were originally intended."[13]

Worldwide, tree-planting is more popular than ever. In 2019, millions of people in Ethiopia planted 353 million trees in just twelve hours.[14] The Ethiopians hope their new trees eventually will become part of the "Great Green Wall of Africa," a proposed corridor of billions of trees planted in a line across the entire 5,000-mile width of the African continent from Dakar to Djibouti. Launched in 2015 by the African Union and funded by an international consortium including the United Nations and the World Bank, the Great Green Wall's advocates hoped to sequester 250 million tons of carbon by 2030.

The Great Green Wall cuts across the Sahel, the hot, dry, and windswept savannah south of the Sahara Desert. The Sahara is creeping southward, encroaching into the Sahel. The freshly planted trees are finding it tough to find enough water to survive in this increasingly hot and arid environment. Millions have died. Only 4 percent of the original target has been met.[15]

"If all the trees that had been planted in the Sahara since the early 1980s had survived, it would look like Amazonia," Chris Reij, a sustainable land management specialist and senior fellow at the World Resources Institute, told *Smithsonian Magazine*. But no one should be surprised about what happened. "Essentially 80 percent or more of planted trees have died," he says.[16]

Planting great numbers of trees in an arid environment is also being tried in China, where a 66-billion-tree fortress known as the Great Green Wall has been planted next to the Gobi Desert, as a commentary in *Nature* said in 2019. The commentary raised doubts about whether these trees will get enough water to survive. "The idea is nice, but it's kind of foolish to plant trees in a desert," Troy Sternberg, a geographer at the University of Oxford, United Kingdom, told *Nature*.[17]

Nevertheless, in 2022 an op-ed in the *New York Times* said large-scale tree-planting projects in arid climates are beginning to show positive results, at least in parts of the Great Wall of Africa. "After years of planting trees and experimenting with methods to capture water, farmers in Niger have begun to see results — soil health has improved, and crops are growing again," the op-ed said.[18]

The World Economic Forum has launched its own global initiative to grow, restore, and conserve one trillion trees around the world.[19] In the United States, President Donald Trump, a notorious denier of climate science, announced support for the tree-planting initiative, possibly his only attempt to combat climate change, though an ineffectual one. In 2021, the U.S. Congress joined the tree-planting jubilee with the introduction of the bipartisan "Trillion Trees Act," calling for planting one trillion trees by 2050. Many other nations in moderate climates, including Ireland, Great Britain, and Mexico, have made similar commitments to planting millions of trees.

It's fair to doubt whether Trump was ever truly committed to growing trees for the environment. In 2019, a county in Virginia cited Trump for illegally cutting down a dozen trees on one of his golf courses. Some had been tossed into a river, creating a safety hazard.[20]

Since the 1980s, the United Nations Environmental Programme (UNEP) has played a leading role in the creation of global climate policies. In 1988, UNEP was a co-founder of the Intergovernmental Panel on Climate Change (IPCC), along with the World Meteorological Organization. The IPCC is the world's leading scientific authority on all things climate. In 2008, UNEP launched a global tree-planting campaign inspired by Wangari Maathai, a Nobel Peace Prize Laureate who is said to have planted thirty million trees in Africa over thirty years. A few years later, the project was renamed the "trillion-tree campaign."

In 2011, UNEP turned the tree-planting campaign over to Plant-for-the-Planet, a non-governmental organization based in Germany. Plant-for-the-Planet was the brainchild of a nine-year-old German boy named Felix Finkbeiner. Today, Finkbeiner is chairman of the board and Thomas Crowther is the scientific advisor. By 2020, Plant-for-the-Planet's website claimed its members had shoveled fifteen billion trees into the ground.[21]

The group pushed children out front to lead the cause, proclaiming on its website, "Children could plant one million trees in every country on the earth and thereby offset $CO_2$ emissions all on their own, while adults are still talking about doing it."

Unfortunately, some of Plant-for-the-Planet's claims are inaccurate and overblown, according to an investigation by the German news magazine *Die Zeit*.[22] The magazine reported that a Plant-for-the-Planet database of the world's leading tree-planters defied reason. For instance, the database listed someone identified only as Valf F of France as the world's greatest tree-planter, crediting them with planting an improbable 682 million trees. The database identified Deekay of Egypt as the second-most tree-planter with 500 million trees to their credit. After *Die Zeit* quizzed Plant-for-the-Planet about the identities of Valf F and Deekay, their names were scrubbed from the database.

More questionable information popped out of the Plant-for-the-Planet website. For example, a map locating freshly planted trees showed many were planted in the South Atlantic Ocean in a straight line between Africa and Antarctica, where the water is thousands of feet deep. Plant-for-the-Planet also gives props to corporations who are clearly greenwashing their nefarious resource extraction activities by planting trees.

Consider, for example, the German coal company RWE AG, which claims to have planted 100,000 trees, according to the Plant-for-the-Planet database. RWE is one of Europe's largest carbon emitters, operating a coal mine near the Hambacher Forest near Cologne in western Germany. After RWE announced plans to cut down the forest to allow expansion of the coal mine, violent clashes erupted between police and environmental activists. Environmentalists say logging the 12,000-year-old forest will be devastating to local biodiversity. *Die Zeit* suggested RWE was planting trees as "atonement" for its misdeeds.

Another German company, Bayer AG, the producer of genetically modified organisms (GMOs) and pesticides, also claims to have planted 100,000 trees, according to the database. Bayer says its tree-planting and other forest conservation projects will offset 200,000 metric tons of greenhouse gas emissions. But as we will see later in this book, forest offset projects do not reliably stabilize the climate. There's not enough spare room on Earth to plant enough trees to fully restore the climate.

When 2019 began, Plant-for-the-Planet claimed to have planted fifteen billion trees. But by January 2021, the number was revised to less than fourteen billion. The missing billion trees appear to be the ones purportedly planted by Valf F and Deekay. But the numbers don't matter. The climate crisis will continue to terrorize humanity no matter how many trees we plant. A tree can be planted in an afternoon, but it won't sequester much carbon for decades.

Then there's the matter of what happens to the freshly planted trees. Almost half of new planted trees have been placed in commercial tree plantations, where they are likely to be logged every few decades, limiting the amount of carbon they will sequester, according to a paper by Simon Lewis, published by *Nature* in 2019 (Lewis is a professor of global change science at University College London):

> The regular harvesting and clearing of plantations releases stored $CO_2$ back into the atmosphere every 10–20 years. By contrast, natural forests continue to sequester carbon for many decades.[23]

Lewis analyzed a German tree-planting initiative known as the "Bonn Challenge," which has a goal of planting more than 350 million hectares of forest worldwide by 2030. Sixty-one nations pledged to join the effort. Half the trees in the Bonn Challenge are planted in tree farms, Lewis writes, noting that tree farms store only one-fortieth as much carbon as a natural forest. He contends planting trees in tree farms should not count as forest restoration under rules set by the IPCC. The rules, which guide compliance with international climate agreements, assume freshly planted forests will remain standing forever, "But there is no guarantee that these forests will be fifty or one hundred years from now, particularly as the demand for land grows." As Lewis told *Science Daily*, "There is a scandal here."[24]

> To most people, forest restoration means bringing back natural forests, but policy makers are calling vast monocultures 'forest restoration.' And worse, the advertised climate benefits are absent.

According to an old Chinese proverb, the best time to plant a tree was twenty years ago, and the second best time is today. But the ancient Chinese did not confront a climate emergency. We now know the best time to plant a tree was a thousand years ago. The best thing you can do today is save a tree.

# Chapter 3

# Guardians of the Climate

In 1962, an obsession over tree size drew the governors of Oregon and Washington into a public spat. Washington governor Albert Rosellini and Oregon governor Mark Hatfield each claimed the biggest Douglas-fir in the world resided in their respective state. They assembled a team of foresters to settle the dispute. The contenders were Queets Fir on Washington's Olympic Peninsula and Clatsop Fir on Oregon's North Coast.

When it comes to the climate, size really does matter: the bigger the tree, the more carbon it stores. But of course, neither governor was concerned about the climate. Though the climate was already on its destructive path, the problem would not attract much attention for decades. Neither governor said anything about ecology or biodiversity, according to newspaper accounts. This contest was strictly a public relations stunt intended to promote logging and tourism. Simpler times.

Each of the two Douglas-firs began life about one thousand years ago during the Middle Ages, about eight centuries before the American Revolution. Each took root in a natural forest, but by the late twentieth century, their fates had sharply diverged. The 221-foot-tall Queets Fir had the good fortune to stand under the permanent protection of the National Park Service in Olympic National Park, about seventeen miles from the mouth of the Queets River on the park's west side. About one hundred fifty miles down the coast, the 225-foot-tall Clatsop Fir stood near Highway 101 in an industrial tree farm east of Cannon Beach, vulnerable to the whims of its owner, Crown Zellerbach, a pulp and paper company. Each tree had a broken top.

*The Oregonian* called the contest the "battle of diameters," treating it like a football game.[1] In this battle, tree height didn't matter. The trophy would go to the thicker tree at ground level.

A panel of three judges sized them up. Oregon's Clatsop Fir measuring nearly 15.5 feet thick, was about one foot thicker at chest height, the critical metric, but thinner up high. By volume, the Queets tree was larger overall, but that didn't matter. The judges declared Clatsop Fir the winner.

Sadly, Hatfield didn't get to savor the victory for very long. Just a few months later in October 1962, a rare typhoon—the Columbus Day storm—whipped into Oregon from the southwest with 120 mph gusts and blew Clatsop Fir to the ground. At the time, Crown Zellerbach promised never to cut down the big tree, but now that it was dead, newspaper photographs hinted at its fate. One photo showed a sign posted next to the tree saying it was big enough to produce 150 tons of paper or ten two-bedroom homes. For the last sixty years, Clatsop Fir—or whatever became of it—has been decomposing, at least some of its carbon blowing in the wind, contributing to climate chaos.

With Clatsop's demise, Queets Fir was suddenly the world's biggest Douglas-fir. However, its reign would not last. In 1998, laser measurements determined that an even larger Douglas-fir was growing on British Columbia's Vancouver Island, northwest of Victoria. Today, this tree, known as Red

Creek Fir, is still the world champion Douglas-fir.[3] Meanwhile, Queets Fir quietly soldiers on, still storing its carbon, and every day sequestering more.

Each of the champion firs—Queets, Clatsop, and Red Creek— fit the definition of an old-growth tree, generally defined as at least 175 – 250 years old. But the ancient forests of the coastal rainforest are much more than just big old trees. They are complex ecosystems featuring trees of all ages and many species. Dappled beams of light filter through their branches, giving life to a diverse universe of younger trees, shrubs, berries, and other vegetation emerging in the understory. Underground, the entire forest is linked into a network of tree roots and mycorrhizal fungi that passes nutrients, water, carbon, and sugars back and forth, tree to tree, even among different tree species, as Suzanne Simard, the noted forest scientist at the University of British Columbia, found in research she conducted in Oregon and British Columbia forests. What's more, Simard discovered trees also share data about their aboveground environment, all transmitted through the fungal links. They communicate information vital to their mutual survival, whispering warnings about things like drought conditions and bug infestations. Yes, the trees are talking to each other. In her wonderful book *Finding the Mother Tree: Discovering the Wisdom of the Forest*, Simard compares the mycorrhizal network to the neural networks in human brains. "The old and young trees were hubs and nodes, interconnected by mycorrhizal fungi in a complex pattern that fueled the regeneration of the entire forest."[4]

A great amount of carbon stored in old forests falls to the forest floor, over time becoming part of the soil or humus. One study calculated that a forest stores up to 70 percent of its carbon in the soil.[5] Another pool of soil carbon accumulates in the canopies, on top of the massive limbs and in the crotches where the limbs connect to the trunk. After centuries, canopy soil, mats consisting of decomposing leaves, needles, and dead branches, can measure one meter thick.

Known among forest scientists as "histosols," these mats contain up to three times more carbon per cubic meter than the soils underfoot, according to research conducted by a team of scientists led by Hannah Connuck, an undergraduate researcher at Franklin and Marshall College. Connuck presented her research at the annual conference of the American Geophysical Union in December 2021.[6]

Although Connuck conducted her research in tropical forests in Costa Rica, histosols are found in ancient forests wherever they exist. "They are especially abundant on the Olympic Peninsula and in Northern California Redwood canopies, accompanying the significant humidity and rainfall," she told us in an interview. It's significant that histosols are missing in younger forests. "It's a good argument for keeping primary and other old-growth forests around, rather than harvesting and replanting with secondary growth forests," Connuck said. Histosols host unique microbiomes consisting of highly diverse microbial organisms and plants like epiphytic orchids while providing nesting material for the endangered marbled murrelet.

Historically, the timber industry viewed old-growth forests as decaying, rotting hulks in need of replacement. The industry has already logged most of the old-growth throughout the Pacific coastal temperate rainforest, replacing it with young plantations to be logged again and again every few decades. Since the time of European settlement, approximately 70 to 80 percent of the original old-growth forest on the Pacific Coast has been cut down. Of the remaining old growth, the Central and Southern Cascades and the Klamath-Siskiyou regions in Oregon account for nearly half.[7]

Traditionally, tree plantations have been monocultures, consisting of trees of only a single age and species. The industry calls them "tree farms," as if to acknowledge they aren't really forests. On a tree farm, the young trees grow in densely packed formations laid out like rows of corn.

A big, old tree like Queets fir sequesters as much additional carbon each year as contained in an entire smaller tree, a 2014 study by the U.S. Geological Survey (USGS) found.[8] The study challenged the industry's claim that once trees reach a certain age, their growth rates decline. Instead, they found that as trees age, their growth keeps accelerating. The study measured tree growth in 403 tree species from six continents, including Douglas-fir, western redcedar, western hemlock, and Sitka spruce from the Pacific coastal temperate rainforest. In one forest in the western United States, 6 percent of the trees measured more than one meter thick at the base, an impressive size. But the big, old trees combined to contribute one-third of the forest's total growth. As USGS ecologist Adrian Das, a co-author of the paper, said, "It is as if the star players on your favorite sports team were a bunch of 90-year-olds."[9]

Although old trees emit carbon when they die, younger, maturing trees will be there to replace them, naturally regenerating the forest and in time replenishing the lost carbon, according to William Moomaw, professor emeritus of International Environmental Policy at Boston's Tufts University. Moomaw told us that sequestering carbon in mature forests, wherever they exist, should be an essential strategy for meeting global climate goals. Moomaw even coined a new word—proforestation—to describe this strategy in a paper published in 2019.[10]

In a telephone interview, Moomaw explained that proforestation has three main components: protecting existing old-growth forests, protecting maturing forests that will become old growth in the foreseeable future, and delaying harvests in younger forests. Proforestation is an ideal climate-mitigation strategy in the Pacific coastal temperate rainforest where the wet climate and highly productive soils maximize tree growth. Unlogged parts of the Pacific coastal temperate rainforest store more carbon per acre than any other forest in the world, with one surprising exception, as we will see.

Moomaw told us proforestation is a solution to the two greatest environmental challenges of our time: the climate crisis and the rapid, ongoing loss of biodiversity. He has the street cred to back up his theory. Moomaw is co-author of five major reports by the IPCC. In 2007, he won the Nobel Peace Prize alongside 2,000 other co-authors for one of the IPCC reports. Moomaw is a retired chair of the Woodwell Climate Research Institute (formerly the Woods Hole Research Center), a leading climate think tank based outside Boston.

Globally, proforestation could significantly reduce the climate threat, according to Moomaw. "If deforestation were halted, and secondary forests were allowed to continue growing," he writes, forests could sequester an additional 120 gigatons of carbon through 2100, capturing some 40 percent of all the excess carbon in the air.

Wayne Walker, director of Woodwell's carbon program, told us that based on his calculations, the Pacific coastal temperate rainforest stores nearly three gigatons of carbon, a "tremendous amount." In his proforestation paper, Moomaw projected forests could double the amount of carbon in storage. If true, the Pacific coastal rainforest could potentially add another three gigatons to its carbon inventory, representing a substantial amount of climate change mitigation.

In recent years, scientists have been collecting data about the carbon storage potential of forests. This information can help guide future decisions about which forests can be logged at minimal risk to the climate, and where logging would do the most harm to the climate.

In 2002, Erica Smithwick, a doctoral candidate at Oregon State University, made a startling discovery: unlogged stands of old-growth Douglas-fir forests in Oregon's Coast Range mountains store on average an astounding 1,127 metric tons of carbon per hectare, more carbon per acre than "any other type of vegetation, anywhere in the world," as far as she knew. And if allowed to keep growing, she said, Oregon's forests could store plenty more.[11]

Smithwick identified a stand of old-growth Douglas-fir near the headwaters of Neskowin Creek in Oregon's central Coast Range as the most carbon-dense stand of trees on the planet. Smithwick measured carbon from the tops of tree canopies down to the soil to a depth of one meter, including roots, brush, shrubs, herbs, foliage, bark, litter, fallen branches, logs lying on the forest floor, and snags still standing upright. Dead and decomposing trees release significant amounts of carbon into the forest soils, where it is stored for centuries or even millennia. In this forest, Smithwick found about one-third of the carbon in the soils.

Smithwick, now a professor of geography at Pennsylvania State University, talked to us via cell phone as she waited for a flight to the 2021 global climate summit in Glasgow. Smithwick told us that transforming tree plantations back into old-growth forests, a process that can take hundreds of years, could double the amount of carbon they store, a conclusion similar to one Moomaw reached. However, she says it would be unrealistic to think all forests should be allowed to become old growth. Younger forests support the local economy while filling an important ecological role. People will still need forests for things like plywood and toilet paper. "Ultimately, we would like to ensure a variety of forests in different successional classes that support different habitats, maximizing biodiversity as well as carbon storage."

Today, scientists no longer consider the Douglas-fir forests to be the most carbon-dense in the world. Less than a decade after Smithwick published her paper, an Australian scientist found an even more carbon-rich forest dominated by flowering eucalyptus trees in southern Australia, near Melbourne.

In 2009, Heather Keith, an ecologist and climate scientist at Australia's Griffin University in Canberra, set out to find the world's most carbon-dense forests. Keith collected previously published carbon-density data from 131 tropical, temperate, and boreal forests around the world, in both hemispheres. She also took some of her own measurements, and published her findings in the *Proceedings of the National Academy of Sciences.*[12] She found the densest forest in the Australasian temperate rainforest north of Melbourne, Australia's second-largest city.

The Australasian temperate rainforest, about a third the size of the Pacific coastal rainforest, surrounds the Tasman Sea in Southern Australia, Tasmania, and New Zealand. This temperate rainforest is home to some of the largest living things on the planet, including the wedge-tailed (*Aquila audax*) eagle, the largest living eagle, and the hulking mountain ash (*Eucalyptus regnans*), sometimes called "swamp gum," one of the seven tree species worldwide known to reach 300 feet in height.[13] Dominick DellaSala, the Oregon ecologist, told us the tallest mountain ash in history exceeded 400 feet in height, though today the tallest living specimen measures just 327 feet.

The data collected by Keith shows that a stand of mountain ash on the Central Victoria Highlands, at a latitude similar to the Northern California redwoods, contains about twice as much carbon per hectare as the Douglas-fir forests of Oregon where Erica Smithwick conducted her research. The precise location of this new world carbon champion is an unlogged watershed known as the O'Shannassy Catchment, the source of drinking water for Melbourne.

Keith measured 1,867 metric tons of carbon per hectare in this forest, plus another one thousand tons per hectare in the soils. "There's a lot more carbon there than people had originally thought mainly because they haven't measured it before," Keith told us in an interview. The tropical rainforest in the Amazon contains up to one-fourth as much. For example, Keith reported that a jungle near San Carlos, Venezuela, contains just 350 tons of carbon per hectare. The forest near Manaus, Brazil, contains only 180 tons. Elsewhere in the United States, Keith found 486 tons of carbon per hectare in the white pine forests of northern Wisconsin, 165 tons in the beech forests of Kentucky, and 117 tons in the oak and sweetgum forests of Indiana. The carbon densities in European forests are just as small, such as in southern Finland, where the Scotch pine forests contain 153 tons.

Australia's mountain ash, one of 700 species of eucalyptus, is the world's largest flowering tree, and found in wood products ranging from furniture to construction beams to hardwood flooring. It is often planted as an ornamental in California, where it is considered an invasive species.

Sadly, in February 2009, a month before Keith published her paper, parts of the O'Shannassy Catchment burned in a major bushfire. In 2020, the hot-burning eucalyptus forest caught fire again, this time in a conflagration that eventually scorched forty-six million acres across southern Australia, killing thirty-four people. The inferno killed or displaced an estimated three billion native animals, including koalas, kangaroos, wallabies, and cockatoos among other species, and released an undetermined amount of carbon.[14] At the time Heather Keith conducted her study, carbon-density data from forests in Africa's Congo basin and in the Northern California redwoods did not yet exist. When carbon-density data from the redwoods finally arrived in 2016, a new world champion forest was crowned.

In the 1980s, Steven Sillett, an undergraduate at Reed College in Portland, Oregon, learned to climb tall Douglas-firs on the heavily wooded campus to relieve academic stress. On a backpack trip to Northern California, he climbed a redwood, a far greater challenge. On a Douglas-fir, the lowest branch might be sixty feet off the ground. The lowest branches on a redwood can hover 250 feet above ground.

Over the following three decades, Sillett climbed hundreds of redwoods, many over 300 feet tall. Sillett often performed death-defying stunts in the canopies, like sleeping on the upper branches and even having sex at those heights. At other times, he walked out toward the end of stiff branches, feats he called "sky walking." Richard Preston, Sillett's biographer, described him as "a science geek trapped within the body of an Olympic athlete."[15] In 2001, Sillett got married near the top of a pair of adjacent redwoods, with bride, groom and minister each dangling in mid-air on ropes strung between the tall trees. In between stunts in the canopies, he had obtained a Ph.D. in botany from Oregon State University.

It's a matter of pride among professional botanists to be the person who discovers a hyper-tall tree. The discoverer isn't the first to see the tree, but the first to measure it or explain its significance. Sillett and his climbing partner, the naturalist Michael W. Taylor, discovered many of the tallest redwoods, including the world's tallest tree, Hyperion. In May 1998, while bushwhacking through a dense thicket in Jedediah Smith State Park in the extreme northwest corner of California, an intact 10,000-acre stand of gigantic redwoods never disturbed by logging, Sillett and Taylor stood face to face with a thick fortress of monstrous redwoods they named the "Grove of Titans."

In 2007, Sillett, now a professor of redwood forest ecology at Humboldt State University in nearby Arcata, returned to the Grove of Titans to find out how much carbon it held. He determined that the Grove of Titans contains 2,596 tons of carbon per hectare, more than any other forest on Earth, and about six times the carbon density of the Amazon. As such, it is the world's foremost forest carbon sink. At the time, the grove was not even on official U.S. Geological Survey maps. Few people knew it even existed. Today, the Jed Smith's world-record setting stand of redwood is attracting a great number of visitors. By 2016, about a quarter acre of sensitive understory plants had been trampled, according to the

Save the Redwoods League, prompting park officials to build an elevated plankway through the grove to prevent further damage. The plankway opened in 2022.

Sillett's research team included Robert Van Pelt, a professor at the University of Washington and author of *Forest Giants of the Pacific Coast*[16] and three other ecologists. They published their data in 2016.[17]

As Preston makes clear, Sillett expected to find a lot of carbon in the Grove of Titan and a nearby forest known as Atlas Grove, and not just in the massive tree trunks. For example, Sillett found tons of decomposing organic matter— carbon—resting on top of the branches, the mats Hannah Connuck calls histosols. As Preston wrote:

> The fern garden in the Atlas Grove (and in the Grove of Titans) are the second most massive collections of epiphytes – plants that grow on other plants – in any forest on Earth. Robert Van Pelt discovered that epiphytes in a rainforest on the Olympic Peninsula in Washington have an even greater mass than the epiphytes in the redwood forest. Both temperate rainforests have far larger and more massive collections of epiphytes than do any rainforest in the tropics. Some of the fern mats in the redwoods weigh two tons when they're saturated with water after a rain.[18]

Sillett mounted LiDAR, an aerial sensing device, on an airplane to measure the forests' carbon densities. LiDAR, an acronym for Light Detection and Ranging, relies on pulsed lasers to measure the amount of carbon held in both the overstory and understory of a forest."

Wherever Sillett's team found an intact stand of old-growth redwoods, they found an extraordinary amount of carbon. They determined that the Grove of Titans is just one of five forests in the world where above-ground carbon densities have been measured in excess of 2,000 metric tons per hectare, and all five are in the redwoods. The others are Prairie Creek Redwoods State Park, Redwood National Park, Humboldt Redwood State Park, and Montgomery Woods State Natural Reserve.

Taken together, the carbon-density studies by Stephen Sillett, Heather Keith, and Erica Smithwick show that the Pacific coastal temperate rainforest is the world's most carbon-dense forest, acre for acre. Only the Australian mountain ash forest near Melbourne comes close. Carbon densities in the Pacific coastal temperate rainforest generally get smaller as you travel further north, but stands of western redcedar on British Columbia's Vancouver Island break the mold. The big B.C. forests hold 1,300 metric tons of carbon per hectare, according to Simard, the forest scientist at the University of British Columbia,[19] somewhat more than Smithwick's Douglas-fir forest on the Oregon Coast. Further north in Alaska's Tongass National Forest, carbon densities are much smaller, but are still on par with densities found in the Amazon. Of course, the Amazon tropical rainforest is much larger than the Pacific coastal temperate rainforest, and thus stores significantly more carbon in total.

Proforestation is already happening in the Pacific coastal temperate rainforest. Though most of the old growth is gone, millions of acres of eighty-to-hundred-year-old trees are growing rapidly, and could become monstrous, carbon-chugging old-growth trees early next century. If left alone, these trees could continue sequestering carbon for hundreds of years. But if logged today, their ability to sequester additional carbon ends today.

The public is getting behind the idea that protecting trees is a smart climate strategy. Oregon Wild, a group with a long history of protecting forests on behalf of biodiversity, is now a leading advocate for protecting forests on behalf of the climate, alongside many other Oregon groups, including the Coalition for a Sustainable Economy. Both sum up this new mission in just five simple words: "Forest defense is climate defense." In 2022, Oregon Wild helped to launch climate-forests.org, a national campaign highlighting forests as a cost-effective climate solution, joining Earthjustice, NRDC, the Sierra Club, 350.org, and the League of Conservation Voters, alongside dozens of other local, regional, and national scientific, legal, and environmental organizations from Alaska to Maine to Georgia.

In British Columbia, the Rainbow Flying Squad is constantly raising the climate issue in protests against logging in old-growth stands at Fairy Creek and elsewhere in the province. In Southeast Alaska, a coalition of twelve Alaska Native tribes is citing climate change in petitions to halt industrial logging in parts of the Tongass National Forest near tribal communities. Clear-cutting old-growth forests on the Tongass has created a "boom or bust" economy, one of the petition's chief backers, Marina Anderson, administrator of Kasaan tribal village on the eastern shore of Prince of Wales Island, told us. Native Alaskans want to receive cultural, traditional, subsistence, and environmental benefits from the forest, not just lumber. As their petition makes clear, climate is among their chief concerns:

The Tongass can no longer be viewed as stands of timber waiting for harvest. It must be viewed as a cultural resource that must be managed for the benefit of its local people, for the long-term productivity of its salmon streams and wildlife habitat, and to help mitigate impacts from climate change.[20]

The state of Oregon, meanwhile, is weighing a proposal to include proforestation as part of its strategy for reducing the state's greenhouse gas emissions by nearly half by 2035. Oregon is also planning to study the benefits of proforestation on the Elliott State Forest (ESF), one of the largest expanses of unprotected old and mature forests outside Alaska. Located between Reedsport and Coos Bay on the South Coast, much of it burned in the catastrophic Coos fire of 1868. About half of the Elliott has been logged over the last seventy years,[21] but none since 2014 when the state canceled all planned timber sales to comply with environmental laws. The state now intends to turn the Elliott over to the Oregon State University College of Forestry for use as a research laboratory. OSU has promised that in fifty years, nearly three-fourths of the Elliott will be one hundred years old or older—nearly a 50 percent increase from today—allowing for long-term studies on long-lived forests. The rapidly growing Elliott can sequester carbon faster than almost anywhere else in the Pacific Northwest, and perhaps in the world, researchers have found.[22] The forest contains more than forty million tons of carbon, according to a 2011 estimate by Ecotrust.[23]

The university plans to cut down 735 acres of the Elliott each year for the purpose of "research."[24] Harvests will happen in sixty-year rotations. But the industry wants OSU to log even more timber. Roseburg Forest Products, one of the largest timber companies in the state, has called for research into salvage logging after fires, and logging in riparian areas, each of which have been shown to cause negative environmental impacts. In a letter to a state agency, the company said:

> With an increasingly constrained timber supply in Oregon due to private, state, and federal forest decisions and regulations in combination with the dramatic 2020 wildfire season which will affect timber supply for decades, timber production from the ESF is more important than ever.[25]

Roseburg Forest Products was among the leading donors to the OSU College of Forestry's new Forest Sciences Complex, contributing $5 million toward the $79.5 million project.[26]

Some environmental leaders in Oregon argue that too much natural forest in the Coast Range has already been logged. Logging even 735 acres per year is too much, says Cristina Hubbard, head of the environmental group Forest Web in nearby Cottage Grove. Hubbard wants the university to protect the entire Elliott for the benefit of biodiversity and carbon sequestration. The university, she suggests, should not treat "this exceptional ecosystem as a harvestable commodity."

> In the face of climate change, the Elliott has greater value than as a site for logging and studying how to extract more commercial timber. Its true value to the environment is as a standing, contiguous forest, sequestering carbon.[27]

Ironically, the idea of protecting forests as a climate strategy is discouraged in the state of Washington. In 2020, Gov. Jay Inslee, who centered his presidential campaign that year on a platform of addressing the climate crisis, signed a timber industry-backed bill[28] formally defining logging as an authorized climate mitigation strategy, despite the strong scientific evidence cited in this book showing it is not. Jay Spadaro, president of the Washington Forest Protection Association, a trade group, argued before a House hearing that as they age, all forests someday will become net emitters of carbon, at best a misleading statement. This, he explained, is why we should cut them down without delay:[29]

> There are some that would have a carbon policy to avoid cutting of trees, extend rotations, grow trees forever and damage our manufacturing sector. We just cannot allow that to happen.

Washington's forests are among the most carbon-rich forests in the world, yet are not protected by the state government for the climate mitigation they would provide if allowed to continue growing. Apparently, Inslee's passion for solving the climate crisis goes only so far.

# Chapter 4

# The Playbook

As a young girl growing up in Minnesota, Beverly Law fed her fascination with nature on lengthy canoe expeditions into the sprawling Boundary Waters Wilderness near Lake Superior, a waterscape of a thousand lakes and tall, elegant, white pine forests. Every young explorer needs a guiding hand, a mentor, and Bev's grandpa, Reuben Walter Law, was hers. As deputy director of state parks in Minnesota, Grandpa Reuben knew his way around the wilderness.

> At age four, I remember him holding my hand and explaining in a way that a little kid could understand. He was a self-made naturalist. I learned bird calls from him, how to walk in the woods quietly so you could see more wildlife. I soaked it up.[1]

Young Bev wasn't interested in individual trees so much as the entire forest. "I've always been interested in the whole system and how everything relies on everything else," she explained. Bev Law would go on to a career as an ecologist, a career shaped by her adventures with grandpa. An ecologist is a scientist who explores the connections between living organisms and their physical environment. In the 1990s, after receiving her Ph.D. in forest science at Oregon State University, she took a position as professor of forest ecology at the university's College of Forestry. Since then, she has published more than

250 papers that peeked into the ecological connections that tie a forest together.

In 2020, sixty years after her first canoe trip with Grandpa Reuben, who lived to be 106, Bev officially retired from Oregon State. These days, she returns home to the boundary waters of northern Minnesota to paddle her canoe and zipline between the white pines. And yet, she still spends more time behind a computer than on a canoe. Her work is far from done.

Today, Professor Law's research focuses on the damage to the climate caused by common industrial forestry practices—a specialty that often draws her into conflicts with the timber industry and its friends in academia alike, though no one has ever found her work to be in error. But nothing approached the backlash she encountered in 2018 when she quantified the industry's impact on the climate.[2] In 2018, Law co-authored a paper showing, for the first time, how much carbon is emitted by logging in Oregon forests, and how decisions to delay or suspend logging could benefit the climate. Her paper appeared in the journal *Proceedings of the National Academy of Sciences*. Law found that logging in Oregon emits more than thirty-four million metric tons of carbon every year, a massive amount. "Even if it's just half that, it's still not good," she told us. Law's paper found that logging emits more carbon than any other sector in Oregon's economy. More than making cement, driving cars, or generating electricity.

Based on Law's data, the timber industry in Oregon emits more carbon each year than any coal plant in the world, except one: the Belchatów Power Station in Poland.[3] Belchatów's emissions are only 9 percent more than the Oregon timber industry's emissions. Law's groundbreaking paper received widespread acclaim within the climate science community. Most notably, in 2019, William Moomaw, the Tufts University professor, cited Law's paper multiple times in his landmark paper on proforestation, the climate strategy we discuss in Chapter 3. Law may have been the first scientist to come up with the idea of proforestation. During a 2017 talk given at a scientific conference in Washington, D.C., Law called this strategy "forestation." Moomaw later added the prefix pro. Law's paper applied the strategy only to Oregon forests. Moomaw extended it to forests worldwide.

Professor Law wasn't the first scientist to show that commercial tree plantations contain significantly less carbon than natural forests. A 1990 study led by OSU professor Mark Harmon found that it takes a plantation two hundred years before it can store as much carbon as an old-growth forest. After a hundred years, the young forest stores only half as much.[4] A 2017 study by the Oregon Coalition for a Sustainable Economy found that for the first 13 years after logging, the logged area is actually a net emitter of carbon.[5]

A tree stops sequestering carbon when a chainsaw tears through its trunk. Once a tree is cut down, between 35 to 45 percent of its carbon—the leaves, needles, bark, branches, snags, and roots—is left on the ground. From there, this material begins to decompose, the carbon returning to the atmosphere. In Southeast Alaska, the carbon emissions from logging are much greater. As many as 70 percent of all logs are left behind, culled by the loggers themselves due to imperfections they see in the wood.[6]

The machinery of logging is also a source of carbon emissions: chainsaws, yarders, bulldozers, graders, and log trucks. Equipment at the sawmill emits even more: lathes, bandsaws, stackers, and chip feeders. Finished wood products—plywood, construction beams, and toilet paper—contain a good amount of carbon, but they will decompose over varied lengths of time. Scientists found that 81 percent of a tree's total amount of carbon is returned to the air within a century.[7]

Law's research also demonstrates that protecting forests is the best carbon-capture technology available. She suggests doubling the number of years between harvests from the current forty years to eighty years, or even to one hundred twenty years, as well as reducing harvests on public lands by half. Doing these things, along with planting trees, she says, would increase the amount of carbon stored in Oregon's forests by at least 56 percent over the rest of the twenty-first century.

In an interview with us, Law explained that cutting down forests every forty years "is just insanity, especially with these forests which live so long." Longer rotations would increase the amount of carbon stored in dead wood and the soil, not just in the live trees.

> For the next hundred years, I would be reserving these big contiguous giant carbon banks. I would be preserving all of those now. They already have carbon they have been storing for hundreds to thousands of years. It only makes sense to keep it there.[8]

Jerry Franklin, a retired University of Washington professor and one of the nation's leading authorities on forest ecosystems, says the OSU professor makes a compelling case for protecting trees as part of our climate-mitigation strategies. "Allowing the forest to go longer between harvests is probably the most important single thing that we could do." The Pacific coastal temperate rainforest, Franklin says, has the potential to store more carbon than "probably any other forest in the world."

The timber companies do not agree with these ecologists. They claim that Oregon's forests sequester far more carbon than they emit. They also claim that Oregon's thirty million acres of forests capture more than half of Oregon's human-caused carbon emissions. No one disputes that, but Law's point is that the forests could easily sequester far more carbon than they do now. Industrial logging is crippling the forest's potential to mitigate climate change, she says. Restoring forests to a natural condition would expand the carbon sink substantially.

The Oregon Forest and Industry Council (OFIC), a trade group based in Salem, is Law's most outspoken critic. OFIC claims young trees are better suited to be carbon sinks than old trees. Its solution to global warming? Cut the old trees down:

> Trees absorb a lot of carbon at a young age as they grow, but at a certain point in their growth cycle, they max out their carbon storage potential. At that point they plateau for a time and then emit carbon as they decompose or burn. The good news is an alternative fate exists for that carbon: storage in wood products. It is, in fact, the sustainable cycle of harvesting and replanting trees that maintains Oregon's forest carbon sink.[9]

Common sense and a number of studies poke sizable holes in these industry talking points. For one thing, a study cited in Chapter 3 found that trees continue sequestering carbon so long as they stay alive.[10] Another study found that that natural forests are forty times better than plantations at storing carbon.[11] A third study found that protecting the Pacific coastal temperate rainforest from logging could increase the amount of carbon it sequesters by 75 to 138 percent.[12] Then there's common sense, which tells us wood products—lumber, toilet paper, and plywood—will never sequester any additional carbon. When the tree dies, that's it. It's dead.

In the end, the industry could not disprove Law's science. So, it resorted to personal attacks.

The attacks came mostly from Oregon Forest and Industry Council, the trade group. OFIC represents forty-five large and small timber companies, including international brand names like Weyerhaeuser, Boise Cascade, and Georgia-Pacific as well as a number of smaller outfits.

A blog post on the OFIC website challenged Law's calculations as "unrealistic at best."[13] The post claimed Law "completely ignored the fact that the forest sector replants its forests after harvest." But in fact Law's paper mentions reforestation, which means the same thing as replanting, a total of fourteen times. We counted.

"Though the underlying data are not wrong," the post continued, "the researchers manipulate those data in a manner clearly designed to produce a contrived outcome." OFIC didn't explain how Law manipulated the data, or show why the outcome was contrived. It also asserted that her assumptions were "entirely untethered from reality," without detailing which of her assumptions needed tethering. What's more, in a move to "cancel" the professor, OFIC encouraged other experts to ignore Law's peer-reviewed paper. OFIC flatly insisted that Law's paper is "unusable in carbon policy conversations in Oregon." Not that everyone is ignoring Law's research. Moomaw, the Nobel Laureate, often cited Law's research several times in his proforestation paper. The Oregon Global Climate Commission, a state agency, cited Law's paper a total of thirty-six times in a major 2019 report on forest carbon.[15] Angus Duncan, the commission's executive director, explained that Law's paper had credibility because it was peer-reviewed.

OFIC rounded up other timber industry insiders to lambast the OSU ecologist. One of them, David Atkins, president of *Treesource*, an industry-friendly magazine based in Montana, wrote an article accusing Law of ignoring many stages of the wood production process, including material and energy substitution.[16] However, he did not explain why incorporating this information would have improved her analysis.

Atkins also claimed the timber industry could double the amount of carbon a forest sequesters without curbing logging. He cited a 2017 policy paper by the European Union, entitled "Climate Smart Forestry." But this paper didn't support his point of view. It called for tripling the amount of forestland strictly protected from logging, a strategy aligning with Law's recommendations but contradict the timber industry's talking points.

To climate advocates, Climate Smart Forestry aligns neatly with Law's prescriptions. For example, Ecotrust, the Portland-based conservation group, says Climate Smart Forestry calls for longer harvest rotations, smaller clear-cuts, and stronger protections for biodiversity.[17] Law laughed off the criticism. She's heard it all before.

> Boy, those guys were just livid. What they are trying to do is create misinformation, so they hired people to punch holes in our paper and are trying to be louder than us. They want to control the conversation. If the timber industry hates it, it means it was really good work. When you are out front, you get chopped down. I've got a bullseye on my head.[18]

We asked Sara Duncan, a spokesperson for OFIC, to explain the rationale behind the personal attacks launched against the ecology professor. "We were insulted," she said.

This wasn't the first time Professor Law got in hot water for producing data the timber industry did not like. In 2006, the peer-reviewed journal *Science* published one of Law's studies that questioned the industry's long standing practice of salvaging burnt timber after a wildfire.[19] The paper, co-written by one of her graduate students, Dan Donato, examined areas burned by the 2002 Biscuit Fire, the worst forest fire in Oregon history. The paper is often referred to as "the Donato Study."

The Donato Study concluded that logging after wildfire kills natural regeneration and increases future fire risk. A forest will regrow more quickly after a wildfire if allowed to regenerate naturally. The timber industry and its allies in academia were not happy, to say the least.

Nine professors at the OSU College of Forestry wrote a letter to the editors of *Science* magazine seeking to block the study's publication, dismissing it as unsupported speculation.[20] "We argue that their paper lacks adequate context and supporting information to be clearly interpreted by scientists, resource managers, policy-makers, and the public," they wrote. One of the nine professors was Mike Newton, who made headlines in the 1970s for his unauthorized experiments with Agent Orange, the notorious military-grade defoliant, in Coast Range forests, as we report in Chapter 7. But the editors at *Science* refused to censor the Donato study. Eventually the university praised the study and scolded its critics, according to the Washington *Post*, which noted that the OSU College of Forestry gets 10 percent of its funding from the timber industry.[21] As Law told us,

> We had people in the college who wanted to keep us from publishing because it turned out some were getting kickbacks. Some were getting paid to come up with really crude estimates of how much wood could be pulled out of the Biscuit fire area. It became a real insidious thing that made news internationally about just how crooked it was.[22]

*Evergreen Magazine*, the aforementioned publication that promotes the industry's point of view, called the Donato paper "shoddy and misdirected work," orchestrated from "the shadows" by scientists with anti-forestry biases.[23] But today, with sixteen years' hindsight, the paper's recommendations have more than held up to scrutiny, and have been confirmed by multiple studies. The Forest Service no longer prescribes salvage logging in national forests after a fire, with exceptions only to protect the public from hazardous or unsafe conditions.

In 2006, the Oregon Legislature investigated the industry's allegations against professor Law. James Karr, a retired professor of forest ecology at the University of Washington, testified that Law's article got it right. In an interview, Karr explained that salvage logging "is not an ecosystem restoration tool." Rather, he said, "post-fire logging damages forests and associated streams and impedes the natural processes normal to post-disturbance situations."

Karr said the industry's reaction to the paper followed a familiar pattern: ignore, overlook, and distort the science. Karr told the Legislature that the "unprofessional response" from Law's colleagues at Oregon State "illustrates that this problem also exists within the halls of academia." Nowadays, the industry claims that wildfires are a major source of carbon emissions. But in her landmark 2018 paper, Law found that is not true. "In fact," she says, "fires are a relatively small carbon source."

Environmentalists have learned to doubt anything the timber industry says. The timber industry, once dominated by large corporations like Weyerhaeuser and International Paper, today consists largely of an assortment of limited liability corporations, real estate investment trusts, and timber industry management organizations.

In 2020, an analysis by the Coast Range Association, an environmental group based in Corvallis, found that Wall Street investors control pretty much everything that happens in Oregon's forests.[24] Their interest is to make money, not protect biodiversity or the climate, Chuck Willer, the group's director, told us. "An investor with $20 million wants to see his or her money grow and provide an annual or final return," Willer said. "Investors expect their money to grow at a compound rate." Strategies friendly to biodiversity and the climate, such as delaying or suspending timber harvests, run counter to an investor's "ballooning money fantasy," he said.

A 2021 investigation by *The Oregonian*, Oregon Public Radio and ProPublica found that Wall Street real estate trusts and investment funds began gaining control over the state's private forestlands in the 1990s. "They profited at the expense of rural communities by logging more aggressively with fewer environmental protections than in neighboring states, while reaping the benefits of timber tax cuts that have cost counties at least $3 billion in the past three decades," their report said.[25]

It's not unusual to see industry groups like the Oregon Forests and Industry Council (OFIC) try to derail the work of scientists by casting doubt. "That is their job," says Mark Harmon, the OSU professor. "Creating doubts rather than advancing understanding." The timber industry is following the footsteps of industries like Big Tobacco and Big Oil, which have long histories of creating doubt by spreading misinformation, lies, and propaganda, as climate scientist Naomi Oreskes and Erik Conway write in their book *Merchants of Doubt*:

> There is deep irony here. One of the great heroes of the anti-communist political right wing—indeed one of the clearest, most reasoned voices against the risks of oppressive government, in general—was George Orwell, whose famous book *1984* portrayed a government that manufactured fake histories to support its political program. Orwell coined the term "memory hole" to denote a system that destroyed inconvenient facts, and "Newspeak" for a language designed to constrain thought within politically acceptable bounds.[26]

Creating doubt as a business strategy was deployed by the tobacco industry in the 1950s, when it established the Tobacco Institute to challenge scientific data linking cigarettes to lung cancer. You know how that went. By casting doubt on the science, the tobacco industry was able to delay any accountability for its deadly products for four decades. Millions of people died. The fossil fuel industry refined the strategy in the 1980s with the creation of the Heartland Institute. As a result, billions of people are likely to die.

On Heartland's website, you will find such canards as *There is no scientific consensus on the human role in climate change. Global warming is not a crisis. The threat is exaggerated. There is no need to reduce carbon dioxide emissions.*[27] The fossil fuel industry has never been held to account for these and other deceptions, let alone for the death and destruction they caused. Today, the fossil fuel industry no longer denies the reality of climate change, but instead simply claims its business-as-usual way of operating is a solution to the climate crisis. We call this "greenwashing."

Since the 1990s, Oregon's timber industry has been working from the same playbook. With funding from the Oregon legislature, the industry created its own (mis)informaton service the Oregon Forest Resources Institute (OFRI). OFRI shares much of its mission and leadership with the Oregon Forest and Industries Council (OFIC), the trade group that targeted Bev Law. Five members of OFRI's board of directors are leaders of companies that are members of OFIC. OFRI is controlled by a thirteen-member board of directors, ten of whom by law must own timberland or work for a forest products company. None can work for an environmental advocacy organization.

OFRI says its job is disseminating "objective information about responsible forest management." On its website,[28] the organization claims that the timber industry in Oregon plants 40 million saplings every year, three for every tree cut down. OFRI claims this carbon "continues to be sequestered even after a tree is harvested and manufactured into wood products." But it does not tell you that few if any of these new trees will be allowed to live beyond their fortieth birthday, and will never contain more than a small amount of carbon. It fails to mention that nearly half the tree's carbon is emitted before manufacturing even begins. And there's no mention of the fact that the carbon in wood products will eventually return to the air. A piece of plywood will sequester no additional carbon. But trees will continue sequestering carbon so long as they live which can exceed one thousand years or more. OFRI believes cutting down trees is an effective climate-mitigation strategy, according to one of its fact sheets:

> When a tree is harvested and made into a house, cabinetry or furniture, the wood continues to store the carbon that the tree had sequestered. So the carbon continues to be kept from the atmosphere.

The OFRI website says nothing about proforestation. So, curious to hear its perspective, we sent an email to Mike Cloughesy, OFRI's chief forester, to ask him what he thought. He failed to respond.

# PART 2

## OREGON

*They took all the trees*
*Put 'em in a tree museum*
*And they charged the people*
*A dollar and a half just to see 'em*
                              *—Joni Mitchell*

# Chapter 5

# The Siuslaw Liquidation

As any forest advocate will tell you, to save a forest, you have to work at it every day. But to liquidate a forest, you only have to do it once. Consider what happened between 1960 and 1990 in the Siuslaw National Forest in Oregon's Coast Range mountains. In the span of those three decades, the timber industry liquidated several hundred thousand acres of old-growth forest on the Siuslaw, possibly the most productive forest on Earth. Almost every square inch of the forest was clear-cut, the appalling but highly profitable system of removing nearly every tree in sight, all at once.

The Siuslaw liquidation was much more just the timber industry's vision for how to manage forests on the Pacific Coast. It was integral to its business plan. The liquidation was also authorized by Congress, thanks in large part to heavy lobbying by the timber industry. It was the law.

The liquidation of an old-growth forest is not complete until a tree farm is planted in its place. The timber industry calls tree farms "forests." Tree farms are a source of valuable wood products, but they do not have the natural qualities of a true forest. They have more in common with cornfields. Ecologists define the act of converting a natural forest into an agricultural crop as "deforestation."

▸

In all, the liquidation spree removed at least two gigatons of carbon stored in the temperate rainforest from Northern California to Southeast Alaska, and probably much more.[1]

The deforestation also overwhelmed a rich biodiversity, driving many species toward extinction. It severely polluted once-pristine mountain streams and crushed their formerly abundant salmon runs. Today, the Oregon Biodiversity Information Center lists 122 birds, fish, mammals, reptiles, and amphibians and 158 vascular plants in the Coast Range as potentially or actively threatened with destruction.[2] Local populations of some species, such as Chinook salmon in the Siuslaw and Coos Rivers, have been extinguished.[3]

The deforestation could have been worse. In his 1990 book *Ancient Forests in the Pacific Northwest*, conservation biologist Elliott Norse predicted all old growth on federal forests in Oregon and Washington would be eliminated by 2023, an ecological disaster he compared to the deforestation of the Amazon:

> The destruction of ancient forests is not confined to desperately poor tropical countries. Precisely the same thing is happening to the ancient forests of our own lush, green Pacific Northwest.[4]

The deforestation finally ended, for the most part, in the mid-1990s when federal courts ordered it to stop. By then, up to 80 percent of the old growth was gone.[5]

This is the story about how the rainforest has been crippled by industrial forestry, with impacts felt around the world far into the future—not just locally—as ecologist Chris Maser wrote in *Clearcut: The Tragedy of Industrial Forestry*.

As we liquidate the natural forests, we are redesigning the forests of the future. In fact, we are redesigning the entire world, and we are throwing away nature's blueprint.[6]

In the dead of winter in 1991, Jim Furnish, a lanky, forty-six-year-old Texan, arrived at the headquarters of the Siuslaw National Forest in Corvallis, freshly appointed as the national forest's new supervisor, its chief executive officer. He landed in the middle of a bitter confrontation between environmentalists and the timber industry over the fate of the forest.

For Furnish, this was familiar territory. In his previous job, he evaluated citizen appeals of timber sales across the country. Working at Forest Service headquarters in Washington, D.C., he heard firsthand the public's deep, pervasive complaints about clear-cutting and the loss of old-growth forests. Dissent was streaming in from every part of the country, he told us in an interview:

> The public was profoundly distressed with how the U.S. Forest Service managed public forests. I came to an inherent realization that the Forest Service was doing it wrong. It adopted an industrial mindset about how national forests should be managed.[7]

It took Furnish only a couple days to figure out what the Siuslaw's previous management team planned to do with the remaining old-growth trees. In the files, he found a fifty-year timetable for liquidating them all, a blueprint for ecological destruction Maser warned about. Liquidating old-growth forests was the policy of the Forest Service, driven from the top. His predecessors at the Siuslaw had drawn up a plan for a final battle against nature, and now Furnish owned it. He was profoundly distressed. He wanted to play no part in the forest's final destruction.

The 630,000-acre Siuslaw National Forest straddles the middle section of Oregon's Coast Range, a mountain chain of steep canyons, heavy rainfall, and modest elevations stretching from the Columbia River to Coos County. The high point is the 4,000-foot Mary's Peak near Corvallis, not far from Furnish's new office. From there, you can see the Pacific Ocean to the west and ten snow-capped volcanoes in the Cascade Mountains in both Oregon and Washington, to the east: Rainier, St. Helens, Adams, Hood, Jefferson, the Three Sisters, Bachelor, and Diamond Peak.

The university's College of Forestry was a hub for research on forest ecosystems and wildlife, featuring the noted ecologists Jerry Franklin and Norm Johnson and many others. Until the mid-1990s, however, they were not the most influential researchers at the college. The influential ones were friendly to the timber industry. Franklin and Johnson were often shunned by their peers, both in academia and in government.

Starting with his first day on the job, Furnish confronted a "timber-driven ideology" which left little room for ecology. Furnish assumed the Siuslaw's foresters would be looking to the ecologists at the university for guidance. Instead, the ecologists "were largely ignored and treated with contempt."

"They were seen as a nuisance and treated as such," he said. "As I started looking at their research, it started making a lot of sense to me." The influence of Franklin and Johnson, however, soon began to rise. Their message, which redefined forestry to include more than just logging, also found popular appeal among the public. A forester must consider the needs of the ecosystem, Franklin and Johnson argued, not just the needs of timber companies. Traditional foresters felt threatened by the young guys, who now had a powerful ally: President Bill Clinton. Clinton's forest-policy advisors decided the rate of logging harvest on national forests in the region must come down dramatically. It was the only way to give endangered species like the northern spotted owl and marbled murrelet a fighting chance.

But Franklin and Johnson also thought a healthy, fully functioning ecosystem could support the well-being of human communities. Some trees could be logged, but not trees in riparian areas, where they are needed to cast a cooling shade over streams to the benefit of salmon. They also recommended placing woody debris in streams, also for salmon. And they also called for leaving dead trees, or snags, in place because of their importance to birds and other wildlife.

At first, most members of Furnish's staff at the Siuslaw's headquarters were not interested in hearing these new ideas about forestry, Furnish writes in his memoir. "We're really not into that," one member of his staff told him. "This is the Siuslaw. We clear-cut here." The Siuslaw Timber Operators Association, a local industry group aligned with the old-school foresters, made sure the gravy train continued, Furnish told us:

> They were effective at getting the Forest Service to keep the timber pipeline full. As long as the Forest Service kept pumping out timber sales, the industry kept pretty quiet.[8]

Things began to change in the 1970s in the wake of severe windstorms that triggered landslides on the Siuslaw's denuded steep mountain slopes. The landslides clogged the streams below, wiping out salmon. Environmental groups sued to block timber sales contributing to the landslides, and won. Logging on steep slopes is no longer allowed on the Siuslaw. It was the first of several court victories that ultimately halted the liquidation.

The Coast Range was never fully carpeted by old-growth trees. Wildfires saw to that. The severe wildfires of today, though horrifying, were common before White settlers arrived in the mid-nineteenth century. Forest fires were an intrinsic part of the natural cycle and only became a threat to human life after people built towns in the heart of the forest.

From 1850 to 1950, one wildfire after another raged through the Coast Range. The greatest fire year was probably 1853, when the Yaquina Burn scorched 500,000 acres (781 square miles) between Eugene and Florence. The nearby Nestucca Burn torched another 350,000 acres. In 1893, President Grover Cleveland signed an executive order that placed many of these burned areas under federal control, creating the Cascade Forest Reserve spanning the Oregon Cascades as well as parts of the Coast Range. In 1907, Congress included these lands within the newly created Siuslaw National Forest, named after a local Indian tribe. This new national forest excluded Tillamook County where four large wildfires burned 350,000 acres from 1933 to 1951, famously known as the Tillamook Burn. In reburned areas, heavy salvage logging contributed to the fire's intensity. For decades afterward, classes of schoolchildren from all over Oregon were bused to help with the replanting.[9]

During the first half of the twentieth century, timber companies were discouraged by the Siuslaw National Forest's rugged terrain and charred landscapes. There were plenty of other easily accessible forests to cut down, as Jim Furnish writes in his memoirs, *Toward a Natural Forest*:

> The Siuslaw held little allure for investors looking for commercial timberland. They passed by the steep forbidding country with its young, dense forests. Better lands lay elsewhere. So, it was left to grow, and in time a great forest emerged.[10]

During World War I, the U.S. military set up shop on Oregon's central coast, clearing out Sitka spruce forests in the tidelands to make warplanes, an enterprise that continued through World War II. In the 1950s, a nationwide boom in home construction took off, initiating renewed interest in the towering stands of Douglas-fir that covered the Siuslaw National Forest's interior valleys, foothills and mountains. The industry deployed modernized logging techniques to extract timber from the rugged canyons, and built a network of roads to transport them to the mills. Before roads, they floated logs down rivers. Our analysis of Forest Service data shows that during the 1980s, loggers cut down more than twice as much timber per acre from the Siuslaw as they did throughout the rest of national forests in Oregon and Washington.[11]

Nothing protects wildlife better than wilderness. No national forest in the Pacific Northwest protects a smaller percentage of its land base as wilderness than the Siuslaw National Forest. Of course, creating wilderness would have interfered with the timber industry's profits.

When Congress passed the Wilderness Act in 1964, it designated more than nine million acres in the United States as wilderness, but none in the Siuslaw. The Siuslaw had no wilderness areas until 1984, when Congress designated 22,000 acres near the coast in the tiny Rock Creek, Drift Creek, and Cummins Creek watersheds. These areas are too small or close to roads to offer primitive backcountry experiences. Neither the Cummins nor Rock Creek forests had any hiking trails at the time of designation. That isn't to say they weren't worth protecting. For instance, Cummins Creek is adjacent to the Cape Perpetua State Park, a thousand-acre gem near the shore where salmon spawn in an ancient forest dominated by Sitka spruce, western hemlock, and Douglas-fir. "We call those pocket wildernesses," says Paul Engelmeyer, who manages natural areas for the Audubon Society and the Wetlands Conservancy near Yachats on the central coast.[121]

In 2019, Congress created another pocket wilderness, the 30,000-acre Devil's Staircase, in the southern part of the Siuslaw forest. Long ago, a number of sizable wilderness areas could have been created on the Siuslaw, Engelmeyer told us, but those areas were logged. The largest natural area on the Siuslaw is Oregon Dunes National Recreation Area, a rare expanse of temperate coastal sand dunes. The dunes are best known for the motorized dune buggies available for rent. People don't go there for a wilderness experience.

The dunes provide important habitat for the endangered western snowy plover, a tiny shore bird. Of the twenty-eight snowy plover nesting sites on the West Coast, five occur on the Siuslaw National Forest and the Oregon Dunes National Recreation Area.

Congress has always been reluctant to set aside areas for wilderness in Oregon. There is twice as much wilderness in Washington and California as in Oregon. For instance, Washington's Olympic National Forest, which is about the same size as the Siuslaw, protects 50 percent more land as wilderness, not counting the million-acre Olympic National Park.

A year after Furnish arrived at the Siuslaw National Forest, the Forest Service hired Martha Ketelle to run the Six Rivers National Forest in Northern California. Ketelle was an outspoken wilderness advocate. She replaced an old-school forester named Jim Davis who saw his job as extracting the maximum amount of timber. Ketelle wanted to change things. Soon after she took the job, she made sure the timber harvest on the Six Rivers plummeted. Davis was devastated. But the quality of wildlife habitat soared. Today, the Six Rivers National Forest contains five times as much wilderness as the Siuslaw.

"It would be fair to say I wasn't a forester," Ketelle told us. Raised as a hiker and camper, she always thought forests have more to offer than just sawlogs. "The only way to protect anything on a national forest from timber harvest was to put a boundary around it and call it a wilderness."[13]

In the 1980s, three square miles of old-growth forests in Oregon were clear-cut every day, enraging environmental activists across the country. The Sierra Club Legal Defense Fund (now Earthjustice) led the fight to stop the slaughter in the courts. Other groups, such as Earth First!, took to the woods to confront the logging companies directly, often clashing with the police while attracting the news media's attention.

The Earth First! Motto—"No Compromise in Defense of Mother Earth"—struck a chord with the public, Mike Roselle, a founder of Earth First!, told us in an interview.[14] Although

Earth First! occasionally filed lawsuits, Roselle favored actions that attracted television cameras: blockading roads, chaining arms and legs to logging equipment, sitting in trees while chainsaws roared below. Roselle thought the war in the woods needed to be won in the court of public opinion, not just in the courtroom. He became an expert at playing the news media.

An early example of civil disobedience in the woods occurred on April 27, 1983, in Southwest Oregon, as the late journalist Kathie Durbin (an esteemed former colleague) recounts in her book *Tree Huggers: Victory, Defeat and Renewal in the Northwest Ancient Forest Campaign*.[15] Roselle and three other activists, Kevin Everhart, Steve Marsden, and Pedro Tama, blocked a logging road at the edge of the Kalmiopsis Wilderness in the Siskiyou Mountains southwest of Grants Pass. They draped an Earth First! banner across the face of the bulldozer that was punching a logging road into the side of a mountain. The Bald Mountain Road would have given loggers access to a one-million-acre block of uncut forest north of the Kalmiopsis. They didn't seem to care that it was the most botanically diverse conifer ecosystem in all of North America, Durbin wrote.

But Earth First! leaders were also aware that the battle in court would ultimately decide the fate of these forests. They joined groups like the Sierra Club, the Audubon Society, and the Oregon Natural Resources Council (now Oregon Wild) in lawsuits against the U.S. Forest Service and U.S. Bureau of Land Management (BLM) for widespread violations of environmental laws. Their strategy was to label the northern spotted owl, an endangered species, as the victim. As one activist said, "If the spotted didn't exist, we would have had to invent it."[16]

Distinguished by the whitish spots on its head and neck, the secretive spotted owl has one major weakness: it lives only in old-growth and very mature forests. This vulnerability gave the owl special status as the "indicator species" of the old-growth ecosystem. As the forest disappeared, so did the owl. By its actions, the Forest Service didn't seem to care what it was doing to biodiversity. It was creating jobs. It claimed to set aside 13,000 acres of "prime older forest" in the Siuslaw National Forest as spotted owl habitat, but, in reality, almost all of this habitat would be logged in fifty years. At the time, the spotted owl did not yet enjoy legal protection under the Endangered Species Act. The Forest Service thought cutting down its habitat was legal, no matter how many owls were displaced or destroyed. Environmental groups disagreed. Lawsuits began to fly.

The groups petitioned the U.S. Fish and Wildlife Service to designate the spotted owl as an endangered species, reasoning that destroying an endangered species' habitat is the same as killing the critter itself. They cited the fifty-year liquidation plans as evidence that the Forest Service was intentionally killing off the spotted owl. They won, forcing the government to add the owl to the endangered species list in 1989. But the lawsuit didn't stop the government from logging the owl's old-growth habitat. So environmentalists filed suit once more.

Finally, in 1991, their litigation came before William Dwyer, a federal judge in Seattle. Dwyer issued a ruling that settled nearly everything in the environmentalists' favor. After uncovering a "remarkable series of violations of the environmental laws," the judge issued a sweeping injunction stopping the liquidation of old-growth forests throughout Washington, Oregon, and Northern California.[17] The Dwyer ruling protected a wide range of biodiversity, not just the owl.

At the time, no one predicted the Dwyer ruling would also benefit the climate, but that is what it is doing. Suddenly, every timber sale that interfered with biodiversity ground to a halt. Timber sales could resume only once the government adopted a scientifically valid plan to prevent extinctions. The timber industry accused Judge Dwyer of unfairly favoring owls over jobs, arguing the injunction "endangered" the survival of the American logger. President George H.W. Bush mused that unemployed loggers would soon be up to their necks in owls. But claims that the environmental litigation harmed jobs were overblown. In 1999, an Oregon State University study found that protecting the spotted owl had "no significant effect on employment.[18] The study noted the industry's greatest decline in timber employment occurred during the 1950s, when a third of Oregon's large sawmills and 85 percent of the small ones closed—long before anyone ever heard of the spotted owl.

Dr. John Osborn, a forest activist from Spokane, said at the time the industry would run out of old-growth forests. "The timber industry is not up against the spotted owl," he said. "They're up against the Pacific Ocean." On April 2, 1993, President Clinton and Vice President Al Gore convened the "Northwest Forest Summit," an extraordinary public conference in Portland, Oregon, to address the human and ecological needs served by federal forests in the region. In the conference's aftermath, the administration commissioned more than six hundred scientists and technicians to develop a scientifically based plan that would protect the spotted owl and over one thousand other species associated with late-successional and old-growth habitat. The effort to develop a new way to manage Northwest forests was led by two familiar faces: Jerry Franklin, now a forestry professor at the University of Washington, and Norm Johnson, still a professor of forest management at Oregon State. They believed industrial-scale logging must give way to a new approach they called "ecosystem management."

These, of course, were the same scientists laughed at by Siuslaw National Forest foresters. Now they were setting forest policy for the entire region. Though most of their plan was based on untested theories, it became official Forest Service policy, Furnish told us. Predictably, their approach did not sit well with the old-time foresters:

> Most of my peer forest supervisors and managers resented this, even if only subconsciously. They very slowly came around. It was a very begrudging act on their part. The foot-dragging was unbelievable. Part of it was incompetence, but it was also full-on obstruction.

The Northwest Forest Plan, which went into effect in 1994, was the first attempt to manage an ecosystem over a broad region under a single set of scientific principles. The plan reduced overall logging levels by 80 percent in an effort to protect one thousand species associated with the region's old-growth forests. After its adoption, logging of mature and old-growth forests on federal lands fell by two-thirds.[19] Originally conceived as a solution to a biodiversity crisis, the Northwest Forest Plan is now sequestering massive amounts of carbon, an ally in the battle to save the climate. The Northwest Forest Plan is considered a global model for ecosystem management and biodiversity conservation,[20] and is now a big laboratory for research on the climate-mitigation strategy known as proforestation.

Today after a quarter century, the Northwest Forest Plan is still in effect, though the Republican administrations of George W. Bush and Donald Trump repeatedly tried to weaken the plan. In January 2021, the Trump administration, during its last week in office, gutted the plan altogether, reopening three million acres of old-growth forest to logging.[21] But a few months later, Joe Biden, Trump's successor, restored the plan.[22] For now, peace reigns in the woods.

# Chapter 6

# "Looters of the Public Domain"

In April 2020, the world is in lockdown as the coronavirus pandemic rages on. But in the foothills at the south end of Oregon's Coast Range mountains, resource extraction is going full speed ahead. On Kenyon Mountain in eastern Coos County, about fifty miles from the Pacific Ocean, a crew of loggers is chopping down fifty-one acres of old-growth and mature trees. Some of these trees have been alive since George Washington was president, based on a count of rings on the stump. Maps say the closest town is the aptly named Remote, Oregon, a town so small it's no longer mentioned in U.S. census counts, yet newsy enough to merit a profile not long ago in the *New York Times*.[1]

At first glance, Remote amounts to little more than a dilapidated gas station, a country store and a post office. But not far from town, a historic covered bridge crosses a small tributary of the Coquille River. A little further away, the tallest Douglas-fir on Earth—329-foot-tall Brummitt Fir— stands beside a popular hiking trail.

On Kenyon Mountain, a modest ridge about ten miles north of Remote, the loggers are clear-cutting a stand of old-growth trees mixed with younger ones. The loggers are not alone. Two environmental activists, Gabe Scott and Francis Eatherington, are hot on their trail, hoping to document the liquidation of some of the last old-growth trees in the entire

Coast Range. They are gathering evidence to feed into potential legal challenges to the clear-cutting as well as to drum up public support for their cause, which is to protect ancient forests. When Scott, an attorney for the environmental group Cascadia Wildlands, and Eatherington, a resident of nearby Roseburg, reached the summit, they found only a field of freshly severed stumps.

Kenyon Mountain is located near the juncture of two ancient geological formations: the Coast Range to the north, which emerged about sixty million years ago during the Paleocene age; and the Klamath-Siskiyou Mountains to the south and east, which originated 400 million years ago in the Jurassic period. Scott's camera captures a massive stump alongside a dirt logging road. "It's old growth," Scott says. "There are more than 200 rings on this one stump." One ring for each year. Scott estimates the tree measured about forty feet around at its base. Trees of this size and age easily qualify as old growth, by anyone's standard.

"There were definitely some trees over 200 years old," Eatherington says. "The majority of the stand was closer to eighty to ninety years. It all got whacked." An eighty-year-old Douglas-fir is a maturing tree, busily inhaling a good amount of carbon dioxide, but won't become old growth for another one hundred years.Eatherington, a veteran of the Northwest timber wars of the 1990s, is accustomed to clear cuts like this. She lives about twenty miles up State Highway 42 at the edge of the 210,000-acre Millicoma Tree Farm owned by Weyerhaeuser. Weyerhaeuser logs each section of the tree farm every forty years, and then sprays the bare ground with chemicals. It's not unusual for Eartherington to begin her day with a fresh whiff of a chemical herbicide.

Over the last 150 years, industrial logging wiped out almost all old-growth forests in the Coast Range that weren't obliterated by fire, like the few scattered patches of old ones on Kenyon Mountain. We asked Sara Duncan of the Oregon Forest and Industry Council, a timber industry trade group, why the timber industry is still cutting down old-growth forests, and drew a sharp rebuke.

"The industry does not target old growth in any way," she told us. To say otherwise, she insisted, "is completely false, and frankly, offensive." But the photographs taken by Scott and Eartherington don't just say otherwise, they shout it out loud. The U.S. Bureau of Land Management (BLM) calls logging the old forests on Kenyon Mountain "regenerative harvests," possibly to avoid drawing too much attention to the carnage.

What does that term mean? we asked Gabe Scott. "Regenerative harvest is just a clear-cut by a different name. It sounds greener," Scott told us. The freshly cut logs will be trucked east to sawmills near Eugene, Cottage Grove, and Roseburg. Soon, the BLM will spray the denuded Kenyon Mountain landscape with herbicides, killing what remains of the understory, and plant a tree farm.

Kenyon Mountain's old-growth forest sits among some 2.1 million acres of timberland under BLM control, all in Oregon between the Cascade Mountains and the Pacific Ocean. Sometimes called the Bureau of Livestock and Mining, BLM's main job is to manage cows and prospectors on 245 million acres of federal land in the arid West and Alaska. But in Oregon, the BLM is also a mini-version of the U.S. Forest Service.

Ever since White settlers arrived in Oregon in the mid-nineteenth century, the ancient coastal forests in Oregon have been targeted by settlers, swindlers, grifters, fraudsters, and now the timber industry. Originally, the forestland was stolen from Indigenous people who were brutalized in a horrific genocide, the darkest period in Oregon history, as we chronicle in Chapter 11. To say the least, these forests have "a sordid past," as Michael Blumm, a law professor in Portland's Lewis & Clark College, explained to us.

Since Oregon's statehood in 1859, these forests have been pawns in various illegal land fraud schemes that yielded a thousand indictments for crimes like bribery and blackmail, as well as hundreds of convictions. This culture of grift extended all the way to the upper echelons of the state and federal governments, as an investigation launched by President Teddy Roosevelt in 1902 found. The investigation ensnared several federal officials whose job was to manage these forests, as well as two sitting U.S. senators, two members of the U.S. House, several members of the Oregon Senate, numerous city and county officials, bankers, attorneys, lumber dealers, hotel owners, real estate agents, and stockbrokers. But the criminal activity did not occur only in the woods. One investigation uncovered an unrelated embezzlement scheme involving an Oregon governor and three secretaries of state. The embezzlement continued undetected for a decade, according to an account in *The Morning Oregonian* newspaper. "Graft is Charged Against Governor," a headline proclaimed.[2] A total of $400,000 was reportedly stolen, an amount worth $12 million in today's dollars. Only one person was ever convicted of the crime—Oregon Secretary of State Frank L. Dunbar. But Dunbar's conviction was later thrown out by the Oregon Supreme Court. The governor, George Chamberlain, was never formally indicted, despite the headline. Later, Chamberlain served two terms in the U.S. Senate.

But whatever crimes were going on in the governor's office were small potatoes compared to the crimes taking place in the forests. The land frauds began after Congress granted vast acreages to railroads in the 1860s as a way to populate the American West. The lands included the 2.1 million acres of forest now controlled by the BLM. Originally, the Oregon and California Railroad (O&C) received this land as compensation for laying tracks for a line running from Portland to the California border. The acreage thus became known as the "O&C Lands." Most O&C lands are located on the south coast, abutting the Siuslaw and Rogue River national forests, extending all the way to California.

The law required railroads to sell the land only to "bona fide and actual" settlers in parcels no larger than 160 acres, and at a price of no more than $2.50 per acre. But the railroads and other grifters found ways around these limitations, enriching themselves and anyone they could bribe. Congress established the General Lands Office (GLO) to supervise the land sales, but someone should have been watching the GLO. In the 1940s, Congress merged the GLO with the U.S. Grazing Service to create the BLM.

By 1888, the O&C's successor, the Southern Pacific (SP) railroad company, had sold about a quarter of its land for an excessive amount. The SP was able to get up to $40 for each acre, or sixteen times the legal limit. In 1902, the Roosevelt administration received a tip about an alleged California-based land fraud ring involving these same lands and sent the GLO in to investigate, but was not aware that the GLO's hands were dirty. Some of the fraudulent schemes involved Binger Hermann, the Commissioner of the GLO. Hermann tried to cover up his crimes by destroying a number of key documents related to the scheme, according to Blumm, who has written several law review articles about the fraud.[3]

Hermann's trial in San Francisco was interrupted by the 1906 earthquake and failed to yield a conviction. Nor did the scandal tarnish Herrman's reputation among fellow Oregonians. He served six terms in Congress before joining the GLO in 1897, and was elected twice more afterward.

"Land fraud scandals infiltrated all levels of Oregon government and business," Blumm wrote in a 2013 law review article.[4] The scandals may have even influenced the outcome of the 1912 presidential election, Blumm says, by helping put Woodrow Wilson in the White House.

The most thorough account of the land fraud scandals comes to us from what seems like a less-than-reputable source. Stephen A. D. Puter, the self-described "king of the land fraud ring," was the government's key witness and lead suspect in many land fraud trials. Puter wrote about the trials and his corrupt dealings with prominent politicians in his 1908 memoir, *Looters of the Public Domain*,[5] where he admits to committing numerous felonies. Writing from the "dismal recesses of a prison cell," Puter provided extensive details about the inner workings of the land frauds. His information alone resulted in more than 100 convictions, including himself. In his book, Puter discussed his trial for bribing Oregon senator John H. Mitchell. Apparently, he paid Mitchell to lean on Binger Hermann to expedite fraudulent land claims. Mitchell had been a lawyer for the Oregon & California Railroad before his election to the Senate in 1873. He was re-elected in 1885, 1891, and 1901.

Francis Heney was the U.S. attorney appointed by Roosevelt to prosecute Michell and other fraud cases. Heney had a colorful reputation, to say the least. In 1891, he shot and killed a plaintiff who attacked him during a civil—or perhaps not-so-civil—trial. In another case, as he was prosecuting the mayor of San Francisco for a crime, a juror shot him in the jaw.

Heney presented evidence in court that Mitchell, a Republican from Portland, took a bribe from Puter. Mitchell was convicted and sentenced to six months in jail—one of only twelve sitting senators ever indicted in the history of the U.S. Senate, and one of only five ever convicted. But Mitchell never went to jail. He died in 1905 while his case was still on appeal, just as the Senate was about to expel him.

Heney also pursued charges against Oregon's other U.S. senator, Charles Fulton. Heney believed Fulton also took a bribe, but failed in two attempts to land an indictment. (In his law review articles, Michael Blumm credits Heney with helping drive Fulton from office by actively campaigning for his opponent in a 1908 campaign.) In another trial in 1905, Heney convicted John Newton Williamson, who replaced Herrman as Oregon's lone representative in the U.S. House. The charge, again, was bribery. Williamson's conviction was later overturned by the U.S. Supreme Court.

Heney also prosecuted John Hicklin Hall, his predecessor in the job of U.S. attorney for Oregon. Heney accused Hall of using his knowledge of illegal activities to blackmail political opponents. Though a jury found Hall guilty of blackmail, he was pardoned by President William Taft. Meanwhile, the railroad companies continued to profit from the illegal sale of land and timber, a clear violation of the law. Few of the sales complied with statutory limits on acreage and price, Blumm says.

In 1916, a frustrated Congress took back the land from the scheming railroads. This is how Oregon's land fraud era finally came to an end. But today, these lands continue to be entangled in legal controversies. This time, elected officials are ignoring environmental laws designed to protect biodiversity and streams on forestlands. And as always, large sums of money are involved.

In 1937, Congress passed the O&C Lands Act, a law spelling out how these lands would be managed in the future. This law handed over a sizable portion of revenues from timber sold from these lands to eighteen Oregon counties. Today, county officials contend that the law requires BLM to maximize the amount of timber sold from these lands. Not even federal environmental laws such as the Endangered Species Act or the Clean Water Act can interfere with the flow of lumber and money. And they found a judge willing to go along with their scheme: Richard Leon, the senior judge in the United States District Court for the District of Columbia, a court some 3,000 miles from the forests in question. Leon was appointed to the federal bench in 2003 by George W. Bush.

Rather than paying property taxes on its forestland, the BLM pays the counties half of all timber receipts. Congress supplements the counties' revenues through a "Payments in Lieu of Taxes" program. In all, the counties receive up to $300 million a year. The property tax rates in the eighteen O&C counties in Oregon are about 40 percent lower than in the eighteen non-O&C counties elsewhere in Oregon.[6] The counties can spend the revenues on roads, schools, and libraries—whatever they like.

Harvests and payments have declined since the implementation of the Northwest Forest Plan in 1994. The counties were not happy to see their payments decline, so they sued.

In 2019, Judge Leon ruled in their favor, saying the BLM has a "mandatory duty" under the O&C Act to manage the land only for timber production. Under his ruling, the BLM cannot protect the forest ecosystem for biodiversity or the climate, unless the counties' demands for timber are met first. "Of this," he emphasized, "there can be no doubt."[7] These forests in western Oregon may be the only places in the United States where environmental laws cannot be enforced.

"It's a shame to see a decision try to turn back the clock on federal forest management out here," says Kristin Boyle, a Seattle-based attorney with Earthjustice, a not-for-profit environmental law firm. If Leon's ruling stands on appeal, Boyle predicts it will destroy salmon and steelhead runs, water quality, and the endangered northern spotted owls, and marbled murrelets that rely on old-growth forest habitat. Sequestering large amounts of carbon in these forests is also out of the question.

Susan Jane Brown, a Eugene attorney who has been battling BLM in court for twenty years, is appealing Judge Leon's ruling. Past and ongoing logging operations have been shown to decrease stream flows during summer by 50 percent, posing a significant impediment to biodiversity. "Judge Leon's reading of the statute is incomplete at best, and completely erroneous at worst," Brown says.

The American Forest Resource Council, an industry group, is the main force behind the lawsuit. The council has called for an immediate 30 percent increase in logging in the BLM's mature and old-growth forests. Such an increase, ecologists told us, would have severe impacts on wildlife and the climate. But the counties are trying to spin their lawsuit as friendly to the environment. In an op-ed published in several Oregon newspapers, three county commissioners claimed Judge Leon's ruling "ensures" the protection of fish and wildlife.[8] But that's not what they say in their in court filings, where they admit the logging could lead to extinctions of fish and wildlife, but nevertheless must continue. "One has to wonder whether the industry really thought through their strategy," Brown says. By allowing the liquidation of old-growth forests to continue on BLM land, Judge Leon may have triggered another war in the woods. Andy Kerr, the long-time forest activist, predicts the backlash could get ugly:

> If big timber and the addicted counties feel besieged now, just wait. They will rue the day they tried to reclaim the bad old days and not adapt to changing times.

As the old trees on O&C lands continue to fall, the damage caused by Judge Leon's order accumulates. But the counties are not willing to stop there. They are now suing the U.S. government for establishing a national monument on the O&C lands.

In 2000, President Bill Clinton established the Cascade-Siskiyou National Monument near the city of Ashland, Oregon, and the California border, a couple hundred miles southeast of Kenyon Mountain. Years later, President Obama expanded the monument. The monument is now a spectacular 114,000-acre natural area (178 square miles) with significant stands of old-growth forests. Logging is not allowed, but most of the monument is within O&C Lands, and the counties are determined to log it anyway. So in 2019, they sued. And once again, they won. And again, Judge Leon was there to give them what they wanted, national monument or not.

The counties argued that monument regulations barring logging violate the 1937 O&C Act. The monument must change its rules to allow industrial scale logging, they said, and Judge Leon agreed. He ruled the Act's logging mandate "cannot be rescinded" by a presidential proclamation creating a national monument.

Cascade-Siskiyou National Monument was established specifically to protect this extraordinary biodiverse ecosystem from damage caused by logging. The monument's unique geography contributes to the area's exceptional biodiversity. Four mountain ranges collide at that location: the Western Cascades, a deeply eroded string of foothills and small volcanoes running alongside the Willamette Valley; the High Cascades, an adjacent string of tall, active and inactive volcanoes extending all the way to the Canadian border, from Crater Lake to Mount Baker; the craggy Klamath-Siskiyou Mountains that reach southwest toward the redwood forest and the Pacific Ocean; and the towering Sierra Nevada to the southeast. The Great Basin, a massive desert ecosystem spanning much of Oregon, Nevada, and Utah, abuts the monument to the east.

Within the monument you can find more than 300 species of birds, mammals, reptiles, amphibians, and mollusks—many rare or endemic—in its forests, grasslands, and meadows. The monument is also home to the northern spotted owl which lives in its old-growth forests. as well as the western bluebird, the western meadowlark, the pileated woodpecker, the flammulated owl, and the pygmy nuthatch.

The monument connects wildlife corridors used by various species to migrate through the monument or disperse. These habitats are resilient to large-scale disturbances like fire, insects, disease, invasive species, drought, and floods—events likely to be exacerbated by climate change. Logging would split the ecosystem into small patches of forest habitat, fragmenting previously connected habitats and corridors. Logging would create pathways for noxious, invasive weeds to infiltrate and wreak havoc.

Before Judge Leon issued his order, the monument protected biodiversity and the climate. But no more. "It is scary that industry has such a grip on our public lands," Francis Earthington, the forest activist from Roseburg, told us.

# Chapter 7

# From Agent Orange to Atrazine

One spring day in 1975, Carol Van Strum watched a helicopter spray fresh clear-cuts near her home in Oregon's Coast
Range mountains with a chemical mist. Within moments, she
felt a burning sensation in her eyes, nose, and mouth. So could
all four of her children. Within days the vegetable leaves in the
garden began to curl. Then their dog died.

She was not ready for this. The previous year, she moved
her family from the urban bustle of Berkeley to the Oregon
rainforest west of Corvallis to write, raise chickens, and grow
organic vegetables for her family. Toxic winds blowing down
the mountain weren't part of the plan. She called the local U.S.
Forest Service ranger district. What was going on? The employee
on the line told her the Siuslaw National Forest was spraying
its clear-cuts to kill off the understory in preparation for the
next planting of young conifers. The spray, she was told, was a
mixture of two compounds: 2,4-D (2,4-dichlorophenoxyacetic
acid) and 2,4,5-T (2,4,5-trichlorophenoxyacetic acid)—the
exact ingredients of Agent Orange, the notorious defoliant
used in the Vietnam War to clear jungle. The most dangerous
of the two ingredients was 2,4,5-T.

This was the Van Strum family's second surprise encounter
with warfare chemicals in the remote section of the rainforest
in as many weeks. Previously, a truck from the county road
department targeting roadside weeds nailed the four Van

Strum children from above while they were fishing in a creek known as Five Rivers, part of an extensive network of tiny streams that drain the rainforest near their home.

The spray, she told us in an interview, caused nausea, cramps, headaches, and diarrhea. Her husband Steve Van Strum tracked down the truck driver to ask what was in that spray. "Just 2,4,5-T," the driver said casually, as though he had hit the kids with a bubble bath.

After the encounters with Agent Orange, Van Strum made it her mission to fight herbicide spraying in forests any way she could. In 1976, she sued the federal government over spraying in the Siuslaw forest, a lawsuit that led to a 2,4,5-T ban in 1979, and began fighting the state of Oregon over aerial spraying on privately owned lands, a battle that continues to rage. Today, as she approaches her 80th birthday, Carol Van Strum is still fighting herbicide spraying in forests.

In 1983, Van Strum wrote about these battles in *A Bitter Fog: Herbicides and Human Rights*,[1] a memoir that has become an environmental classic in the tradition of Rachel Carson's take-down of DDT in her 1962 book *Silent Spring*.[2] Years later, Van Strum updated *A Bitter Fog*[3] and then posted all her herbicide research, a giant trove she calls the "Poison Papers," to the internet.[4]

The controversy over herbicide spraying did not end with the banning of 2,4,5-T. Timber companies found alternative herbicides that work nearly as well, such as atrazine, which unlike 2,4,5-T is not a carcinogen. Instead, atrazine is an endocrine disruptor which can cause serious reproductive health problems in animals and humans.

Nationally, exposure to pesticides has resulted in count-less poisonings and more than fifty thousand deaths a year. And yet, historically, the state of Oregon showed little concern for health risks associated with herbicides. For decades, state law allowed aerial spraying right up to homes and schools, and within seventy-five feet of a stream. In 2016, the Oregon Legislature tightened the rule by banning spraying within sixty feet of any home or school, roughly the distance between the pitcher's mound and home plate in baseball. A three mile-an-hour breeze can carry pesticides sixty feet in less than a second, a Virginia study found.[5] These new sixty-foot buffers are incapable of protecting anyone.

Many people living near sprayed forests still complain of nausea, vomiting, dizziness, bloody noses, skin rashes, and piercing headaches, just as the Van Strum children did a half century ago. Pesticides also accumulate in wildlife, where their biological impacts magnify over time. Herbicides can damage the ecosystem down to the root level. Glyphosate, a commonly used herbicide in these forests, has been found to affect interactions between essential soil organisms such as earthworms and symbiotic mycorrhizal fungi. As one study in a *Nature* publication pointed out, earthworms are valuable ecosystem engineers because they shred and redistribute organic material in soil and increase soil penetrability for roots, thus improving overall soil fertility.[6] The study found Glyphosate decreased earthworm activity. It also found amphibian species and other wildlife were detrimentally affected by glyphosate-based herbicides.

Pesticide usage in the forest also has a measurable impact on the climate. Agricultural activities contribute approximately 30 percent of all greenhouse gas emissions in the United

States, mainly due to the use of chemical fertilizers and pesticides. In Oregon, forestry accounts for about 4 percent of all pesticide use. The tiny alders, shrubs, and grasses underneath the tall conifers—the part of the forest known as the understory—constitute less than 1 percent of the carbon in a forest.[7] Killing the understory releases carbon into the air.

A military biological weapons program originally developed 2,4,5-T for use in World War II. After the war the chemical was marketed for civilian purposes. Forest scientists, or silviculturists, found 2,4,5-T helped timberland owners squeeze more production, jobs, and profits out of their prized Douglas-fir tree plantations. Helicopters and fixed-wing aircraft could spread it over large areas quickly. From around 1950 until 1979, 2,4,5-T combined with 2,4-D—the formulation for Agent Orange—was an integral part of industrial forestry.

The objective was not necessarily to kill competitive vegetation, but to increase the amount of light, moisture, and nutrients reaching the conifer without harming it. Oregon State University tested hundreds of herbicides for this task, but 2,4,5-T did it best and was used in 75 percent of forests in the region.[8] (A minor health threat, 2,4-D has also come under scrutiny; its use declined in the 1980s.).[137] Multiple treatments for each site increased the rate of growth.[9]

Of course, the Douglas-fir doesn't need herbicides to grow big and tall; as we saw in Chapter 1, it grows taller than almost any other tree on Earth entirely on its own. Herbicide treatments supersize the tree, especially during its early years. One OSU study found spraying herbicides could yield a 454 percent increase in a Douglas-fir's volume in just 15 years.[10]

Unfortunately, according to the EPA, every batch of 2,4,5-T ever made was laced with a form of dioxin known as TCDD—the most carcinogenic industrial poison in the environment. [11]

TCDD is an inevitable byproduct of the 2,4,5-T manufacturing process and persists intact in the environment for long periods of time. No one has ever manufactured TCDD intentionally; it has no beneficial use whatsoever. In the early years, TCDD concentrations of forty parts per million (ppm) in 2,4,5-T were common. By the 1970s, TCDD levels decreased to below one ppm.[12] In 1964, federal researchers found as much as 75 percent of the 2,4,5-T spray drifted in the wind away from its intended target, often in the direction of nearby populations and wildlife.[13]

Upon learning her children were exposed to 2,4,5-T, Carol Van Strum thought back to an article she read in *The New Yorker* magazine a few years earlier about its use in Vietnam. The article reported that researchers linked it to miscarriages and birth defects in laboratory animals. It unearthed health information the federal government has gone to great lengths to conceal.[14]

But with the secret exposed, military leaders went public with concerns about the use of 2,4,5-T. They worried using it in warfare may have been a war crime, as it endangered the health of Vietnamese civilians and American soldiers, *The New Yorker* reported.

The article resulted in an uproar in Congress, leading directly to Senate hearings.[15] On April 15, 1970, the Pentagon stopped using Agent Orange in Vietnam, a full four years before the war ended. The U.S. Veterans Administration now associates fourteen severe health problems found in Vietnam vets exposed to Agent Orange, including heart disease, Parkinson's disease, diabetes, liver dysfunction, and six types of cancer.

But in 1973, Agent Orange, a chemical too dangerous for use in war, was being deployed in the Oregon temperate rainforest. That spring, the *Eugene Register-Guard* newspaper broke the news that Michael (Mike) Newton, an Oregon State University professor (now emeritus) obtained five fifty-five gallon barrels (about a half-ton) of Agent Orange from the U.S. Air Force's 1.37 million-gallon stockpile.[16] He was using it in forestry experiments in Oregon's Coast Range mountains. The Air Force turned down his request for an additional 5,500 gallons.

"Field testing with Agent Orange, the controversial military herbicide banned for use in Vietnam, has actually been underway on some 350 acres of western Oregon brushlands," the article, by Jerry Uhrhammer, the *Register-Guard's* chief investigative reporter, began. Uhrhammer reported that Newton was testing Agent Orange on 220 acres in Lincoln County owned by two timber companies, Starker Forests and Publisher's Paper, and another 128 acres in Douglas County owned by Roseburg Lumber (now Roseburg Forest Products). Newton told Uhrhammer he sprayed Agent Orange no closer than three miles from any home and an unspecified distance "away from any streams."

The EPA previously warned Newton he needed an experimental use permit to legally use Agent Orange, but Newton had no permit. At first, Newton denied he was conducting any experiments with Agent Orange, but three days later abruptly changed his story when Uhrhammer pressed for more details. Newton told Uhrhammer that Oregon State University had no involvement in his experiments but was vague about where his funding came from. "I'm doing this as a consultant for, well, I don't know," Uhrhammer quoted him as saying. "In this sort of thing, I'm a liaison man. Basically, I'm a consultant for western Oregon forests."

Newton claimed the dioxin content in the Agent Orange was "low enough to permit its safe usage." However, there is no acknowledged safe threshold level for TCDD. Now eighty-eight years old, Newton's tenure career at Oregon State began in 1959, a few years after graduating from the University of Vermont with a bachelor's degree in animal and dairy husbandry. He received his Ph.D. from OSU in 1964.

Despite Newton's record of conducting unauthorized experiments with Agent Orange in the Oregon rainforest, he is "one of the most respected forest scientists in the nation," according to a profile published in 2014 in *Evergreen Magazine*, a pro-timber industry publication based in Missoula, Montana.[17] Few scientists have more experience with 2,4,5-T. In 1967, he led an international symposium that brought together many of the world's foremost scientists, and teachers of vegetation science and herbicide technology.[17] The symposium included a promotional presentation by a representative from Dow Chemical, the manufacturer of 2,4,5-T, but a summary of the proceedings offered no hint that the world's most dangerous dioxin might harm human health. The symposium ignored health issues even though at the time, the health and ecological impacts of pesticides were a hot topic worldwide, with the recent publication of *Silent Spring*.

In 1972, Newton was among seventeen scientists appointed to a blue-ribbon National Academy of Sciences (NAS) panel that investigated the health impacts of Agent Orange usage in Vietnam. Their report, released in 1974, said the scientists did not find "any definitive indication of direct damage by herbicides to human health."[18] However, the report left open the possibility people were harmed, as subsequent health studies eventually showed. Many health conditions associated with Agent Orange take decades to appear, such as cancer.

Nevertheless, as evidence of health impacts accumulated, Newton continued to insist that 2,4,5-T is safe. In 1999, he wrote that herbicides work better at clearing brush than alternatives like manual removal both "in terms of safety and effectiveness."[19] Newton also claims that Agent Orange has "about half the toxicity of caffeine,"[20] according to a video about Agent Orange posted to the OSU website. Of course, the implication that spraying Agent Orange is about the same as spraying tea or coffee is ludicrous. The university posted Newton's video as a "research update" on its media portal without any mention of National Academy of Sciences research linking 2,4,5-T to cancers and other health problems.

And in 2016, he wrote a personal testimonial touting Agent Orange as posing no risk to anyone's health:[21]

> I've had more exposure to Agent Orange than anyone. Since my experience in Southeast Asia, I've lived another 44 years, despite receiving dose after dose of 2,4-D and 2,4,5-T, each being far greater than any that could have been experienced by field troops. Now 83 and still in perfect health, I can say definitively that at no time have I experienced any health problems that could be attributed to TCDD. I am a very healthy guinea pig after huge and nearly continuous exposure to herbicides, including a lot of TCDD.

Newton was not the only one spraying the dangerous herbicide in Coast Range forests. From 1972 to 1977, the Forest Service sprayed about 10,000 pounds of 2,4,5-T—almost exclusively by helicopter—on 7,000 acres near Alsea in western Benton County, the EPA revealed at one time. No one notified the one thousand people living in the area about the spraying. In researching this book, we found no evidence that the state of Oregon, the EPA, or anyone else attempted to assess the potentially serious health impacts from the spraying. As a result, we know a lot more about the impacts of spraying Agent Orange over eight years in Southeast Asia than we know about the health impacts over 30 years in Oregon.

The Alsea River basin receives up to 140 inches of rain per year. Ground zero in the forest spraying controversy is the small town of Alsea, located thirty miles southwest of the Oregon State University campus in Corvallis, thirty miles north of the Van Strum farm in the town of Deadwood, and thirty miles from the coast.

In the mid-1970s, an unusual number of miscarriages turned up in the Alsea area. Bonnie Hill, a schoolteacher who had a miscarriage in 1975, began asking around to see if anyone else had a similar experience. While taking a college course at the nearby University of Oregon, Hill learned that dioxin caused spontaneous abortions in monkeys. Was it also being sprayed near her home? She began to investigate. She counted nine women in the Alsea area, including herself, who had a total of thirteen miscarriages between 1972 and 1977, around the time when heavy amounts of dioxin were being sprayed in the area.

Hill analyzed spray data supplied by the federal government and a private timber company along with the location of each woman's home. She discovered each miscarriage closely followed (within six weeks) a 2,4,5-T application in a nearby forest. She drew a map showing a close spatial correlation between spray sites and the dwellings—evidence of a link, she later testified in court, that was "too strong to ignore."

She sent her research to the EPA, which contacted Colorado State University to look into the question of whether the miscarriages might be connected in some way with 2,4,5-T. The EPA was already suspicious of the herbicide's ability to cause health problems. The Colorado State researchers found "statistically significant" correlations between the timing of sprayings and a "subsequent increase in spontaneous abortions."[22] They submitted the results of their investigation, known as the "Alsea II Study," to the EPA on February 27, 1979, which can be accessed today via Carol Van Sturm's Poison Papers archive as well as an EPA website.[23]

The next day, the EPA issued an emergency declaration banning the use of 2,4,5-T in forestry, just before the start of the spring spraying season.[24] EPA said it acted quickly because pregnant women exposed to the chemicals "faced an immediate unreasonable risk of spontaneous abortions." Dr. John Griffith, a senior EPA researcher who supervised the study and edited the final report, wrote in a memo that he believed the women were exposed by drinking contaminated water, not by air inhalation.[25] The EPA found TCDD levels in sediments at a drinking water source greater than one part per billion, rendering the water unsafe to drink, in Griffith's opinion. He later wrote:

> The facts are that we don't know the minimal dosage of TCDD necessary to kill or damage a human embryo. It did not ... seem inconceivable that TCDD residues could be transported on such sediment directly to the waiting embryo.

The Alsea II study also noted TCDD was highly toxic to the ecosystem. Dioxin was found in animal fetuses as well as in adult deer and elk. However, the study added this important caveat: "For all its complexity … this analysis is a correlational analysis, and correlation does not necessarily mean causation." The study was never formally published in a scientific journal or even peer reviewed, though it generated a flood of controversy. Many scientists found several serious flaws with the study, including a team of six OSU scientists who wrote that it relied on "incomplete and inaccurate data" and that it failed to recognize that the rate of "spontaneous abortions" was not greater than would be expected.

> When corrections for some of these problems are applied, we find the rate of spontaneous abortions in the study area does not appear to be related to the use of 2,4,5-T.[26]

Dow Chemical also disputed Alsea II, arguing in court that the study's conclusions were supported "only by speculative opinion."[27] The company also said it is "inconceivable that these women could be exposed to levels of TCDD significant enough to cause reproductive damage."

Right or wrong, it is clear Alsea II led directly to EPA's decision to ban 2,4,5-T. Dow's appeal of the decision failed, and in 1983 the company halted its production altogether. It no longer makes 2,4,5-T. In researching this book, we found the EPA vastly underestimated the amount of 2,4,5-T that had been aerially sprayed in the Alsea area. Its reports account only for the spraying occuring in the 1970s, but we found records showing the spraying may have been going on for nearly thirty years—starting as early as 1950. We also found unpublished data collected in 1964 by the aforementioned Mike Newton showing 2,4,5-T contaminated streams at levels up to sixteen times greater than the EPAs reported in Alsea II.[28]

We also located state records showing that 2,4,5-T was sprayed in forests far outside the Alsea watershed, sometimes with disastrous effects. In 1977, for example, an errant 2,4,5-T spray appeared to kill fish in a salmon and steelhead hatchery on Gnat Creek near Astoria. The incident prompted the Oregon Department of Forestry to enact its first regulations controlling the use of pesticides.[29]

The National Academy of Sciences (NAS) conducted twelve major studies over the years on the health impacts of Agent Orange usage in Vietnam. The most recent came out in 2018. Molly Kile, an associate professor at the Oregon State University School of Biological and Population Health Sciences, served on the 2018 panel. Kile is also a member of the Oregon Environmental Quality Commission. In its report, the panel found "sufficient epidemiologic data" to associate exposure to 2,4,5-T with several types of cancers, she told us.[30] To her knowledge, no similar study has ever been attempted in Oregon.

According to the NAS, Alsea is one of three places globally where people had an "extraordinary environmental exposure" to TCDD.[31] The others are Times Beach, Missouri, a town so severely contaminated with dioxin it eventually had to be abandoned; and Seveso, Italy, where a chemical plant that produced 2,4,5-T exploded.

In 2007, a woman called into the Eugene headquarters of the environmental group Beyond Toxics with a familiar complaint: helicopters were broadcast spraying toxic pesticides on timberlands all across western Oregon and people were getting sick. Chemicals were seeping into homes, schools, bus stops, and churches. Lisa Arkin, Beyond Toxics' executive director, took the call.

The caller, Lynn Bowers, had mapped toxic hot spots based on interviews with possible victims and information coughed up by the state of Oregon. But her data was severely limited. A state law in effect at the time made it illegal for the state to release timely information about aerial herbicide spraying to the public, researchers, or even doctors.

One community mapped by Bowers was the Triangle Lake area between Alsea and Eugene in western Lane County. Dozens of Triangle Lake residents, calling themselves the Pitchfork Alliance, were so concerned about their levels of herbicide exposure they tested their own urine and sent the lab results to the EPA.

In all, forty-three residents—including several children—tested positive for atrazine, an herbicide known as a "gender-bender" chemical. Atrazine earned this nickname after scientists discovered it disrupts endocrine systems in animals and humans. The most important studies were conducted by Tyrone Hayes, a biology professor at the University of California, Berkeley, who found atrazine chemically castrated male frogs, turning some into females. After dissecting frogs exposed to atrazine, Hayes noticed some could not be clearly identified as male or female: they had both testes and ovaries. Others had multiple testes that were deformed. Even very low doses of atrazine disrupted estrogen and testosterone in fish, amphibians, birds, reptiles, laboratory rodents, and humans, Hayes found.[32]

Atrazine, the second-most heavily used herbicide in the U.S., behind glyphosate,[33] has been banned since 2004 in the European Union. Its manufacturer, Syngenta, deployed heavy-handed tactics to avoid a similar ban in the U.S., including making personal attacks against Hayes, who formerly worked for the company, as Rachel Aziz reported in *The New Yorker* in 2014.[34]

Mike Newton claimed in a letter to the Corvallis *Gazette-Times* newspaper that Triangle Lake residents had nothing to worry about from atrazine and were exaggerating the threat:[34]

> If there were risks, the hundreds of millions of dollars spent on toxicology and exposure would have found higher residues on roadsides, utilities, croplands and lawns, where 99 percent of these products are used each year. Yet the reported products have long histories of safe use close to humans, as on mega-corn crops, nurseries, lawns!

The Oregon Forest and Industry Council, the trade group, doubled down on Newton's claim, saying in a statement to the Oregon Health Authority (OHA) that "aerial application is often the safest, fastest, most efficient and cost effective way to apply herbicides, especially on remote, steep and rough forest terrain."

Despite these assurances, the EPA launched an investigation into what happened at Triangle Lake, with the Oregon Health Authority taking the lead. In its own sampling, OHA confirmed the presence of atrazine in urine, though at levels not nearly as high as the residents found in their own sampling. In its report, the agency said it did not have access to lab equipment that could test for most other herbicides used in Oregon forests. It did not assess the health threat posed by atrazine, contending not enough was known about the chemical, even though it's been around since the 1950s.

To no one's surprise, OHA's study failed to satisfy members of the Pitchfork Alliance, who pointed out no urine samples were collected in the spring, when spraying is heaviest, or within a day or two of aerial applications, when atrazine levels in urine would be greatest. Instead, it collected samples in August and September when spraying had all but ceased.

OHA also declined to investigate similar herbicide poisonings elsewhere in western Oregon, including Florence and Gold Beach. These and other towns spent millions of dollars on water purification plants protecting drinking water from forestry operations. The Oregon Legislature responded to these controversies in 2016 by giving the public far greater access to aerial spraying information by posting data to the internet and by banning aerial herbicide spraying within sixty feet of any home or school.[35] But it refused to take action limiting the public's chemical exposure. In 2019, conservation groups attempted to force the state to tighten pesticide spraying rules with three ballot measures. Timber companies countered with three additional ballot measures requiring the state to pay them compensation if it enacted any new regulations. But the following January, both sides agreed to drop their ballot initiatives and begin negotiating a settlement. In the end, they agreed to expand aerial no-spray zones next to structures from 60 to 300 feet—a five-fold increase over the existing buffers. The agreement was signed by twelve timber companies or organizations[36] and thirteen conservation organizations.[37] It was later enshrined in state law by the Legislature.

In the end, the environmentalists were eager to compromise, as Mary Scurlock of the Oregon Stream Protection Coalition, one of the conservation groups, told the Legislature:

Countless hours have been spent marshaling science and policy arguments in favor of increased protection for water and against positions taken by timber industry representatives. It is rare for legislation to be so strongly supported by both conservation and timber interests, and this bill represents sincere and hard-fought compromise on both sides.

"On the whole, we're coming into the twenty-first century," said Sean Stevens, executive director of Oregon Wild, one of the thirteen eco groups signing on to the deal.

But not everyone agreed the new 300-foot buffers would be enough. They won't adequately protect the health of people living near clear-cuts, Carol Van Strum explained to us. Now seventy-nine and still living on her Alsea area farm, Van Strum suffers from deep battle scars earned from fighting aerial spraying over the better part of five decades. Her greatest anguish stems from the staggering loss of all four of her children in a 1978 house fire she believes was set by an arsonist—though arson was never proved. Someone wanted to shut her up, perhaps someone associated with the spraying, she surmises.

Van Strum's trauma was so great she couldn't bring herself to mention the fire, or the loss of her children, in her book *A Bitter Fog*, either when it was first published in 1983 or in the second edition in 2014. These were the same children who were sprayed in 1975 with 2,4,5-T when they were fishing.

No-spray buffers of 300 feet won't protect anybody in the wet and windy Coast Range forests, she told us:

You can smell and taste these chemicals from a mile away. The 300-foot buffers are a sop to the ignorant and to industry, because there's no safe distance or level of exposure to these poisons, they move far and wide on air and water currents, which is why they're found in polar regions thousands of miles from application. I am appalled that any so-called environmental group agreed to that. The 300-foot buffers are total, total bullshit.

This fight is far from over, if Carol Van Strum has anything to say about it.

# PART 3

## THE KEYSTONE SPECIES

*One of the complexities of being a biologist today is that we don't know how much time an ecosystem under siege has left before it collapses.*

*—Alexandra Morton*

# Chapter 8

# The Invasion

A quarter century ago, an extended family of orcas on the southern coast of British Columbia vanished. The missing orcas, known among whale biologists as the "A5 Pod," lived year-around in the Broughton Archipelago, a wild, untamed enclave near the northern tip of Vancouver Island. The archipelago, known for the fjords that cut deeply into the surrounding Pacific coastal temperate rainforest, typically offers the orcas a rich buffet of salmon to eat. But the salmon were vanishing, too.

No one knew these orcas better than Alexandra Morton, an American biologist who set up a research station in the archipelago to study their language, culture, and habits. She followed the A5 Pod around on a twenty-two-foot cabin cruiser named *Blackfish Sound*, often with a child, dog, crayons, and Legos in tow. She photographed the black-and-white patterns on the orcas' sleek bodies, unique markings comparable to a fingerprint, and gave each a name: Stripe, Yakat, Kelsy, Saddle, Top Notch, and Eve (the pod's matriarch).

Orcas, often called killer whales, are actually dolphins. They resemble humans in that they can be quite talkative. Using an underwater microphone, Morton eavesdropped on orca clicks, calls, whistles, and chatter. In time, she developed a good idea of what many vocalizations meant. She authored several books about the A5 Pod, most notably *Not on My Watch* in 2021, *Beyond the Whales* in 2004, and *Listening to Whales* in 2002.[1]

Morton noticed one of the families in the A5 clan stopped coming around. Today, as she reflects back, she realizes that "a quarter of a century has passed since this whale family—two sisters and their kids—have been seen in the Broughton archipelago."[2] One by one, the remaining families in the A5 Pod quietly slipped away, until all were gone.

With her research subjects now on the lam, Morton could have turned her attention to any of several other nearby orca pods. But the A5 Pod's mysterious behavior raised serious questions in her mind. She needed answers. Why did they leave? Where did they go? Did they relocate further up the coast, perhaps as far as Alaska? Or did they die?

And yet, she had no doubt *why* they left. Salmon runs in the archipelago were crashing. At the same time, multinational seafood companies were setting up salmon farms in the archipelago. Were the two developments linked? By the end of 1993 there were four net pens. Noise-making devices installed on the net pens generated loud noises to discourage harbor seals from stealing fish. The devices are capable of producing 198 decibels of noise, as loud as a jet engine up close.

The acoustic harassment was supposed to be an improvement over the previous method of restraining the thieving seals. Shooting them. But the devices clearly interrupted orca communications.

So, Morton surmises, the orcas went away, but the seals stuck around. Apparently, they would rather go stone deaf than miss out on salmon.[167] Besides being ineffectual, the noise-making machines were probably illegal. In Canada it's against the law to harass orcas. Nonetheless, no charges were ever filed. The devices were dismantled in 1999, but by the end of 2020, the A5 orcas were still missing.

Why did they stay away? To figure out what happened, Morton decided to take a closer look at the fish farms. Were the fish farms wiping out wild salmon to the point the archipelago could no longer feed its orcas? Orcas could easily find plenty of salmon to eat elsewhere.

"At the whim of this corporate-controlled industry, 80,000 years of whale history in the archipelago came to an end," Morton wrote in *Listening to Whales*.[3]

Three major groups of orcas live on the British Columbia coast. One group, consisting of about 200 orcas known as the Northern Residents, patrol the 600 miles of coastline from the Broughton Archipelago to Southeast Alaska. The A5 Pod is a subgroup of the Northern Residents. A second group of about seventy-five orcas, the genetically distinct Southern Residents, stay mostly in the Salish Sea straddling the United States and Canada border, encompassing Puget Sound, the Strait of Juan de Fuca and the Georgia Sea. Some Southern Residents stray as far down the coast as San Francisco. Both groups eat primarily wild salmon. A third genetically distinct group, known as transients, keeps mostly far from shore near the Continental Shelf. Numbering around 320, these orcas prefer marine mammals like seals and porpoises and avoid salmon.

Both the United States and Canada consider all orcas, the ocean's top predator, to be at high risk of extinction. With the A5 Pod no longer around, and salmon runs in free fall, Morton needed to find a new topic to study. She switched her attention to the ecosystem, documenting its collapse as it unfolded over the ensuing decades in real time. She found extensive damage from the marine waters up into the Great Bear Rainforest ringing the archipelago. And, as Morton explained to us in an interview, even the global climate took a hit.

Upon her arrival in the Broughton Archipelago in 1984, Alexandra Morton settled into a floathouse in Echo Bay, a small fishing village on the north side of Guilford Island, the largest island in the archipelago. Previously, the native of Connecticut studied orcas at Marineland of the Pacific near Los Angeles, where she witnessed the birth and death of the first orca ever conceived in captivity. At Marineland, she eavesdropped on its two captive orcas using the same underwater microphone technique.

Alex, as her friends call her, traced the lineage of Corky, the captive female at Marineland, to the A5 pod in the Broughton. Corky was captured near the British Columbia coast in 1969. Corky's mate, Orky, a member of another Northern Resident pod, the A4s, was captured there the year before. Morton was astonished to hear orcas in the Broughton vocalize sounds in a dialect that sounded exactly like Corky's vocalizations at Marineland. The captive orcas at Marineland had preserved their dialect precisely while in captivity. Alex felt right at home in Echo Bay.

Echo Bay, a small fishing and logging town, has a post office with thrice weekly seaplane mail service, a church, a community hall, but no phone, water, or electric service. The community had a small school but it burned down. The giant ferries traveling the Inside Passage to Alaska come nowhere near.

The area is the ancestral homeland of the Musgamagw Dzawada'enuxw First Nations (pronounced MOOSEga-ma dzou-wa-DAY-nek). The Musgamagw never gave the fish farming companies permission to develop their net pens in the Broughton, raising questions about their legality under Canadian law from the start.

In Echo Bay, Morton established the Salmon Coast Field Station, where she housed a team of researchers to document the ecosystem's decline. A traditional scientist in Morton's shoes might have written papers about the collapse of the Broughton ecosystem, and left it at that. But to be true to her heart, Morton decided she must also save the ecosystem, as well as expose the "ruthless industrialization" that was breaking it.[4] So she became a scientist/activist who came to public hearings with armfuls of her own peer-reviewed research.

Morton also stepped to the forefront of peaceful occupations, marches, and protests, alongside leaders of First Nations. She once helped lead a march the entire length of Vancouver Island to rally political support for the cause in the provincial capital of Victoria. She filed five lawsuits against the Canadian government over its many failures to protect wild salmon, and won them all. In 2021, she recounted these battles in her memoir, *Not on My Watch*, a best-seller in Canada that reads like a top-notch investigative thriller.

*Not on My Watch* tells the story of Alexandra Morton's bitter fight against the destructive practices of the fish farm industry. Powerful forces in government and industry humiliated her, stalked her, lied to her, lied about her, arrested her, excluded her from meetings, shut her down, but could not stop her. "I am part of the resistance movement against extinction," she writes. "The movement spans the globe. We are a force of nature. Like a river, we well up, slip around, bore through and dive under obstacles. We don't stop."[5]

"This is an industry that has slandered me continuously since the mid-'90s," she told us. And she wasn't the only scientist who was perceived as a threat. Other scientists who dared investigate the impacts of fish farming practices were also muzzled, even ones working for the very government agencies supposedly looking out for the interests of the wild salmon.

In the early 1990s, several seafood corporations based in Norway, including Marine Harvest (later renamed MOWI), Cermaq, and Grieg Seafood, exported millions of Atlantic salmon, an alien species on the Pacific Coast, from northern Europe to British Columbia. They set up some 130 salmon farms in the midsection of the Pacific coastal temperate rainforest, from Seattle to Bella Coola on British Columbia's central coast, including thirty farms in the Broughton Archipelago.

Each farm raised up to one million Atlantic salmon in square net pens resembling cattle feedlots. In our interview, Morton told us a "simply enormous" mountain of evidence linked the fish farms with the destruction of wild salmon stocks. Despite this evidence, she said the companies decided early on to never admit to doing anything wrong. And as of 2021, they still haven't.

The industry enjoyed the protection of the Canadian federal government, led by the Department of Fisheries and Oceans (DFO), though several other federal and provincial agencies have a say. The DFO is also in charge of protecting wild salmon. Morton says the DFO has a long history of coddling its fish farming industry while dismissing its impacts on wild salmon. The Canadian government has also never acknowledged the ecological damage done by the fish farms.

The industry claims to have a yearly economic output of $1.6 billion and employs 6,500 full-time workers. The government decided the fish farming companies could plop their net pens right into the path of migrating wild salmon, where they can do the maximum amount of damage. This decision, Morton discovered, was what triggered the ecosystem's collapse. Morton sent letter after letter to DFO bureaucrats hoping to alert them to the problems she was seeing, but rarely received much of a response.

"Dear Ms. Morton, there is no evidence … " the replies to her letters often began, if a reply came at all.[6] Her persistent mailings keep the local postal station solvent, even as the bureaucrats found it convenient to ignore them. The DFO was hesitant to send scientists to the Broughton to inspect impacts. When DFO did send scientists, they often botched the research, perhaps intentionally, Morton says.

The DFO even threatened to send Morton to jail for conducting research without a license. One day, a DFO official on Vancouver Island telephoned Morton to ask her to send diseased salmon to the agency's biologists to study. So she sent five. A few days later, the cops showed up at her door and charged her with poaching. She faced a potential penalty of $500,000 and two years in jail. Morton was puzzled by the fact that the government never took legal action against fish farms for killing wild salmon by the million, yet nicked her for taking just a handful. Eventually, the charges were dropped.

Since the 1980s, Morton and her team of scientists have written more than 100 peer-reviewed research papers documenting impacts of fish farms on the health of wild salmon. These papers, with titles like, "Heavy sea louse infection is associated with decreased foraging success in wild juvenile sockeye salmon," appeared in peer-reviewed journals like the *Proceedings of the National Academy of Sciences*, *Virology Journal*, *Canadian Journal of Fisheries and Aquatic Sciences*, and *Science*, almost always in collaboration with professors at institutions like the University of British Columbia, Simon Fraser University, the University of Victoria, and the University of Washington.

The papers presented hard evidence that the fish farms were the source of deadly bacterial infections, viruses, and parasites spreading into the wild salmon population. The sea louse, a nasty parasite, attaches itself to wild juvenile salmon as they swim past the fish farms, munching on brains, eyeballs and flesh.[168] The researchers determined that even a single louse can kill a fish. Some young salmon were covered with dozens of lice, head to tail. They had no chance.

The researchers found that heavy sea lice outbreaks were decimating the wild salmon population. A paper they published in 2007 in *Science* warned that if the outbreaks were allowed to continue, "then local extinction is certain."[7]

The Salmon Coast researchers identified a half dozen viruses that kill wild salmon: salmon alphavirus, which attacks the pancreas; piscine reovirus, which causes a dangerous syndrome known as heart and skeletal muscle inflammation; the flu-like infectious salmon anemia virus, which causes lesions; and salmon leukemia virus, which causes cancerous tumors.

The team suspected infectious salmon anemia virus (ISAV), the most feared of these pathogens, may have been behind a mysterious die-off of massive numbers of sockeye salmon in the Fraser River, their research shows. ISAV is transmitted among salmon populations by the sea louse.[8]

In 2002, the Salmon Coast Research Station linked the collapse of a once-massive run of pink salmon in the Broughton's Knight Inlet to these diseases.[9] A half-dozen fish farms were sited on Knight Inlet, a popular destination for tourists to view grizzly bears. In the fall of 2002, some of the grizzly bears were reportedly so hungry they ate their cubs.[10] The pink salmon run in Knight Inlet, the Broughton's deepest fjord, collapsed again in 2019. That year, photographs of emaciated bears walking the beaches of Knight Inlet went viral on Facebook. As Rolf Hickel, the photographer, told a local newspaper, "Many felt, as I do, that the low salmon runs were the cause of the bears' starvation and this worst salmon run ever was the result of fish farming."[11]

On the British Columbia coast, orcas have six varieties of wild salmon to choose from: king, pink, chum, sockeye, coho, and steelhead. The orca's favorite is the king, the fattest of the six species, weighing up to fifty pounds, and sometimes one hundred. The five-pound pinks are the tiniest and most abundant.

Born and raised in rivers, wild salmon spend as many as seven years at sea. When they are ready to spawn, they return to their native rivers. The hatchery-bred salmon return to their native hatchery. Farmed salmon never go anywhere, other than circling around and around in their cages. For thousands of years, salmon returning from the ocean traveled south along British Columbia's Inside Passage, the channel between the coast and Vancouver Island, the largest island on the Pacific coast of North America. As they circle around the island's northern tip, some enter the Broughton Archipelago's seven rivers to spawn, but first they must swim through toxic effluent from the fish farms.

Many of the salmon bypass the Broughton and head down Johnstone Strait, the main north-south thoroughfare. Soon, they will enter the Discovery Islands, with its twenty-two fish farms. As they travel south, the next stop is the Fraser River, the largest river in the province and the second most productive salmon fishery on the west coast of North America, after Alaska's Bristol Bay. By the time the salmon reach the Fraser, they will have circumvented up to sixty fish farms.

But for many salmon, the journey has barely begun. Some of these fish continue south into Puget Sound, while others turn west into the Strait of Juan de Fuca and head for the

Columbia River and even California. The number of salmon on this journey has dwindled remarkably over the years, especially those headed for rivers in the United States. Data shows the number of wild salmon returning to American rivers has been declining steadily for more than a century, from around forty-five million to less than two million.[174] About 40 percent of distinct salmon populations have gone extinct, while hundreds of others are barely hanging on.[12]

In British Columbia, the wild salmon runs were considered to be in "relatively robust" condition as recently as 1997.[13] But now, wild salmon populations there are collapsing too. One way of viewing the collapse is to look at commercial fishing data. Between 1925 through 1993, the commercial fleet netted an average of twenty-four million salmon per year off the British Columbia coast. In 1994, around the time fish farms began moving in, harvests began to fall steadily. In 2019 and 2020, the catch dropped to two million. And then, in 2021, the federal government closed the ocean fishery almost entirely.

Bernadette Jordan, Canada's minister of fisheries, explained why in a news release:

> Pacific salmon are in a long-term decline, with many runs on the verge of collapse. We are pulling the emergency brake to give these salmon populations the best chance at survival.[14]

The loss of sockeye salmon was felt most acutely in the Fraser River. At one time, the Fraser's sockeye salmon run exceeded forty million. By the mid-2000s, the run had fallen to about one million. Yellowed sockeye carcasses littered the Fraser's shorelines and streambeds, possible victims of infectious salmon anemia virus, Morton says. Many female salmon died with unfertilized eggs still in their bellies.

The collapse was so steep the federal government ordered an investigation led by Bruce Cohen, a retired federal judge. In his report, "The Uncertain Future of Fraser River Sockeye," published in 2012, Cohen recommended seventy-five actions for solving the crisis.[15] One recommendation called on the DFO to phase out of fish farms unless it was satisfied the farms "pose at most a minimal risk of serious harm to the health of migrating Fraser River sockeye salmon."

A decade later, the fish farms were still operating, and the Fraser River sockeye run was still dropping. It lost another 80 percent, placing its future even further in doubt. In 2020, the Fraser River sockeye run was the lowest on record. Not all wild salmon populations on the British Columbia coast are failing. Wild salmon that avoid fish farms during their migrations are thriving. For instance, sockeye spawning in the Harrison River, one of the Fraser's main tributaries, are doing well. The Harrison's salmon migrate on a course leading away from fish farms.

An experiment conducted in 2003 demonstrated that removing fish farming in migration routes reduces the wild salmon's death rate.[16] And yet, the government of Canada refused to allow the scientists to repeat the experiment in 2004, or any year after that.

Sometimes, farmed fish escape from their net pens. The largest escape occurred in 2017, when an estimated 253,000 Atlantics broke out of a net pen on Cypress Island operated by Cooke Aquaculture in Washington's San Juan Islands. Biologists tracked down escapees as far away as Broughton Archipelago, 300 miles up the coast. It's anyone's guess how many parasites and pathogens they encountered along their heavily-used migration route. The escape from Cypress farm was not an isolated incident. One study found up to 1 percent of the ten million or more farmed salmon in the province escape from net pens every year, or an annual total of 10,000 or more escapees.[17] As Morton noted in *Not on My Watch*, the disappearance of 10,000 wild salmon from a river would be an ecological disaster. But on a fish farm, it's business as usual.

The Canadian government was not eager for the public to learn about health problems in its salmon populations, and even muzzled one of its own scientists whose research shed light on them. That scientist was Dr. Kristi Miller-Saunders, the DFO's lead scientist in its molecular genetics laboratory in Nanaimo, B.C. Miller-Saunders found a "powerful genomic signature" that showed wild salmon were infected with salmon leukemia virus.[18]

After Miller-Saunders published her data in 2011 in *Science*, the Canadian government sought to quash news coverage of it.[180] Reporters who asked for permission to talk with the DFO's star scientist were ignored. There would be no interviews.

"There was clear evidence of a cover-up," Morton told us. Undaunted, the media began to dig. Margaret Munro, a reporter with the *Vancouver Sun*, obtained 792 pages of emails and memos under Canada's Access to Information Act. Munro's article in the *Sun* disclosed that the emails showed DFO brass "deliberately muzzled" Miller-Saunders, preventing her from answering media questions about "one of the most significant discoveries to come out of a federal fisheries lab in years."[19] What's more, the DFO also threatened to shut down her lab and the type of "innovative research" she was doing, Munro reported.[20]

Miller-Saunders suspected, but could not prove, that fish farms were spreading viruses into the wild salmon population. The DFO denied her request to look into this question. The leash tightened. Miller-Saunders' research also offended the BC Salmon Farmers Association, an industry group, which called it "speculative" and "problematic" in a news release.[21] Sea West News, a pro-fish farm industry publication, attacked the scientist personally. "Her science is fishy. Her claims are baseless. But Dr. Kristi Miller-Saunders keeps accusing her colleagues of collusion with the aquaculture industry to suppress research."[22]

DFO, however, could not keep a lid on Miller-Saunders forever. In 2012, she testified for three days before the Cohen Commission and clearly influenced its recommendations. Finally, in 2021, things changed dramatically. Bernadette Jordan, Canada's minister of fisheries, decided to phase out all fish farms in marine waters by 2025, except in the Discovery Islands, where the phase-out must be completed by 2022. In her announcement, she did not acknowledge fish farms ever harmed a single wild salmon.

We asked the DFO to respond to criticism of its management of wild salmon. "The protection of wild Pacific salmon is a priority for the government of Canada," Alexandra Coutts, a DFO spokeswoman, told us. "The Department does not have the resources to review all external publications, including scientific papers and books." The salmon farming industry is not going away without one last fight. Industry lawyers are challenging Jordan's decision in the courts in a last-ditch attempt to hang on. As Morton told us, the fish farming industry is "dying a messy death."

Meanwhile, the Washington Legislature has told Cooke Aquaculture it cannot raise Atlantic salmon at its four fish farms in Puget Sound after 2025. However, the state is permitting Cooke to grow steelhead in its net pens instead. Some fish farms on the coast have already shut down, giving coastal ecosystems a breather from the non-stop onslaught of pathogens and parasites. Meanwhile, the orcas seem hopeful. In January 2021, a member of the missing A5 Pod was seen in the Broughton area for the first time since the mid-1990s, Morton told us. A second orca was spotted in June.

The wild salmon Alexandra Morton is trying to save are vanishing throughout the Pacific coastal temperate rainforest, not just in the Broughton Archipelago. A wide variety of factors are devastating the salmon, including climate change, logging practices, dams, overfishing, beaver trapping, interactions with hatchery fish, and fish farms. The loss of Pacific salmon has left a gaping hole in the rainforest ecosystem. Salmon feed more than 138 species, including orcas, grizzly bears, eagles, migrating birds, seals, wolves, and humans.[23] Because so many species depend on a reliable, abundant supply of wild salmon, scientists call them the "keystone species" in this ecosystem.

The wild salmon need to put on weight at sea if they hope to reach their spawning grounds, which can be a thousand miles from the ocean. At sea, they ingest nitrogen-15, an isotope of the nutrient commonly used in garden fertilizers. Nitrogen-15 does not occur naturally in the relatively nutrient-poor forest soils. Scientists are finding nitrogen-15 in trees, and they know how it got there. By the time salmon reach the spawning grounds, their bodies have become big bags of organic fertilizer. Bears, wolves and eagles carry carcasses deep into the forest for later consumption. Forest soils absorb the nutrients from decomposed salmon parts and animal wastes. The trees take it from there.

Nitrogen-15 has been found in trees as far as seventy-five feet from the stream, way beyond the riparian fringe. Trees within that perimeter grow three times faster than trees further away, a 2001 paper by Jim Helfield and Robert Naiman of the University of Washington calculated.[24] It takes trees far from a salmon stream more than 300 years to reach a diameter of fifty centimeters (20 inches). But when salmon are near, the tree can reach fifty centimeters in less than ninety years.

Helfield and Naiman conducted their study in southeast Alaska, where salmon runs are relatively healthy. In places where salmon have been depleted (which is most places), the forests receive just 6 to 7 percent of the nitrogen they once received, another study found.

Salmon provide a keystone link between biodiversity and the climate. Restoring salmon in the rainforest does much more than revitalizing an undernourished ecosystem in one corner of the globe. Restoring salmon restores the climate, benefitting the entire planet, a connection Alexandra Morton explores in *Not on My Watch:*

> The growth of trees is linked to the health of the climate. The more trees grow, the more they absorb carbon dioxide, drawing down the deadly level of this greenhouse gas that is putting our entire civilization at risk.

# Chapter 9

# Mayhem on the Nehalem

One December morning in 1923, as coho salmon prepared to spawn in the Nehalem River in Oregon's Coast Range mountains, a herd of milk cows waded across the river in search of fresh pasture. Just upstream, a pile of freshly cut logs waited in a reservoir behind a small wooden dam, weighing several tons apiece. In a flash, the dam opened its gates. With the power of a hundred-year flood, a rush of water vaulted the logs downstream toward the terrified cows.

The logs were headed for a sawmill some twenty miles away in the coastal town of Wheeler. Before the advent of logging trucks, rivers provided the only means of transporting logs from the mountain to the mill. The Nehalem was too small a stream to easily float logs, so a dam was built to give them the needed boost. Hundreds of dams like it were erected in small streams throughout the temperate rainforest. Everyone called these structures "splash dams."

The cows, owned by Olive Moore, a local dairy farmer, scrambled to safety atop a gravel bar, but the salmon had nowhere to go. Before impact, Moore saw "millions of salmon" in the river. The projectiles slammed mercilessly into the helpless fish, squishing some under their massive weight while bouncing others onto shore. A neighbor filled several gunny sacks with dead salmon.

Several months later, Olive Moore recounted this harrowing episode in testimony at a public hearing before the Oregon Public Service Commission (PSC) in Wheeler. A larger splash, she surmised, would have wiped out all of her cows. A neighboring dairy farmer lost two, according to a transcript of the hearing preserved in state archives.[1]

Three or four times a year, the splash dam on the Nehalem unleashed a load of logs, Moore told the commission. After each splash, the logs creamed everything that happened to be in their path—streambeds, boat docks, and salmon. The logs also cleared out salmon spawning redds, obliterated beavers, beaver dams and lodges, and yes, even cows.

In June 1924, the PSC heard Moore and twenty-four of her neighbors spell out the hazards of splash dams in the Nehalem. A 1917 law called the Log Boom Act gave the commissioners the authority to enact splash dam regulations, resolve disputes, and impose sanctions. The neighbors demanded action.

But the PSC had other ideas. At the time, the PSC was also weighing an application to build another splash dam further upstream in the Nehalem. The neighbors protested that this new dam would only escalate the destruction. But the PSC approved the new dam anyway, and even permitted four additional dams. For the PSC, this was business as usual, as Jessica D. Phelps, a University of Oregon student, noted in her doctoral thesis in 2010. The PSC's decisions, Phelps wrote, "generally favored the logging companies."[2] It's always been that way. Today in Oregon, the logging companies still get what they want.

Splash dams, first introduced centuries ago in Europe and North America, became common in western Oregon and Washington starting around 1880. In all, more than three hundred splash dams were built throughout the region, transforming bucolic rivers like the Nehalem into giant log chutes, driving perhaps a billion logs to the mills, according to one estimate.[3] Incredibly, about seventy of them were built in one tiny stream, Mill Creek in the Coast Range west of Salem.[4]

The first splash dam in Oregon was erected on the North Fork of the Coos River. Eventually, logging roads rendered the splash dams obsolete. The last splash dam in Oregon was torn down in 1957, but today the state is still dealing with the legacy of this destructive technology. By all accounts, the impacts of splash dams have been felt most acutely by the region's iconic coho salmon runs. The coho is one of six salmon species native to the temperate rainforest (the others are Chinook, sockeye, chum, pink, and steelhead trout). The coho are born in the fresh, cold waters of a mountain stream, then migrate a thousand miles in the ocean. Around the time the adult coho reaches the age of four, she returns to her native stream to spawn, now weighing about ten pounds.

Before the splash dam era, more than two million coho returned each year to Oregon's coastal streams, one study estimated, based on an extrapolation of cannery data. By 1950, the coho population had almost completely disappeared, battered to near extinction by the splash dams. In many river systems, the loss exceeded 99 percent. The Coquille River, one of the most splash-dammed rivers in the state, lost 99.3 percent of its coho run. The Nehalem lost 99.5 percent of its run. It's a wonder any of them survived at all.[5]

Historically, the state fishery departments in Washington and Oregon each blamed the salmon crisis on splash dams. In 1955, the Washington Department of Forestry reported that salmon runs in one river fell sharply soon after a splash dam was built.[6]

On the day prior to the splashing of one of the large dams on the Humptulips River, an observer noted a large number of steelhead appeared below the apron of the dam. After splashing, no fish were seen, nor were any seen the following day. In case a log jam blocked the stream, dynamite was on hand to clear the obstruction. Any fish in the river were blown into smithereens. Sometimes the logging crew used an excessive amount of dynamite, as the Department of Forestry noted:

> In those days the policy seems to have been that if two boxes of powder would suffice, four were used. In some areas below dams in the lower Humptulips region, an average of five boxes of powder a day were used to break up log jams. Great numbers of salmon and steelhead trout were reportedly killed by these blasts.

In Oregon, splash dams were so destructive they caused "almost complete annihilation of the salmon and steelhead," M.C. Davis, Oregon's director of fisheries, said in a 1956 memo to the Public Service Commission.[7]

Splash dams and log drives were "two of the most effective destroyers of salmon habitat ever devised by humans," Jim Lichatowich, another fishery administrator in Oregon, wrote in 1999 in his book *Salmon Without Rivers*.[8]

> Each splash of logs and water left behind a devastated river with fewer and fewer of the ecological attributes the salmon needed in their habitat. Hiding places under overhanging banks were gone. Spawning gravel had disappeared, and the danger of being killed by yet another load of logs was just a few hours or days away. Splash dams made life particularly dangerous for Chinook salmon,

because they spawned and reared in the mainstems —
directly in the path of every log drive.

"I have seen streams that are largely just bedrock sluices as a
result of historic log runs," Bill Bakke, a longtime advocate for
wild salmon in Oregon, told us.

In 1998, coho salmon gained legal protection under
the Endangered Species Act. And yet, the coho population
continues to slide. In the Pacific coastal temperate rainforest,
salmon are the keystone species.[9] The sharp decline in the
coho population has heavily impacted the entire ecosystem.
As many as 138 species of wildlife feed on salmon, including
humans. The salmon also nourish the forest, as we saw in the
previous chapter. The presence of salmon can triple the size of
trees located near the stream. Larger trees store more carbon.
Thus the destruction of the salmon, in some modest way, has
contributed to the climate crisis.

For decades after splash dams were banned in the 1950s, their
environmental legacy was largely unknown. That changed
in 2010, when Rebecca Miller, then a doctoral candidate at
Oregon State University, decided to investigate.[10] Miller found
the ecological damage caused by splash dams is still evi-
dent after all these years. What's more, splash dams are still
killing salmon.

In her research, Miller found damage throughout the Coast
Range. She called for extensive and intensive stream restoration measures, but has seen no concerted effort to repair the
pernicious damage splash dams left behind. Miller consulted
with Jim Sedell, a veteran fish biologist who played a central
role in the development of the Northwest Forest Plan in the

1990s. Sedell, author of a history of splash dams, was one the first of few scientists to document their troubling legacy.[11]

"It still amazes me that no one really picked up the trail," Miller told us. Now a fishery biologist with the National Marine Fisheries Service, Miller is still concerned about saving salmon. Miller determined that the impacts of splash damming were not all caused by the rush of logs. Streams needed to be straightened, or else all the logs would leave the streambed at every turn. Re-engineering streams dried up adjacent wetlands, meadows and swamps. These areas were prime salmon habitat, but in many splash-dammed rivers, they no longer exist.

In her research, Miller compared healthy streams with those damaged by splash dams. "I found statistical differences in splashed and not-splashed reaches," she told us. Miller found a fully intact splash dam in Little Fall Creek east of Eugene. Throughout the western Oregon mountains, she found footings, winches, and Lincoln-log style cribbing, the detritus of the splash dam era.

Miller located 232 splash-dam sites in western Oregon. Many remain visibly damaged. On heavily splashed reaches of the Nehalem River, such as near Olive Moore's cow pastures, Miller found half were scoured to bedrock. Areas normally covered with gravel were bare. In the Nehalem's unsplashed reaches, only 5 percent of the river was bare bedrock and almost all of the spawning gravels were still in place.

Deep pools in the Nehalem—the refuges where juvenile salmon chill out and hide from predators—have been filled with sediment stirred up by logs in the heavily splashed parts of the river. In the unsplashed sections, deep pools are still in good condition, Miller found. Restoring salmon habitat damaged by splash dams could be a key to restoring the salmon itself, Miller told us. It could also be a cost-effective climate solution.

Splash dams usually gave some warning that a splash was imminent. A splash dam on the Coquille River splashed daily with a five o'clock whistle. When a splash dam released its logs, Jack Flitcroft, a retired splash dam operator, told Miller, you could hear "a good roar." But people downriver might not know what was coming.

In 1925, a splash on the Coos River sent a wall of water toward a film crew working on the silent movie *The Ancient Highway*, a tragic event Coos Bay author Lionel Youst recounts in his book, *Lost in Coos*:

> A stunt man named Renald D. Jones, doubling for star Tim Holt, was in a canoe below the Sugarloaf Dam. The scene called for him to be paddling ahead of a rush of water and logs. When the dam was opened, the wall of water immediately capsized the canoe and Jones was drowned in the sight of hundreds of spectators. Filming stopped, the search was on, and his body was found the next day.[12]

Splash dams were not imposing structures, often rising only a few feet above the water. The largest splash dam ever in Oregon, Tioga Dam on the South Fork of the Coos River, stood fifty feet tall. The largest splash dam anywhere in the region might have been Big Dam, a 100-foot-tall structure built in

1900 on a flimsy bed of gravel in a steep canyon in Southwest Washington. Big Dam collapsed with the first splash.

Built in 1944 by the local Coos River Boom Company, Tioga was later owned by the Menasha Corporation, a multinational timber company based in Wisconsin. Tioga was constructed of logs placed vertically in the water, end on end, shore to shore. Other splash dams were little more than logs piled horizontally across a streambed. Engines known as "steam donkeys" skidded felled trees into the reservoirs behind the dams.

The head of operations at Tioga Dam was a former schoolteacher, Dow Beckham, who later chronicled life on a splash dam in a 1990 memoir, *Swift Flows the River*.[13] In the book, Beckham claims splash dams were law-breakers from the start. For instance, splash dam operators routinely skirted laws requiring shipping channels in navigable rivers like the Coos to remain open at all times. But the regulators with the Public Service Commission didn't seem to care.

"We could not have handled the volume of logs otherwise," Beckham wrote in *Swift Flows the River*, the first of four books he penned after his eightieth birthday. "If they had enforced the rules, splash dam logging would have been terminated."[14] The dams also appeared to violate an Oregon law from prestatehood that required all dams to provide fish passage, Bill Bakke told us. "Obviously splash dams did not provide fish passage. The state did not enforce the issue." We learned a lot about the history of splash dams from Dow Beckham's son, Stephen Dow Beckham, now a retired history professor at Lewis & Clark College in Portland.

The PSC approved Tioga Dam only after a lengthy, contentious public hearing, citing national security concerns during World War II while dismissing the concerns of fish biologists,

Stephen Dow Beckham told us. In his opinion, the PSC realized the importance of Tioga Dam to the war effort:

> It operated at full tilt during the war as a highly efficient and affordable means of bringing tens of millions of board feet of logs to the sawmills for construction of barracks, docks, and other military facilities along the West Coast and in the Pacific theatre of war operations. Because my father's position was deemed critical in a war-related industry, he was not called for military service nor were the men on his crew. Virtually no heavy equipment was available to construct logging roads nor trucks for log hauling between 1941 and 1946. Water transportation thus proved vital.

Tioga Dam's contribution to the war effort lasted just a couple years. After the war ended in 1945, Tioga continued operating for another twelve years. As Miller reports in her study, salmon habitat in the river below the dam remains damaged. Tioga continues to kill salmon. Tioga was the last splash dam in Oregon to cease operating.

Today, some timber industry executives regret the damage splash dams caused to salmon. Scott Starkey, a former vice president of Coos County operations for the Menasha Corporation, acknowledges that splash dams were "detrimental" to fish runs. Starkey is now an executive for Campbell Global, a timber management consulting company. In an email, he told us:

The splash dams on the Coos, while in operation, most likely wiped out all native fish runs at the time. They not only totally blocked the rivers for many years, but also wiped out much of the habitat below them during the splash. In hindsight, we now know that those logging practices at the time were quite harmful. I wish it had never happened. However, over the years with new scientific knowledge, forest practice laws have evolved that now provide for excellent stream protection.

To mitigate the impact of splash dams, the state of Oregon built hatcheries. The state hoped to save salmon without restricting the logging practices that were killing them. But hatcheries have not worked out as hoped. Jim Lichatowich told us that a hundred years of hatchery production has not increased the size of salmon populations at all.

Logging has contributed to the salmon's demise in other ways as well. For example, the common practice of logging next to some streams has caused stream temperatures to increase to levels harmful to salmon. The Oregon Department of Forestry has refused to enact regulations that would ban this practice on privately owned lands, where it exercises regulatory authority.

Two federal agencies contend that by failing to act, Oregon is violating two federal laws, the Clean Water Act and the Coastal Zone Management Act. The Environmental Protection Agency (EPA) and the National Oceanic and Atmospheric Administration (NOAA) have each penalized the state for failing to enforce these laws.

The agencies began issuing fines of about $1 million a year in 2015. By 2022, more than $8 million in fines had accumulated, according to documents we obtained via Oregon's public records laws. EPA and NOAA say they will cease penalizing the state only if it strengthens the forestry regulations. In late 2021, an agreement between industry and environmental groups called for stronger regulations, potentially resolving the issue.

In Oregon, enforcement of forestry regulations is controlled by the Board of Forestry, a seven-member panel. Three of its members can, by law, receive a significant portion of their income from the timber industry. It's an arrangement devised by the Oregon Legislature. In Oregon, candidates for the Legislature can receive unlimited campaign contributions from corporations, one of only five states that allow this, according to an investigative report in 2019 by Rob Davis of *The Oregonian*, the state's largest newspaper.

From 2008 to 2017, the timber industry contributed an average of $2,000 per year to each of Oregon's ninety legislators, more than it gave to legislators in any other state, as the newspaper reported in an award-winning series, "Polluted by Money."[15]

"Corporate cash has corrupted one of the greenest states in America," the newspaper proclaimed. In one article, *The Oregonian* reported that timber industry lobbyists "repeatedly attacked the reporting as incorrect. Without providing evidence, lobbyists said we twisted the truth. We didn't," the newspaper retorted. It claimed to have the facts backing up its reporting. "And the receipts."[16]

# Chapter 10

# The Blue Carbon Zone

In the 1990s, as salmon runs on the Oregon Coast slipped perilously close to extinction, an army of volunteers stood up against the clear-cutting that was ravaging spawning grounds in Coast Range streams. After a century of logging, the streams became inhospitable to the fish, and were getting worse.

Led by Paul Engelmeyer, manager of an Audubon wildlife sanctuary near Yachats, the volunteers began patrolling one million acres of forestland from mountain summits to the ocean. At the time, Engelmeyer was best known for his conservation work on behalf of birds in western Oregon. One of his wards was the marbled murrelet, a tiny, endangered seabird that had also fallen victim to heavy logging. The campaign to save salmon was his next challenge.

In the 1980s, Engelmeyer was part of a group of ornithologists who discovered a marbled murrelet nest in the mountains west of Corvallis. No one had found a murrelet nest in Oregon before. Their nests are hard to find. The murrelet prefers to nest in the most secluded place it can find, ideally in the canopy of an old-growth tree far from the forest's edge. There's no safer place for the murrelet to hide its babies from crows and other predators.

Engelmeyer, a skilled tree-climber, found the nest in a Douglas-fir canopy near Corvallis some forty miles from the ocean. Many more nests were soon found. The murrelet's nesting habits revealed the seabird's unorthodox pattern of behavior: after spending its days in the ocean bobbing for fish, the murrelet races back home at dusk at speeds approaching 100 mph. At dawn, it returns to the ocean for another day of fishing. Few species on Earth commute further each day from home to work than the marbled murrelet.

Engelmeyer pressed the federal government to stop the logging that was demolishing the murrelet's nesting trees. The effort paid off in 1992, when the U.S. Fish and Wildlife Service gave the seabird protection under the Endangered Species Act. The government eventually banned logging throughout 3.6 million acres of old-growth forests in California, Oregon, and Washington, protecting each murrelet nesting tree on federal land, plus every tree in the immediate vicinity. The government also set aside an even greater amount of forest for the northern spotted owl, another endangered bird that nests only in old-growth forests. In addition to protecting biodiversity, these decisions also protected trees on behalf of the climate.

With these victories in hand, Engelmeyer turned his attention to the wild salmon, a fish that is born in a river, as opposed to one born in a hatchery or a fish farm. Like the murrelet, restoring salmon will depend on finding better ways to manage forests, such as banning logging in the riparian zones next to streams. Riparian trees provide a cooling shade needed by salmon. Fewer shade trees means higher stream temperatures that can be deadly to salmon. But protecting forests, if that's all we do, will not be enough to restore the salmon. Salmon face additional perils throughout their life journey, which takes them thousands of miles from native streams to the ocean and back again. After leaving their place of birth as a young smolt, they head to the estuary—the flat, wet, coastal plain where they spend a significant part of their young life. Sadly, almost every estuary on the Pacific Coast is degraded, a factor that depresses the salmon's chances of survival.

Restoring estuaries is seen as critical to restoring salmon populations, and is likely to have an important side benefit: it will help mitigate climate change. Rescuing an endangered fish, Engelmeyer soon realized, would be far more complicated than rescuing an endangered bird, and could potentially yield much greater rewards.

When the baby salmon reaches the estuary, it enters a zone where freshwater flowing down the mountain mixes with the salty tidewater washing up from the sea. The salmon will spend days, weeks, or even months in the brackish estuary while their bodies add weight in preparation for a future life in the ocean.

There are nearly seven hundred estuaries in Washington, Oregon, and California.[1] Over the last 150 years, humans have dramatically altered almost all of them with urban development and agriculture. Most of them have been drained, logged, filled, and diked.[2] Few remain intact.

Of the seven species of salmon on the Oregon Coast only three are present in significant numbers: coho, Chinook, and steelhead. The Chinook, being the bigger fish, often weighs in excess of twenty-five pounds, and spends a greater amount of time in the estuary, often as long as six months.

Barely 1 percent of the salmon survive their stay in the estuary, but their odds of survival increase if the estuary is in good condition. For the Chinook, especially, a healthy estuary can dramatically increase the odds. One study found that Chinook salmon traveling through degraded estuaries are three times more likely to die.[3] The quality of habitat in the estuary does not seem to affect the coho as much, likely due to shorter estuary visits.

Most Chinook salmon return to their native coastal rivers in either the spring or fall, though a few arrive in summer. The spring runs are in the most trouble. In Oregon, spring Chinook inhabited almost every estuary at the start of the twentieth century, but today only a handful still remain, according to Conrad Gowell of the Native Fish Society, a conservation group in Oregon. Spring Chinook no longer exist in the Siuslaw, Coos, and Salmon estuaries, Gowell says. Very small populations remain in the Tillamook, Nestucca, Siletz, Alsea, and Coquille estuaries. But no one knows the exact numbers. The Oregon Department of Fish and Wildlife has documented a steep decline in the abundance of coho salmon since 1900, but has no similar data on Chinook populations.

There are fifteen major estuaries on the Oregon Coast, and Laura Brophy, an ecologist from Corvallis, has mapped them all.[4] She charts the twelve-foot tides that inundate Oregon's estuaries twice a month; only seven areas in the western hemisphere have high tides that great.[5] In other parts of the world, tides rise a foot or two, or maybe just a few inches, Brophy says, "but that's not the Oregon Coast."

Brophy divides estuaries into three different ecosystems: tidal marshes, tidal shrub wetlands, and forested tidal wetlands. The tidal marsh, located closest to shore, is covered with grasses, sedges, rushes, and broadleaf plants. Further back, the tidal shrub wetland is occupied by woody bushes and a few small trees. Forested tidal wetlands, located furthest from shore, are dominated by towering Sitka spruce forests.[6]

The most intriguing part of the estuary may be the forested tidal wetlands, which Brophy refers to as "tidal swamps."

About 85 percent of tidal wetlands on the West Coast have been lost, Brophy says.

> Tidal swamps are some of the most beautiful places I have ever seen. To see the forest floor moving with a foot of moving water was a real turning point in my understanding. We don't really think of forests as having the tides flow through them.

Hiking in a forest flooded by high tides can be dangerous, she says. Swift currents can sweep you off your feet. Where they still exist, tidal swamps provide excellent habitat for all species of salmon, not just coho. They offer deep and complex channels, a rich and abundant supply of food, large woody debris, beaver ponds and the opportunity for them to gradually acclimate to saltwater. At low tide, you can see the shallow channels spanning the tidal swamp. At high tide, the channels fill up with water. Some of this water spills into the forest. "We're only beginning to learn what tidal swamps do for us," Brophy says. "We expect they fill lots of functions, but we don't have a lot of data yet."

Centuries ago, the temperate rainforest stretched all the way from mountain summits to the ocean, with long arms frequently reaching far into the tidal zone. Almost all of these long arms of the rainforest have been cut off, though you can still find tiny remnants of this venerable ecosystem. In Oregon, at one time more than 80 percent of the Coquille River estuary south of Coos Bay was forested. Today, less than 1 percent remains. About 63 percent of the Tillamook Estuary was forested, but only 8 percent remains.

Tidal swamps can also be found in the Nehalem, Siuslaw, Yaquina, and Columbia River estuaries. You can still find a relatively intact tidal swamp in the Columbia estuary, in a mysterious place known as Secret River.

The lost tidal forested wetlands are not only disappearing from the landscape, they are slipping from memory. They've even been expunged from the scientific literature, as though they never existed. The Oregon Estuary Plan Book, the authoritative guidebook for restoring estuaries, doesn't mention forested tidal wetlands at all.[7] Nor are there any mentions of tidal forests in *Oregon Wild: Endangered Forest Wilderness*, a definitive book on Oregon forests by Andy Kerr, the veteran environmental advocate.[8] When we asked Kerr about tidal forests, our questions perplexed him. Later, he mused in his blog, "What the hell is he talking about? While I had long occasionally heard reference to 'tideland spruce,' it never made any sense to me."

Kerr said he should have paid more attention to guidebooks on forest ecology, such as *Natural Vegetation of Oregon and Washington*, by University of Washington professor Jerry Franklin, which offers this brief description:[9]

> *Picea sitchensis* is, of course, the characteristic tree species of tideland areas and has been referred to as 'tideland spruce' almost since its discovery. Sprawling, open-growth (Sitka spruce) border tidal flats and channels all along the Oregon and Washington coasts.

"One likes to learn something every day," Kerr said, "but this is at least a week's worth of learning." Cottonwoods and ash can thrive in the brackish waters of some tidal swamps, but most are anchored by Sitka spruce. The Sitka spruce is the temperate rainforest's answer to the tropical mangrove.

In forested tidal wetlands, the fast-growing Sitka spruce also qualifies as a keystone species. In the tidal swamp, the roots of Sitka spruce form platforms looming several feet above the channel, providing shelter where salmon can hang out until the high tide returns. These dense, multi-layered ecosystems also provide exceptional habitat for waterfowl, songbirds, raptors, owls, warblers, fly-catchers, and thrushes.

Estuaries and other intertidal zones are more than hubs for biodiversity. They are also important carbon sinks. Known as "blue carbon" ecosystems, estuaries store carbon in soils down to a depth of ten feet. Blue carbon ecosystems occupy the intertidal margins of shorelines and estuaries. Forests are green carbon. Oil fields and coal mines are black carbon.

Even in a degraded state, the blue carbon ecosystem alongside the Pacific coastal temperate rainforest stores more carbon per acre than any other intertidal zone on Earth, according to a 2020 study by J. Boone Kauffman, an Oregon State University ecologist.[10] Laura Brophy was one of the study's co-authors. Restoring blue carbon ecosystems is considered to be a vital natural solution to both the biodiversity and climate crises. When we spoke in 2021, Kauffman was preparing a report on blue carbon ecosystems for the Intergovernmental Panel on Climate Change.

Climate scientists have been studying the carbon content of estuaries in the tropics for more than a decade, but carbon data from tidal ecosystems in the temperate zone did not exist until 2020, when Kauffman published his research in the peer-reviewed journal *Global Change Biology*. There is still a dearth of data. Even in their current tattered condition, blue carbon ecosystems along the Pacific Coast are an "exceptional carbon sink," he says. Kauffman's measurements show the tidal forests contain about 1,000 tons of carbon per hectare, just under the 1,100 tons of carbon found in the Douglas-fir forests in the Coast Range.

In the Pacific coastal tidal zone, Kauffman found large amounts of carbon in dead and alive vegetation above the ground, and in roots and soils down to about ten feet. Kauffman analyzed the carbon densities of every segment of the Pacific Coast's blue carbon ecosystem—seagrasses, wetlands, marshes, and forests. Each contains more carbon per acre than comparable ecosystems in Brazil, Mexico and elsewhere in the tropics.

On a surprisingly warm February day, we visited a tidal forest in Southwest Washington known as the Secret River—a place so secret neither of us had heard of before. We found the GPS coordinates in the Kauffman study that showed its extraordinary value to the climate. Located at the head of an estuary next to the Columbia River upstream from Astoria, the Secret River flows through an ancient Sitka spruce forest, providing important habitat for salmon and storing massive amounts of carbon. The Secret River estuary contains 20 percent more carbon than any other blue carbon ecosystem on earth, so far as we know.[11] It's not much of a river, measuring no more than a mile or so in length. It runs through a marsh with tall grasses, ducks, a proliferation of invasive blackberries, and an abandoned rock quarry. It is a small remnant of a lost ecosystem of extraordinary value to the planet.

The Columbia Land Trust, a non-governmental organization based in Vancouver, Washington, is buying the land in an effort to protect and restore the Secret River, Ian Sinks, the trust's stewardship director, told us. "It is a special place," he said.

One sign of a healthy estuary is the presence of the North American beaver (*Castor canadensis*), the furry, fifty-pound rodent with a funny tail, big teeth, and no neck.

"Whenever I see a beaver dam out in the tidal marsh I always take a picture because it's fascinating," Brophy says. Beavers are ecosystem engineers, best known for the work they perform in rivers. Beavers build dams that create ponds, alcoves, and side channels—ideal infrastructure for juvenile salmon to feed, rest, and hide from predators. They also create and maintain upland meadows and wetlands.

Few people know beavers also build dams in the estuary. The aforementioned Oregon Estuary Plan Book says nothing about beavers. But the beaver's work down in the estuary is important. Though beavers are not particularly fond of brackish water, they will build dams in the estuary if they can find the right building materials: sticks, mud, branches, and logs.

Beavers perform important functions in estuaries, as ecologist Greg Hood discovered about a decade ago while collecting data in the Skagit River Delta in Puget Sound for a research project. When Hood looked down at one of the channels crossing the estuary, he saw masses of branches and twigs. Beaver dams. At first, he didn't believe his eyes. "They looked suspiciously like beaver dams," he told us. "I never heard of beaver dams in tidal marshes."

He searched Google for scholarly papers on beaver dams in estuaries, but turned up nothing, save for one paper on the European beaver, a different species, in the Rhine River Delta.

So Hood decided to start his own research, and eventually challenged the conventional view of beavers as residents of only non-tidal, freshwater habitats. What's more, he found that beavers perform a vital service in the estuary for the salmon—and the climate.

In 2012, his groundbreaking paper, "Beaver in Tidal Marshes: Dam Effects on Low-Tide Channel Pools and Fish Use of Estuarine Habitat," appeared in the peer-reviewed journal *Wetlands*.[12] In tidal marsh and shrub tidal wetlands, Hood found that Chinook salmon[13] were three times more abundant in beaver dam pools than in other tidal channels.

In the estuary, high tides cover the beaver dam with a foot or more of water. As the tide recedes, the dams impound some of the outflow in channels where juvenile salmon can hide from predators like the great blue heron, or feed on insects. In areas lacking beaver dams, a swift tidal outflow can sweep the juvenile salmon out to sea, regardless of whether their bodies are ready to go on to the ocean and survive in saltwater. The channels behind a beaver dam never empty out, enabling the young fish to remain on shore, potentially saving its life, Hood told us. A salmon spending more time in the estuary will have a better chance of surviving into adulthood.

The beaver is a keystone species in the blue carbon ecosystem. Habitats altered by beavers are biodiversity hotspots. Beavers occupy 1 percent of the landscape, yet support dozens of species. Keystone species tie the ecosystem together. Without them, things would fall apart. As Greg Hood's research shows, beavers measurably boost the population of salmon. The more salmon in the river, the larger the trees. Larger trees store and sequester more carbon from the atmosphere, a clear win for the climate.

Beavers also help to increase the amount of carbon sequestered in soils. Beavers can create peatlands, where large
amounts of carbon is stored. Carbon is also stored in the
sediments of beaver ponds and beaver meadows. One report
calculated that, globally, beaver ponds, meadows, and peatlands store 378 million metric tonnes of carbon.[14] And yet,
no matter their importance to the ecosystem and the climate,
beavers receive no special protection under state or federal
laws. A determined group of Oregonians is out to change that.

At one time, there were millions of beavers in North America,
but fur trapping nearly left them extinct by the time Oregon
became a state in 1859. In the twentieth century, their numbers rebounded, but today they remain at less than 10 percent
of historic levels.[15]

You would think the public would want to protect an
animal that can help an endangered salmon survive, especially
if that animal also contributes to the fight against climate
chaos. "There is nothing you could do today that would be a
better cost-effective climate change mitigation strategy than
to eliminate trapping beaver," Kauffman told us. And yet in
Oregon, beavers are still hunted down like criminals. The
beaver trapping season begins in November and continues
until March, coinciding with their breeding and pregnancy.
Trappers kill about 2,500 per year. Beaver pelts go for $10
to $21 each. Landowners can kill beavers on their own land
without getting a permit or filing a report. Nobody knows how
many they kill.

At one time, the beaver was Oregon's most iconic species.
Beavers are Oregon's official animal, the mascot of Oregon State
University, and the supplier of the state's nickname, as author

Ben Goldfarb writes in his wonderful book *Eager: the Surprising, Secret Life of Beavers and Why They Matter.*[16]

> When, in 1848 the Oregon Territory defied the federal government by creating its own mint, beavers featured on the coins; today, a golden beaver, waddling across a navy field, adorns one side of Oregon's flag. Yet for all its iconography, the Beaver State remains notably hostile to its eponymous rodents, classifying the herbivores, ludicrously, as predators.

In 2020, Suzanne Fouty, a retired hydrologist with the U.S. Forest Service and one of the state's leading beaver experts, spearheaded a campaign to stop the hunts. She filed a petition with the Oregon Fish and Wildlife Commission, and several conservation groups signed on. Some of the most vocal supporters of the petition were volunteers with the Midcoast Watershed Council who fought alongside Engelmeyer to save coastal coho salmon decades ago. Now they are beaver believers.

At public hearings, they argued that beaver hunting depresses the animal's population at a time when their labors are urgently needed. "There are not enough beavers in each of our watersheds to create the ecosystem benefits we know they can create," said Fran Recht, a resident of Depoe Bay and a Midcoast council board member. "Beavers contribute more to the economy when they are alive than when they are dead," said economist Hans Radtke of Yachats.

But Derek Broman, the state of Oregon's main beaver expert, insists the harvest rate on beavers is low. However, Broman acknowledges he has no data to back that up. He does not know how many beavers are out there. Nor does anybody else. Broman did not respond to our request for an interview.

Fouty, for one, isn't buying Broman's talking point. "Areas that at one time supported beaver dams can no longer do so," she says. She cites as evidence some twenty years' worth of data, from 1999 through 2019, collected from seventeen coastal streams. During this time, the total area inundated in these watersheds by beaver ponds shrank by 92 percent. This was prime salmon-rearing habitat, and it has been lost. As a result, nearly 40,000 adult coho salmon, or about one-third of the entire coastal coho run, have vanished, according to Steve Trask, a coastal fish biologist. Even federal agencies argued in favor of banning beaver hunts. A coho salmon recovery plan devised by the federal National Marine Fisheries Service (NMFS) said restoring beaver populations is essential. Killing beavers is not part of the plan.

"Unfortunately Oregon stands out nationally and internationally as a dark spot on the map of science-based management of our natural resources when it comes to beavers," says Chris Jordan, a NMFS biologist. Bob Sallinger, conservation director of Portland Audubon, which owns the sizable wildlife sanctuary near Yachats run by Paul Engelmeyer, said the state has failed to show that beaver hunting does no harm to the ecosystem. This failure, he said, violates the Precautionary Principle, the idea that no action should be taken before all the facts are in. "We need to start first with the health of our ecosystem and then figure out what can be extracted from it," Sallinger says. In the end, the state Fish and Wildlife Commission rejected Fouty's petition. The beaver hunts will continue.

A small lake on Prince of Wales Island, as seen from the air.
Photo by Jessica Applegate.

A logging truck on Prince of Wales Island hauls the latest harvest for
export to China. Photo by Jessica Applegate.

Dominick DellaSala of Wild Heritage Institute stands next to a pile of logs at the Viking Lumber Mill on Prince of Wales Island. Photo by Jessica Applegate.

A muskeg (a type of wetland) on Prince of Wales Island. Photo by Jessica Applegate.

Paul Koberstein standing in a clear-cut known as the Big Thorne timber sale on Prince of Wales Island. Seventy percent of the logs cut go to waste and are left on the ground. Photo by Jessica Applegate.

The cargo ship *Global Striker* sits at a dock on Prince of Wales Island, where it is loaded with logs headed for China. Photo by Jessica Applegate.

Aerial shot from a bush plane over clearcuts on Prince of Wales Island.
Photo by Jessica Applegate.

Heading into a roadless area north of Juneau, Alaska. Photo by Jessica Applegate.

Fog over Juneau, Alaska. Photo by Jessica Applegate.

A forested wetland north of Juneau, Alaska. Photo by Jessica Applegate.

Fishing boats in Sitka, Alaska's busy harbor. Photo by Jessica Applegate.

A totem pole in Sitka National Historical Park, Alaska. Photo by Jessica Applegate.

Dying yellow cedar on Chichagof Island, as seen from a ferry boat transiting Alaska's Peril Strait, northeast of Sitka. Photo by Jessica Applegate.

Tlingit master carver Tommy Joseph carving yellow cedar log in Sitka, Alaska.
Photo by Jessica Applegate.

Maple trees in the Hoh Rainforest in Olympic National Forest drip with moss; this area is known as the Hall of Mosses. Photo by Jessica Applegate.

Western hemlock nurse log in the Hoh Rainforest. Photo by Jessica Applegate.

Port Angeles lumber mill sits in the shadow of the Olympic Mountains in northwest Washington. Photo by Jessica Applegate.

A charred redwood tree in the Grove of Titans, Del Norte County,
Northern California. Photo by Jessica Applegate.

A person strolling through redwoods at the Jedediah Smith Redwoods State Park
in Northern California. California. Photo by Jessica Applegate.

A nurse log nurturing new life in the rainforest of Northern California.
Photo by Jessica Applegate.

The Ghost Forest of Neskowin: remnants of a Sitka spruce forest in Neskowin, Oregon. Photo by Jessica Applegate.

Clear-cut debris on the side of the road in Oceanside, Oregon, mere miles from the most carbon-dense forest north of California.
Photo by Jessica Applegate.

The Big Spruce, one of the largest Sitka spruce trees in the world, is at Cape Meares National Wildlife Refuge in Oregon. It is 144 feet high and 48 feet in circumference, with a crown spread of 90 feet by 88 feet. Photo by Jessica Applegate.

Jessica and Paul in a bush plane over Prince of Wales Island, Alaska.
Photo by Paul Koberstein.

Paul preparing for an interview in Juneau, Alaska. Photo by Jessica Applegate.

# PART FOUR

## THIS IS THEIR FOREST

*Suppose a White man should come to me and say, "Joseph, I like your horses. I want to buy them." I say to him, "No, my horses suit me; I will not sell them." Then he goes to my neighbor and says to him, "Joseph has some good horses. I want to buy them, but he refuses to sell." My neighbor answers, "Pay me the money and I will sell you Joseph's horses." The White man returns to me and says, "Joseph, I have bought your horses and you must let me have them." If we sold our land to the government, this is the way they bought them.*

*—Heinmot Tooyalakekt (Chief Joseph),*
*Nez Perce Tribe*

# Chapter 11

# Stolen Ancestral Homelands

September 8, 1855, should be celebrated as the day peace came to Oregon's coastal temperate rainforest. Representatives of the United States government and sixty-one coastal tribes met that day at the old Empire Hotel on the Coos Bay waterfront to wrap up the sweeping Oregon Coast Treaty. After two months of talks, they agreed on language to end a long, bloody war between settlers and Indians. But hardly anyone remembers. The treaty was never ratified. There was no peace. Instead, the tribes lost their ancestral homelands in the midst of a brutal genocide.

Violent conflicts between Whites and Indians on the southern Oregon coast erupted after gold was discovered there in 1852. Miners streamed into the region, seizing whatever they wanted, but Indians fiercely resisted. In response, miners burned down villages and slaughtered hundreds of people. (In this book, we honor the preferences of Indigenous people. In the United States, they identify themselves as "Indians" and their communities as "tribes." In Canada, they identify themselves as "First Nations.")

Joel Palmer, representing the federal government at the treaty talks, began the proceedings with a hopeful homily to the chiefs and headmen in attendance, representing the Chinook and Tillamook tribes on the northern Oregon coast, and the Coos, Lower Umpqua, and Siuslaw nations to the south:

> I present you with the peace pipe. It is the pipe I take
> with me to all my Councils. I first smoke it, and then

give it to your Chief, and then to the people, and every
man that smokes is, it is expected, will be a good man. If
he has a bad heart, he must put it away until he smokes
it. I want none to smoke it who has a bad heart. From
this day on, I want you to be at peace among yourselves,
as well as with the Whites. I have written out a Treaty,
a bargain for their country from the Columbia to the
California line. No Whites will be allowed to live on the
Reserve but the Agents and employees.[1]

In the words of the treaty, the tribes cede their ancestral
homelands in the Coast Range from the summit to the Pacific
Ocean, and from the Columbia River to the California border—a 7.2-million-acre landscape densely forested with gigantic conifers, by far the most productive timberland in the world.
The treaty called on them to relocate to a 1.1-million-acre reservation on the central coast, as well as "be friendly" with all
of the citizens of the United States:

This treaty shall be obligatory on the contracting parties
as soon as the same shall be ratified by the President, and
Senate of the United States.[2]

In return, the government promised to build a fort on the reservation to protect the Indians and provide them with about
$120,000 in cash and supplies. But the treaty was not sub-
mitted to the Senate until February 1857 and was never put
up for a vote. Instead, the government unilaterally claimed
ownership of the land while paying little compensation, eventually selling it off (or giving it away) to settlers, railroads, and
timber companies.

The next four chapters of *Canopy of Titans* tell the story of how the theft of ancestral homelands enabled the timber industry to wrest control of much of the Pacific coastal temperate rainforest on both sides of the U.S.-Canada border, and how Indigenous people in both countries are reclaiming some of their lost heritage.

The timber industry later compounded the larceny by defying attempts by native people, other citizens, legislatures, and regulatory agencies in each country to protect the rainforest's water quality and fragile biodiversity, including world-renowned salmon runs. This defiance continues to this day. And now, the industry is fighting efforts to preserve the rainforest as a carbon sink as climate mitigation for the benefit of all of humanity. The injustice of their actions, and the horrific consequences of climate change, are being felt most acutely by Indigenous people.[3]

The Indians held up their end of the bargain, but the U.S. government did not. The government never came through with the promised money, supplies, or protection. Instead, the U.S. Army initiated a brutal siege. In 1860, they forcibly marched the Indians to the Oregon Coast Reservation near present-day Yachats, imprisoning some 2,000 people for seventeen years. Half died in the first decade.

The massive reservation was to be a little larger than the entire state of Rhode Island, stretching about 100 miles from Cape Lookout to the Sea Lion Caves in the central coast. Starting in the 1860s, the government began allowing White settlers to occupy the reservation, in contradiction to the specific language of the unratified treaty. All the settlers were White. A state law enacted in the 1840s, a decade before statehood, made it illegal for racial minorities to live in Oregon. The specific intent of this law was to ban Black people. Native Americans could still legally live in the state, though they were often brutalized and murdered. The 14th Amendment to the U.S. Constitution, ratified in 1868, invalidated that racist law, though it remained on the books until 1926.[4]

In 1865, President Andrew Johnson signed an executive order dramatically reducing the size of the reservation, now known as the Siletz Reservation. Ten years later, Congress reduced it some more. Today, the formerly million-acre reservation encompasses just 3,500 fragmented acres.

In 1892, the federal government agreed to pay $142,000 for the Siletz Reservation, a total rip-off, according to Steven Puter's book, *Looters of the Public Domain*. From his cell in a Salem prison, Puter wrote:

> What the Indians were coaxed into giving for this comparatively insignificant amount represents an area equivalent to about 1,300 homesteads of 160 acres each, or practically 200,000 acres in round numbers, and is worth today at a conservative estimate more than $8,00,000. If Uncle Sam could do this well on all his real estate investments, he could afford to retire, satisfied with his sagacity, if not his conscience.[5]

The tribal members imprisoned at the reservation lost their right to hunt, fish, and gather food at their traditional places. These rights were not even mentioned in their unratified treaties, unlike treaties with many other tribes in the region, where these rights were specifically reserved forever.

"Ten treaties negotiated on Puget Sound and in the interior of the Pacific Northwest had 'reserved rights' clauses," Stephen Dow Beckham, professor emeritus of history at Portland's Lewis & Clark College, told us. Beckham is author of *The Indians of Western Oregon: This Land Was Theirs*,[6] a definitive book on the subject, and the son of Dow Beckham, the operator of splash dams in Coos County whom we met in Chapter 9. "These people lost everything," Beckham told us. "They left behind their baskets, obsidian blades, dugout canoes and plank houses."

"For each tribe, their removal was a time of sadness," David G. Lewis, a former tribal historian at the Grand Ronde Reservation in Oregon's Yamhill Valley and currently a professor of history at Oregon State University, told us.

> People gave up all their lands, sold everything that they may survive the constant onslaught from the Americans. All promises made of a better life for tribal people on the reservations went unrealized. In fact, the opposite occurred for many tribal families, and many today suffer from this differential history of the lack of resources, of racist treatment by the White Americans, and from some 160 years of repression by the federal government.

In a paper published by Oregon Historical Quarterly in 2019, Lewis traced the conflict between Whites and coastal Indians back to 1832, when two fur trappers with the Hudson Bay Company were killed in the central Coast Range near Alsea. The company retaliated by slaughtering about 400 members of the Yaquina Tribe, which "effectively ended the Yaquina people as a nation."[7]

"Ultimately," Lewis writes, "the coercive power of violence was the decisive factor of the ascendancy of Whites in the West." The Oregon Coast Treaty of 1855 was long forgotten and remained hidden until 1916, when dozens of autonomous tribal groups came together in an attempt to resurrect the treaty. Meeting again at the Empire Hotel, the Coos, Lower Umpqua, and Siuslaw tribes collectively represented 1.6 million acres of ancestral homelands extending across much of the Coast Range. At the meeting, they formed the new Confederated Tribes of the Coos, Lower Umpqua, and Siuslaw, and hired a young attorney, George Bundy Wasson, a tribal elder of both the Coos and Coquille (also spelled Coquelle) nations, to investigate what happened to the treaty document.

A few years earlier, Wasson discovered the document while "digging through the dusty tomes" in the U.S. Department of the Interior in Washington, D.C. He saw it as the legal weapon the tribes needed to win compensation for their losses, as well as a symbol of unity he could use to "whip up interest" among Oregon tribes for suing the government, Beckham said.

Much of what we now know about Wasson comes to us through the writings of his son, the late George Bundy Wasson Jr., a tribal elder, writer, anthropologist, archeologist, historian, and musician. Wasson Jr. compared the misery that his ancestors suffered on the Oregon coast with the Holocaust.[226] "Many tragic tales could be told about the conflicts and atrocities suffered by Oregon Indians," he wrote in his dissertation for a doctorate in anthropology at the University of Oregon, which he received in 2001.

We can't change the course of history, but we have imminent power to change our reactions to it. We can't undo the atrocities of the bloody 'holocaust,' but we can honor the memory of our ancestors and become better people today than ever before. We may never regain the daily use of our old languages, but we can learn much about our heritage by studying them.

The effect on the tribes of Southern Oregon was an American holocaust just as suffered by the Jews during World War II in Germany. Just as the holocaust in Germany must be taught and remembered, so must the holocaust in Oregon be taught in our schools so Oregonians and other Americans will know the true history. That knowledge might better ensure that such a Holocaust never happens again.[8]

No book on the coastal temperate rainforest can be complete without acknowledging the genocide that occurred there 150 years ago, or the heroic efforts of many generations of the Wasson family—alongside many other families with similar experiences—to reclaim what was lost. As Wasson Jr. explains,

Not one square mile of Coos, Curry, Josephine, Jackson or Douglas counties has been spared the awful impact of murder, human torture, desperation, and anguish spilled out of the people who experienced the vulgar onslaught of the mid-nineteenth century.[9]

In his research, George Bundy Wasson Jr. felt that tribal culture, traditions, and history had disappeared into "a cultural black hole" from which they did not escape.[10] He discovered many important historical documents and artifacts

languishing in national repositories and research institutions at the Smithsonian, the National Archives, and the Bureau of Indian Affairs. But much has been lost:

> Very little knowledge through scientific research was collected and preserved for posterity. Federal policies of acculturation thoroughly decimated the cultural integrity of small Oregon tribes.[11]

In 1995, he launched the Southwest Oregon Research Project (SWORP), a collection of widely scattered and overlooked original documents and artifacts preserving the traditions and history of Indians of greater Oregon. The collection is housed at the University of Oregon. Tragically, Wasson was murdered in 2014 at age eighty-two (the rate of violence against Native Americans in the United States is disproportionately high), but the project continues to gather material of historical significance.

The silence of highly traumatized Native American survivors also kept these facts hidden, according to a history written by Don Whereat, tribal historian for the Coos, Lower Umpqua, and Siuslaw tribes.

> My parents and grandparents, like many others of their generations, did not speak of their culture and heritage. The abuses and horrors suffered by our ancestors to recent times caused multi-generational trauma. Silence was one of the many consequences.[12]

Thousands of years ago, the first Americans came from Asia over a land bridge between the continents. No one knows when the first migration occurred, but the last one is thought to have taken place some 12,000 years ago. Migrants arrived on the Oregon Coast some 8,000 years ago, a date set by two archeological digs, one in the Upper Rogue Valley and one in Lake Tachenitch north of Coos Bay.

Before the arrival of Europeans in 1774, as many as 200,000 Indigenous people lived within 100 miles of the Pacific Ocean from Northern California to Southeast Alaska, roughly the borders of the temperate rainforest, making it one of the most densely populated nonagricultural regions of the world, according to the authoritative *Handbook of North American Indians*.[13] The Indians started dying in large numbers in the late 1770s when a massive smallpox epidemic spread by early explorers and fur trappers wiped out one-third of the population. As settlers populated the region over the next century, five more major smallpox epidemics erupted, along with outbreaks of malaria and measles, further decimating the Indigenous population.

The settlers and their descendants were also responsible for the nearly complete demolition of the Indians' most important food resource—the coast's legendary runs of salmon. By the end of the twentieth century, the salmon were reduced to 5 percent of their historical abundance. Without a treaty, the coastal Indians were powerless to halt this decline, unlike tribes on the Columbia River who leveraged their treaties to protect salmon from the deadly impacts of massive hydroelectric projects in the late 20th century.[14]

Wasson believed the absence of a ratified treaty did not mean the coastal tribes had no legal rights. In fact, several federal laws expressly guaranteed legal rights to Native people throughout U.S. history. A pre-constitution law, the Northwest Ordinance of 1787, required the United

States to exercise the "utmost good faith" toward protecting Indians and their property, human rights, and liberty. (First passed by the Continental Congress, it was reaffirmed by the newly created U.S. Congress in 1789 and signed into law by President Washington.) The Organic Act of 1848 establishing the Oregon Territory said Indian land could not be taken away without their consent. Native claims to land in Oregon could be extinguished only by treaty. The Oregon Donations Land Act in 1850 put in motion the treaty-making machinery.

Language barriers made the negotiating process difficult. Neither Joel Palmer, the federal agent who signed several treaties, nor his interpreter had any mastery of the languages of the Oregon Coast, Beckham told us. Local interpreters lived among the Indians only for a year or two before 1855. Whatever rudimentary communication occurred, Beckham said, was expressed in the Chinook Jargon or Chinook Wawa, a patois incapable of conveying understanding about such concepts as "land cession," "payment of annuities," and other subtleties in the document. As a result, it's unlikely coastal Indians understood they were signing away the title to their ancestral homelands. "The treaties were not negotiated," Beckham explained. "They were dictated."

In 1854 and 1855, the U.S. Senate was flooded with twenty-three treaties, the Oregon Coast Treaty being the largest, each involving Indians in coastal Oregon. None were ratified. They simply fell "by the wayside" while the Senate worked through a large number of hearings on other treaties and other legislative work, Beckham said. Seven treaties with western Oregon Indians were ratified, however, but these applied only to lands east of the Coast Range. The government hoped the treaties would quell tensions between gold miners who felt threatened by the Indians, who were irate at being displaced from their lands—a hope dashed by the Senate's inaction.

From 1851 to 1856, settlers waged what became known as the Rogue River War. The war began when miners burned an Indigenous village next to the Pistol River in Curry County. The nineteen survivors were chained together and marched forty miles north to Port Orford, where they were shot to death by vigilantes. In another assault three years later, a mob of forty miners slaughtered an entire village known as Nasomah near the mouth of the Coquille River. On the day of the attack, sixteen Indians were killed. Another six were later found dead in the woods.

A federal agent named F.R. Smith reported his observations from the scene:

> The Indians were aroused from sleep to meet their deaths with but a feeble show of resistance; shot down as they were attempting to escape from their houses. Fifteen men and one Squaw were killed, two Squaws badly wounded. On the part of the White men, not even the slightest wound was received. The houses of the Indians, with but one exception, were fired and destroyed. Thus, was committed a massacre too inhuman (sic) to be readily believed.[15]

The U.S. military rounded up the survivors and imprisoned them in line with its policy to keep the Indians "safe" from the marauding settlers by physically separating the groups from each other. Significantly, no settlers were imprisoned; the soldiers kept only Indians in chains. In 1860, the U.S. Army marched the surviving Indians from Coos Bay sixty miles up the coast to a camp on the Yachats River, Wasson Jr. wrote:

> Yachats was nothing more than an extermination camp, and many of those people were the survivors of village massacres, just like the villagers who were slaughtered in My Lai during the VietNam War.[16]

This long trek was their *Trail of Tears*, according to the official history of the Confederated Tribes of the Coos, Lower Umpqua, and Siuslaw:

> Within a short time at the reservation, many died of hunger, exposure, mistreatment, and sheer exhaustion. Once there, they were imprisoned for seventeen years and forced to give up their traditional culture for farming, on a coastal plain ill-suited to agriculture. Fifty percent of the Tribal members died during this period due to the deplorable conditions including starvation, mistreatment, and disease.[17]

In his doctoral dissertation, George Bundy Wasson Jr. tells the story of how three generations of his family fought White settlers, federal bureaucrats, the United States Army, the U.S. Court of Claims, and ultimately the U.S. Supreme Court for the right and title to their sacred ancestral homelands.

In 1860, his great-grandmother, Gishgiu, (or "Gekka," as she was fondly called), was among the Indians forcibly marched by Army soldiers from Coos Bay to Yachats. Gishgiu compared the Yachats camp to a prison. But for many, the reservation was a death camp, as half the population died in the first ten years. Somehow, she escaped by jumping into the frigid Pacific Ocean and swimming several miles around Cape Perpetua and Sea Lion Caves with soldiers in hot pursuit. During the day, she hid in the bushes. At night, she walked the long beaches and sand dunes, finally arriving at her home in the South Slough near Coos Bay to be reunited with her daughter, Susan Adulsah.

> Even though she was now blind, her presence in the home added immeasurably to keeping up a large house and raising a big family. There have been many stories and anecdotes about Gishgiu, which the family all told in remembering the feisty little woman who defied the U.S. Government and outwitted the soldiers who sought to capture and return her to the concentration camp at Yachats. Most of them have been lost and forgotten, but some are well embedded in family memory.

Gishgiu was deemed a runaway and wanted by the authorities. Though she was home, she was not safe. Soldiers frequently roamed the area to round up "runaway" Indians and return them to the reservation up north. "This was especially difficult for the mothers with small babies, as rushing madly would frighten them and cause them to cry," Wasson Jr. wrote. Mothers who couldn't muffle the screams of their children were quickly found and taken away.

By then, Gishgiu was already a widow. Her husband, Kitz-un-ginum (Elk Skin No Meet In Middle), chief of the Coos Tribe, was killed in battle in 1853. He signed his name as "Kitchen" on an 1851 treaty with the federal government.

Some thought of him as the most prominent chief in all of Southwestern Oregon.

Susan Adulsah, their daughter, spoke ten languages and was the "bahsic" of the Coos tribe, or the keeper of the tribal legend. She was an authority on the history of the Coos Indians, as well as their languages, traditions, stories, and medicines. She made a point of describing in detail the losses her people suffered, and the injustice inflicted upon them by the Whites who took their homelands.

Susan married a Scottish immigrant and miner named George R. Wasson. They both became U.S. citizens on Feb. 14, 1859, the day Oregon became a state. As George Bundy Wasson Jr., wrote in his dissertation, Susan's marriage to the White settler likely saved her from being taken away to a prison camp like her mother Gishgiu.[19]

> Susan Adulsah and her husband George (the Scottish immigrant) were an excellent combination of different cultures, Indian and EuroAmerican. It seems that their unbounded respect for each other provided strength and fortitude for survival, achievement, and success in an ever-changing frontier world. Their combination of Indian traditional knowledge in Native survival, hunting and gathering, and New England knowledge and expertise in the maritime trade and logging/lumbering abilities, provided the perfect union and melding of cultures in the "frontiers" of Oregon.[20]

George R. Wasson tried to see both sides of the conflict. He was greatly disturbed by the atrocities he saw perpetrated against Native people. At the same time, he was also concerned about the welfare of the settlers who were also being attacked by the local tribes in fierce defense of their homelands.

The couple had ten children. George Bundy Wasson Sr., born in 1880, was the youngest. George grew up in Coos County, but spent his teen-age years in the 1890s in neighboring Curry County, in a village known as Chet-Less-Chunn-Dunn that had been there for 3,000 years. It was the same village that miners burned down in 1851. George was a graduate of Chemawa Indian School in Salem, Oregon, and Carlisle Indian School in Pennsylvania where he studied law and music.

In 1916, as the new attorney for the Confederated Tribes of the Coos, Lower Umpqua, and Siuslaw, George's first order of business was to unite coastal tribes in a legal battle to reclaim their ancestral homelands. As his son wrote in his dissertation:

> He wanted to get their land back or obtain compensation for those who had their land taken with no ratified treaty or reservation. I'm sure he would like to have practiced private law and made a halfway decent income to support his wife and five children, but that was not his preordained destiny.[21]

George Bundy Wasson Sr. began traveling regularly to Washington, D.C., to meet with lawyers, senators, and representatives. But progress on the lawsuit was slow, leading to frustration that threatened to divide the tribes. To make his case, he interviewed the oldest living Indians as they answered questions about their history, who was related, where they were born, where the old customary fishing places were, and much more.

It was a losing battle from the beginning, but he could not stop working on it. It must have been as though his grandmother was standing alongside him urging him to "get it back."[22]

Under a federal law in effect in the early twentieth century, it was illegal for an Indian to file suit against the federal government. In 1929, Wasson Sr. persuaded Congress to pass a special law allowing his case to proceed. Wasson then filed a lawsuit, *Coos (or Kowes) Bay, Lower Umpqua (or Kalawatset), and Siuslaw Indian Tribes v. the United States of America*,[229] with the U.S. Court of Claims, a five-judge panel established to settle claims against the federal government.

In 1931, court-appointed clerks took testimony from Indians who survived the Oregon Coast Reservation. Seventeen members of the tribes spoke about their brutal treatment, going all the way back to the day it opened, seventy-one years earlier. Several spoke only in their native tongues. At first, they were happy to relocate to the reservation, if only to escape the violent settlers. But settlers also moved onto the reservation, in violation of the treaty, and eventually claimed it as their own. The government allowed this to happen. The Indians lost their lands twice: they lost their reservation, and never got their old lands back.

Testimony suggests the Army soldiers could hardly have been more brutal. Frank Drew, a member of the Coos tribe, compared the treatment his people received with slavery:[23]

My people were compelled to go out and work, both in pleasant or the severest kind of weather for the Government and in return they received nothing for their labor. There was an Indian agent by the name of George Collins who was very cruel to the Indians. He would compel the Indians to work for him without allowing them any rations to live on.

Annie Miner Peterson, who also lived on the reservation, testified that she was forced to watch government agents tie Indians who escaped the reservation to posts and flog them.[24]

> (That) may seem unreasonable but that is just what they did. There were many of them who the agent would gather together to see the performance carried on. The object of the spectators at this place is to teach the other Indians that they may not run away again from the agency without the consent of the agent.

Non-Indians also testified on behalf of the tribes. But Wasson Sr. felt there could be no better evidence of "aboriginal sovereignty" and "territorial occupation" than the elders' own words, Wasson Jr. wrote in his dissertation.

Wasson Sr. introduced the testimony as evidence in court in the early 1930s but had to wait until 1938 to get a final ruling on the case. When the court finally ruled, it made the astonishing assertion that the United States never recognized the plaintiff Indians as the owners of the lands they claimed, and had never consummated a treaty.[25] Oral testimony as to facts and traditions, by witnesses many of whom have a direct interest in the outcome of the case, is insufficient to establish Indian title to a vast acreage of lands; it does not afford a degree of proof sufficient to overcome contemporaneous documentary and historical evidence to the contrary.

The Court of Claims didn't even acknowledge the tribes ever lived on these lands. And it ignored the brutal treatment of Indians at the hands of the U.S. Army and White colonists.

> An unratified Indian treaty is not evidence of Government recognition of Indian title to land. The fact that the United States did make treaties with other Indians in the

same area falls short of establishing individual title to a described area in an unratified treaty.[26]

The tribes, it concluded, had "no right, title or interest to the coast of Oregon whatsoever." As for the testimony collected from tribal elders, the court dismissed that as "hearsay," Wasson Jr. wrote:

> Those old Indians couldn't even speak English. Hearsay! My dad hadn't been there when those things happened. He just heard about them from his elders. It was all just declared hearsay, time after time, in the court records.[27]

"It was a legal lynching," Wayne Shammel, a former legal counsel to the Cow Creek Band of the Umpqua Tribe, told us. In his book *The Indians of Western Oregon*, historian Stephen Dow Beckham wrote that the court "totally ignored the records of the Office of Indian Affairs," as well as numerous maps and other documents. "It was as though these Indians of the Oregon coast really did not exist."[28] But the litigation did not end there. In 1946, the Clatsop, Nehalem, Tillamook, and Coquille tribes filed another lawsuit, *United States v. Alcea Band of Tillamooks*,[29] in the Court of Claims. This time, the court ruled in the tribes' favor, thanks in part to evidence submitted by John Peabody Harrington, a linguist and ethnographer with the Smithsonian Institution. Harrington submitted two million pages of transcripts of interviews with western Oregon Indians, plus many other documents, most of which have been archived by the Southwest Oregon Research Project at the University of Oregon.

In 1946, the U.S. Department of Justice appealed the ruling to the Supreme Court, but lost. The nation's top court ruled that the Indians were, in fact, the true descendants of the aboriginal occupants of the land and had a right to compensation. Indians had to wait ninety-one years after the Oregon Coast Treaty was signed for the U.S. government to finally recognize that Indian land claims in western Oregon were valid.

In 1947, George Bundy Wasson Sr. died of a heart attack while surveying Indian land claims several miles north of Port Orford near Cape Blanco, the westernmost point in North America outside Alaska. He was sixty-seven. His decades-long work enabled Clatsop, Nehalem, Tillamook, and Coquille tribal members to receive an award from the court totalling $3,128,000, but after numerous deductions, each member of these tribes collected just $2,000. No money went to the Coos, Lower Umpqua, and Siuslaw tribes.

The unequal treatment applied to the Coos and Coquille peoples by the two court cases sparked a rift in the tribal community. The two tribes, who once enjoyed a close kinship split into two separate, federally recognized tribes. Today, many western Oregon Indians still feel burned by the decisions.

In the 1950s, as if a century of brutalizing Native Americans hadn't been enough, the federal government found a novel way for it to continue. During the Eisenhower administration, Congress enacted three assimilation programs that terminated tribal sovereignty, relocated Indians to urban areas, and transferred federal law enforcement jurisdiction on Indian reservations to the states. In all, the government terminated 109 tribes.[30] Many years of anguish and economic, social and cultural disruption followed. In 1972, the Nixon administration recognized the termination policy's failure, and decided to restore each tribes' status, one by one, subject to approval by Congress.

In 1984, Congress restored the Coos, Lower Umpqua, and Siuslaw tribes, and restored the Coquille tribe in 1989. To the tribes, restoration meant they could regain access to federal assistance for health and education programs and economic development. It also presented them with an opportunity to reclaim their forests. In 1996, Congress gave back about 5,400 acres of forestland in eastern Coos County to the Coquille tribe, a small portion of their ancestral homelands. Every year, the Coquille tribe logs about 3.6 million board feet of timber from the land, enough to employ 200 workers, as the Coquille Tribe says on its website:[31]

> Sustainable production of natural resources on these lands promotes Tribal self-sufficiency, while providing jobs and revenue to local economies. Because these places always have been and always will be part of our home, we feel a unique calling to cherish them. We honor our responsibility to keep our forest ecosystems forever healthy.

But Andy Kerr, the author and conservationist, is skeptical. He contends forest practices on tribal lands are no different than those on industrial timberlands, and thinks the tribes should have been compensated with cash, "not the irreplaceable and precious public lands that belong to all of us."

> I completely understand Native American tribes wanting America's public lands. But the currency of compensation by the United States to Native American tribes ought to be the currency of the dollar.[32]

But tribal members say it's unfair to equate their steward-ship of the land with industrial forestry. "I see us guardians of resources when we are allowed to do so," says Esther Stutzman, an elder in the Kalapuya, Coos, and Siletz tribes of western Oregon who works as a cultural consultant, artist-in-residence and lecturer for museums, libraries, and universities, including the University of Oregon. "We are not always allowed to do that. There was a lot of Native land that was taken away and logged." To Stutzman, stewardship of a forest means a lot more than just logging:

> The forest is an absolute resource for food and shelter and clothing and everything we needed, so we didn't see a necessity to kill the forest. It provided things we needed to live every day.

Tribal leaders have been criticized for clear-cutting forests, but so has almost everyone else. In 2018, Congress returned nearly 15,000 acres of forest to the Confederated Tribes of the Coos, Lower Umpqua, and Siuslaw, a tiny sliver of their one million-acre ancestral homeland.

Nearly one-third of the stolen ancestral homelands in the Coast Range are publicly owned, including land owned by two federal agencies, the U.S. Forest Service, the Bureau of Land Management, and land owned by the state of Oregon. The rest is owned by timber companies, partnerships, trusts, hedge funds, and individuals.

The largest privately held piece of property in the Coast Range is a 210,000-acre tree farm north of Coos River owned by Weyerhaeuser Corporation, the world's third largest timber company.[33] The site is part of the ancestral homelands of the Miluks, one of two language groups in the Coos tribe.

Weyerhaeuser bought the land in 1902 from the Northern Pacific Railroad, which obtained it a few years earlier from the federal government in a trade for timberland near Mount Rainier that became part of Mount Rainier National Park.

Weyerhaeuser named its property the "Millicoma Tree Farm'" after a Coos word that means "near the Miluks." Millicoma is also the Indigenous name for the North Fork Coos River, which runs through the property. Interestingly, the first splash dam in southwestern Oregon was erected in 1884 on the Millicoma River, long before Weyerhaeuser came on the scene. Weyerhaeuser had no involvement in splash dam logging in southwestern Oregon, though it depended extensively on rivers to drive logs on the mill, Stephen Dow Beckham told us.

In 2000, Weyerhaeuser published *Millicoma: Biography of a Pacific Northwest Forest*, a history of the tree farm. This book, written by Arthur V. Smythe, a former forester for the company, dismisses tribal titles to the land as "vague." The first chapter, entitled, "Whose Woods These Are," justifies the company's right to the land by quoting John L. O' Sullivan, the editor of the New York *Democratic Review*, who is given credit for coining the term "manifest destiny":

> Away with all these cobweb issues of rights of discovery, exploration, settlement, contiguity – our title is by the right of our manifest destiny to overspread and to possess the whole of the continent which Providence has given us.[34]

In the 1940s, Weyerhaeuser expanded the tree farm by purchasing an adjacent 48,000 acres from the Pillsbury family of Minnesota, famous for the baking company of the same name. In 1951, Weyerhaeuser began clear-cutting the tree farm's dense old-growth forest, a liquidation it completed in just forty years. The company built a large sawmill in nearby North Bend to process the logs, but in 1989, when it cut down the last tree, it closed the mill, throwing hundreds of people out of work.

Much of the vast amount of carbon once stored in the forest has been released back into the atmosphere, contributing to the climate disaster. Weyerhaeuser has been replanting its tree farm, but the new trees are not reabsorbing much of the lost carbon. Instead, the company is logging the tree farm every forty years or so, preventing much carbon accumulation. But these days, the logs don't go to the North Bend mill for processing. In the 1990s, Weyerhaeuser sold the mill to the Coquille Indian Tribe, which redeveloped it as The Mill Casino and Hotel.

David G. Lewis, the Oregon State University professor and former Grande Ronde tribal historian, told us the tribes must continue to press for a return of their land or some other equitable solution.

> Unless a portion of those lands is returned to tribes we will always have problems. They were never fairly paid for, even those that were paid for under Indian claims, and so I feel that the tribes deserve to have returned millions of acres of land.[35]

Roberto Mukara Borrero, CEO of the Tribal Link Foundation, a group that supports the empowerment of Indigenous peoples worldwide, says in general, forests are healthier when they are returned to their original, Indigenous owners.

Many current studies affirm that when Indigenous peoples have control over their forests, and by control what I mean is secure title, respect for their rights, recognition of our traditional territories, that's where we see forests largely intact and biodiversity thriving. Indigenous people are the best guardians of the forest.[36]

# Chapter 12

# A Resilient Community

*(This chapter was written by Terri Hansen, a journalist who focuses primarily on environmental and scientific issues affecting North American tribal and worldwide Indigenous communities. Terri is an enrolled Native American citizen of the Winnebago Tribe of Nebraska.)*

Walter Ward swept his arm over a pebbled beach, backed by a tight wall of evergreens and strewn with logs tossed by passing storms. Ward grew up on this piece of Washington coast, in a thriving Hoh tribal village that was here "forever," he said. "The houses used to be along the top of the hill, and all along the beaches." Tribal artifacts in the area date back 12,000 years. Today, all that's left of his childhood home are two vacant houses and a road nibbled away by an ever-encroaching ocean.

Four tribal nations inhabit low-lying land along the west coast of Washington's Olympic National Park in the Pacific coastal temperate rainforest. The Hoh, Quinault, Quileute, and Makah Tribes coped with threatening storms and tsunamis for thousands of years. Now, they have become some of the West's earliest victims of climate change, as rising sea levels and other impacts endanger their villages and history.

"The area is relatively vulnerable," said Patty Glick, global warming specialist and author of a National Wildlife Federation report, "Sea Level Rise and Coastal Habitats in the Pacific Northwest."[1] Tectonic rise—an uplifting of land along the coast—makes it difficult for scientists to determine just how much of a rise will affect the region, she said, but higher wave action, wave force, and destructive storm surges will increase.

Destructive storms are another manifestation, and will become more frequent, Glick said, speaking of climate change. Researchers with the University of Washington Climate Impacts Group predict a rise of fourteen inches by mid-century and thirty-five inches by 2100. "If we lose the clam beds, well, that is who we are," said Larry Ralston of the Quinault Indian Nation. "The cultural and subsistence significance of this is dramatic." Quinault people speak of "clam hunger," a physical, emotional, and spiritual craving that connects them to their ecosystem, their ancestors, and to their very existence.[2]

Ralston likened the peril to "a slow-moving tsunami." The Quinault have a large land base, but their main village, called Taholah, is already experiencing the effects of sea level rise.

Taholah, their main population center, is just a stone's throw from the beach. In 2014 the seawall that protects the town was breached by a storm surge that flooded half the town. Less than a year later, intense rains caused flooding, landslides, culvert failures, and washouts, closing roads and threatening their sewage treatment plants. The U.S. Army Corp of Engineers repaired their seawall, but it's a temporary fix. The Quinault will have to move the lower half of the town to higher ground.[3]

The Makah Tribe, located on the northwest tip of the Washington coast is also witnessing the negative effects of climate change, said Michael Chang, Makah Tribe climate adaptation specialist. The fact the tribe needs a climate adaptation specialist says it all. "For the Makah, whose traditional area is the northwest Olympic Peninsula and marine waters in Washington state, the environment, the culture, and the community are all interconnected," he said.

And the Makah have started planning and preparing for climate change adaptation. They began with an ocean acidification impacts assessment back in 2015 that snowballed. In the assessment, they found they couldn't talk about impacts to ocean resources without also talking about impacts to land and air, and about the impacts on tribal cultural resources. Chang said, "So instead of one specific project, we are viewing this as an iterative planning process."

Now, the tribe is completing multiple related projects, including impact assessments, community engagement plans, an adaptation plan, carbon footprint analysis, and a carbon mitigation plan.

The Hoh and Quileute Tribes were allotted only tiny slivers of their original ancestral land along the coast. To cope with the looming climate changes both tribes needed higher ground to move a school and residents out of harm's way. Therefore, the Olympic National Park had to return a portion of its land—a first. Even wilderness preservationists understood the dilemma.

"On the one hand, you have the big supporters of national wilderness, then you have these tribes whose lands they were given are not going to work for them in the long term," said Bonnie Phillips, president of the local Olympic Forest Coalition. The 135-mile Olympic coastline is a national marine sanctuary, and adjacent Olympic National Park is a United Nations World Heritage Site and International Biosphere Reserve.

Ninety-five percent of the Olympic Peninsula is designated wilderness. The remote wilderness is home to four Indian reservations and 13,000 non-tribal residents. The Quinault Indian Nation at the park's southern end encompasses

200,000 acres of magnificent, productive forests, swift-flowing rivers, gleaming lakes, and twenty-three miles of pristine Pacific coastline. The Quinault River flows from deep in the Olympic Mountains through a lush temperate rainforest to Lake Quinault before emptying into the Pacific Ocean. It's a short hike from the Lake Quinault Lodge to visit some of the tallest hemlock, Douglas-fir, and western redcedar trees, and the largest Sitka spruce tree in the world.

The Quinault own and manage forests from Lake Quinault and the Quinault River to the Pacific Ocean, and co-manage the fisheries—inland and at sea. They are especially involved in ocean acidification research. The runs of salmon in the Quinault River have supported generations of the Quinault people. The villages of Taholah and Queets are located at the mouth of two great rivers that flow into the Pacific Ocean, which is the source of salmon, halibut, crab, razor clams, and many other species that are part of the Quinault heritage.

"Since the summer of 2006, Quinault has documented thousands of dead fish and crab coming ashore in the late summer months, specifically onto the beaches near Taholah," Quinault marine resources scientist Joe Schumacker said. "Our science team has worked with NOAA scientists to confirm that these events are a result of critically low oxygen levels in this ocean area."

The great productivity of this northwest coast is driven by natural upwelling, in which summer winds drive deep ocean waters, rich in nutrients, to the surface, Schumacker explained. This cycle has been happening forever on the Washington coast, and the ecosystem depends on it. But now, "due to recent changes in summer wind and current patterns possibly due to climate change, these deep waters, devoid of oxygen, are sometimes not getting mixed with air at the surface," Schumacker said.

The deep water now comes ashore, taking over the entire water column as it does, and we find beaches littered with dead fish – and some still living – in shallow pools on the beaches, literally gasping for oxygen. Normally reclusive fish such as lingcod and greenling will be trapped in inches of water trying to get what little oxygen they can to stay alive.

The Quinault, working with the University of Washington and NOAA scientists, determined these hypoxia events were also related to ocean acidification, Schumacker said:

Now Quinault faces the potential for not just hypoxia impacts coming each summer, but also those same waters bring low-pH acidic waters to our coast. Upwelling is the very foundation of our coastal ecosystem, and it now carries a legacy of pollution that may be causing profound changes unknown to us as of yet. The Quinault Department of Fisheries has been seeking funding to better study and monitor these potential ecosystem impacts to allow us to prepare for an unknown future.

Schumacker noted that tribes are in a prime position to observe and react to these changes:

The tribes of the west coast of the U.S. are literally on the front line of ocean acidification impacts. Oyster growers from Washington and Oregon have documented year after year of lost crops as tiny oyster larvae die from low pH water. What is going on in the ecosystem adjacent to Quinault? What other small organisms are being impacted, and how is our ecosystem reacting?

We have a responsibility to know so we can plan for an uncertain future.

The tribal nations in the Pacific coastal temperate rainforest depend on their environment for subsistence as well as cultural identity. The cultures of these tribal nations are deeply connected to their ancestral lands, waters, and natural resources. There is a need to protect the viability of their economies and livelihoods as the changing climate impacts hunting, gathering, fishing, forestry, agriculture, energy, recreation, and tourism enterprises.

Salmon, crucial for nearly all the tribes in the region, are projected to lose 22 percent of their habitat by late century due to warming stream waters if nothing is done to stop or slow carbon emissions, according to the National Climate Assessment.[4]

On the whole, Native Americans experience poverty at a higher rate than any other group in the country. Some reservations lack health care facilities, grocery stores, social services, and transportation resources. This has made tribal communities particularly vulnerable to the effects of climate change, and adaptation strategies are crucial to building resilience.

Under the leadership of Chairman Brian Cladoosby, the Swinomish Indian Tribal Community on Puget Sound developed the first comprehensive climate change adaptation plan in 2010. Today, it's the template for climate resilience planning throughout Indian Country and beyond.

The azure waters around the Swinomish community are breathtaking, especially at sunrise and sunset, and have provided salmon and shellfish for people there for 10,000 years.

Rising waters pose a great threat to the fifteen-square-mile reservation that sits at or near sea level. The U.S. Geological Survey estimates that sea levels in this region will rise four to eight inches by 2050.

Using climate projections available in 2009, the Swinomish analyzed the highest predicted risks and the tribe's priorities. They categorized the level of risk to infrastructure, human health, and natural resources from low to high, and estimated the time needed to develop strategies for adapting to those impacts.[5] Using a unique model based on an Indigenous worldview, the tribe updated its adaptation strategy in 2014 with environmental, cultural, and human health impact data. It now views health on a familial and community scale, and includes the natural environment and the spiritual realm, said Jamie Donatuto, Swinomish community and environmental health analyst.

The innovative report provides a model for other tribal communities looking to understand how predicted climate changes will affect their people and homelands in practical ways specific to Indigenous life. The tribes throughout the Pacific coastal temperate rainforest are leaders in climate adaptation and have mounted multifaceted responses to the threats they face. They are also leaders in coalitions that have blocked proposed projects that would have increased the transfer of raw fossil fuels to proposed ports on the Pacific coast, dubbed the "gateway to the Pacific," for export to lucrative Asian markets.

The Lummi Nation and the Quinault Nation joined a growing coalition of other tribal and local governments and allies to form a resistance to fossil fuel expansion along the West Coast, at the heart of which is hundreds of years of treaty rights and case law, said Fawn Sharp, president of the Quinault Nation.

> We are a fishing, hunting, gathering people who care
> deeply about our land, water, and resources, as well as all
> life dependent on a healthy ecosystem. These proposals
> threaten our economy, our environment, and our culture.

Sharp, who is also president of the National Congress of American Indians, said the best solution to the challenges created by what she called "the temperament of greed in this country," is the grassroots momentum that rises when the people—both tribal and non-tribal—share a common vision and take action in their votes, voices, lifestyles, and the lessons they convey to their families. "We know the country can't break its addiction to oil overnight," she said. "But we know that, over time, it has to be eliminated from use, and we know that process of elimination is a task that must be undertaken now."

Treaties, according to the U.S. Constitution, are the supreme law of the land, and do not expire. Many agreements between the federal government and tribal nations affirm a tribe's right to hunt and fish on its ancestral land beyond current reservation boundaries. In addition to clear-cuts, oil spills and coal train derailments pose threats that could infringe the tribes' treaty-protected rights to hunt and fish their lands. These treaties have proven to be a potent legal mechanism in environmental protection in the Pacific Northwest, already racking up victories based on industry violations of generations-old government-to-government agreements.

The Coquille Indian Tribe in southern coastal Oregon purchased 3,200 ecologically and culturally significant acres of forestland in Oregon's Siskiyou National Forest in 2015, naming it Sek-wet-se, their peoples' name for the river and their ancestors who lived there, said Coquille chairwoman Brenda Meade.

Our ancestors have lived on these lands since time began. Hunting, fishing, and traditional food gatherings are all abundant on this land. Coquille people will again be able to gather in these same places in the same ways as our Grandparents before us. We will be able to utilize these places to teach our children their history and the importance of caring for these lands and its resources in a sustainable way.

"The Coquille people are a strong and tenacious people who never gave up even through assimilation and termination policies," Meade said. She said that after regaining federal recognition, the Coquille Tribe wrote a self-sufficiency plan that declared their destiny must be self-determination by regaining self-sufficiency.

> Our Elders believed that they had a sacred trust obligation to meet the needs of our current tribal members and future generations. The priorities were then and still are today: To attain economic self-sufficiency, attain social self-sufficiency and to attain self-determination through a strong and healthy Tribal Government that protects the sovereign rights of Coquille People, today and for future tribal members. We are unique in our cultural and historic heritage and we must preserve that for all Coquille People.

Tribal nations managed the Pacific coastal temperate rainforest sustainably prior to European contact. The most important tool the tribes had to manipulate their environment was anthropogenic fire, also known as cultural burning. It allowed the tribes to manage the land for big game such as deer and elk, and maintain habitats for food, medicinal and weaving plants, and forage for wildlife.

The ancestral homeland of the Yurok Tribe in northern California encompasses 7.5 percent of the California coastline and is home to the coastal redwoods and other woodlands and the Klamath River, the lifeline of the Yurok people.

Like all the tribal nations along the coast, the federal government took most of the Yurok's land from them in the mid-to-late nineteenth century. And in tandem with the other tribes, their forests were clear-cut by industrial timber companies. Hundreds of miles of logging roads scarred the land, and slash piles were left behind. The forest degradation devastated culturally valuable fish and wildlife populations. In 2006, the tribe partnered with Western Rivers Conservancy to buy back ancestral lands from Green Diamond, a timber company. The tribe completed the deal in 2019, regaining ownership of 50,000 acres, including the watershed of Blue Creek, a vital cold-water refuge for salmon.

The Yurok tribe has also obtained a cache of carbon credits from the state of California that it sells to polluters to offset some of their carbon pollution. However, as we learn in Chapter 16, forest carbon offsets rarely benefit the climate. The Yurok's management of the forest earned them the United Nations Development Program's Equator Prize in 2019. The Prize committee praised them for forming an unprecedented alliance with the government of California to auction carbon credits from their sustainably managed forests through the state's cap-and-trade program, allowing the Yurok Tribe to finance the purchase of over 54,857 acres (22,200 hectares) of their ancestral lands.

The Yurok put tribal citizens to work re-creating the diverse ecological conditions that existed on their lands for millennia. They manage their forests to produce traditional foods, medicines, and basket materials, and to store and sequester carbon. What they call the centerpiece of their holistic project is the development of the "Yurok Old-Growth Forest and Salmon Sanctuary" in the Blue Creek watershed, an important tributary on the Klamath River for salmon and for their sacred ceremonial practices.

Yurok Chairman Joseph L. James said their approach combines traditional ecological knowledge and western science to rebuild biodiversity in their forests and to restore resilience within their community. He called it a "time-tested strategy for rehabilitating critical habitats that can be duplicated all over the world to reduce the impact of climate change."

The most effective tool they have to protect the forest "is the use of cultural burning," Yurok vice-chairman Frankie Myers told the Select Committee on the Climate Crisis to explore natural techniques to keep carbon out of the atmosphere.[6] Myers also recommended using logging techniques that create uneven-aged stands of forest that go back to more of a traditional forest landscape.

## Chapter 13

# Husduwach Nuyem Jees
# (Land of Milky Blue Waters)

In August 1991, a seaplane carrying the American conservationist Spencer Beebe and three others landed on Gardner
Canal, an arm of the Pacific Ocean near the mouth of the
Kitlope River, some 350 miles north of Vancouver, Canada.
A founder of Conservation International, Beebe had been
working to save the Amazon rainforest in South America.
Restless, he wondered whether other rainforests worldwide
might also be in danger. That led him to the Kitlope, the
largest contiguous unlogged rainforest watershed remaining
on Earth. "We were there to take a look around the place,"
Beebe told us.

On a sandy beach near the mouth of the Kitlope River,
he met with Gerald Amos, the elected chief of the Kitamaat
Village Council, and Cecil Paul, an elder with the Haisla First
Nation. In 1948, the Haisla merged with the Xenaksiala First
Nation, who lived there for thousands of years. Cecil, whose
Xenaksiala name was Wa'xaid, was one of the last fluent
speakers of the Xenaksiala language until his death in 2020.

The Xenaksiala call the Kitlope "Husduwach Nuyem Jees,"
or the "land of milky blue waters," in reference to the azure
hue of water flowing through glacial till. As a ten-year-old
child, Cecil was among thousands of victims of a genocidal
Canadian government policy that removed Indigenous children from their culture and sent them off to boarding schools

for assimilation into the dominant White culture, or as a Canadian prime minister once put it, "to kill the Indian in the child." Years later, Cecil returned to the Kitlope as a young man. The intact Kitlope somehow managed to avoid the industrial logging that tore through other productive, low-elevation coastal forests on the Pacific Coast of North America. It faced an immediate threat posed by West Fraser Timber Co. Ltd., the world's largest timber company, which had been clearing ancient forests in British Columbia for some time.[1]

West Fraser had an eye on 247,000 hectares (800,000 acres) of the Kitlope's old-growth trees. The company saw the forest for the timber, but the Haisla First Nation saw much more. Before the logging could begin, the Haisla people demanded a say.

Though the British Crown claims ownership of the Kitlope, the Haisla people never ceded an inch of it to anyone—not to the provincial government, not to some queen in far-off England, and certainly not to the timber company banging at the door. Like all of British Columbia, the Kitlope was the unceded ancestral homeland of an Indigenous people. When British Columbia became part of Canada, the provincial government illegally handed it over to White settlers without treaty or compensation. The fight for the Kitlope was a fight for Indigenous rights.

Just a few days before Beebe's plane touched down, Cecil was hiking in the forest. He found bright orange ribbons and stakes along the path, marking the route for West Frazier's first logging road into the narrow valley, a sure sign the loggers were on their way. The road would push right through the exact location of Cecil's birth. In a quiet act of civil disobedience, he stuffed the markers into his pack, as he wrote in his memoir, *Stories from the Magic Canoe of Wa'xaid*, published in 2019:

> These survey markers are what I dread. These ribbons
> are sharper than arrows. They cut deeper than knives.
> I knew logging was coming, but not this soon.[2]

Even if he had to fight alone, Cecil was ready to defend the
Kitlope from the loggers, but that would not be necessary.
A potential ally was sitting right next to him at the campfire.

As Cecil, Amos, and their American guest chatted into the
night, a worried Cecil brought up the orange ribbons stuffed
in his pack. "They're going to log our valley. How are we going
to stop them?" In Beebe's opinion, an international effort
based on science, coupled with lots of organizing, would be
necessary. Beebe had expertise on both fronts. He mapped
temperate rainforests worldwide and was painfully aware this
forest type, located outside the tropics in both the northern
and southern hemispheres, was vanishing. Beebe could tap
into a vast global network of ecologists. But as he writes in his
memoir, *Cache*, science wouldn't be enough. The community
needed to present a strong, cohesive front in opposition to the
logging.[3]

> Though it's taken me a long time to learn this, I've come
> to see Gerald is right: culture is more powerful than data,
> science, money, and technology. Indeed, culture shapes
> all these things, and the landscape as well. It is our inter-
> dependence and the character of our relationships with
> each other and environment that matter. I call this "reli-
> able prosperity." Cecil Paul calls it the "magic canoe."

The Xenaksiala needed to show that protecting the Kitlope is
vastly important to their well-being, providing food, medicine,

and peace of mind. The Kitlope is also valuable to the entire planet as a bulwark against the twin global crises of shrinking biodiversity and climate disaster.

The Kitlope's main rivers, the Kitlope and Kowesas, are home to five species of Pacific salmon: coho, chum, sockeye, steelhead, pink (sometimes called humpies for their hump-back shape), and huge summer Chinook (some weighing eighty pounds).

In summer, the watershed is home to a population of harbour seals feeding on the rich supply of salmon migrating into the Kitlope River. The landscape also teems with river otters, mountain goats, moose, ptarmigan, peregrine falcons, cougars, the occasional mountain caribou from the interior, more than one hundred bird species and two kinds of bear: black and grizzly. Nearby along the nearby British Columbia coast, a third type of bear, the rare and mysterious kermode, lives nowhere else on the planet. Often called spirit bear or ghost bear, the kermode is actually a black bear with a reces-sive gene that turns its fur into a snowy white, giving it the cuddly appearance of a stuffed polar bear, not that you'd dare hug one. Only one in ten black bears in the area possesses the white coat.

The Kitlope is a land of towering snow-capped mountains, pristine alpine lakes and formidable granite cliffs shooting straight up thousands of feet. Dramatic waterfalls tumble from domed peaks pock-marked with colorful mountain ponds, giant caves, and cirques—the amphitheater-like craters formed by glacial erosion. The old-growth forest gives way at higher elevations to alpine tundra and glaciers. In recent years, these frozen icescapes have been steadily shrinking, the localized impacts of climate change. Periodic violent flooding inundates the valley floor.

The Kitlope marks the northernmost point in the range of Douglas-fir, the most commercially valuable tree in the entire Pacific coastal temperate rainforest. Impressive stands of western hemlock, western redcedar, Sitka spruce, Pacific silver fir, and red alder also blanket the Kitlope landscape.

That a rainforest of such size and grandeur could still exist intact intrigued Beebe. He was one of the first environmentalists to see the Kitlope as much more than just a single, isolated forest. In the 1980s, on a flight from Anchorage to Portland, he perceived it as the midpoint of a spectacular coastal rainforest ecosystem between San Francisco and Anchorage. This large rainforest reminded Beebe of the Amazon, but within the temperate zone in the planet's upper latitudes, far from the tropics. A temperate rainforest.

During the flight, Beebe saw with "deadening frequency" one massive clear-cut after another. He imagined a mythical time when an unbroken, ancient forest stretched along the entire coastline, an expense interrupted only by the Salish Sea and great rivers like the Copper, Taku, Tatshenshini, Stikine, Skeena, Fraser, Hoh, Chehalis, Columbia, Siuslaw, Umpqua, Coos, Coquille, Rogue, Smith, and Klamath, each overflowing with the world's most abundant runs of salmon. Every winter, river banks swell from heavy rains in the Pacific coastal temperate rainforest. After the meeting with Gerald Amos and Cecil Paul, Beebe returned to his home office in Portland to launch a scientific inquiry into the entire temperate rainforest in collaboration with colleagues at Conservation International (CI). The result was a book entitled *The Rain Forests of Home: An Atlas of People and Place*, offering a new way of thinking about the Pacific coast's ancient forests. The first step in saving the temperate rainforest was to define it, a task taken up by Paul Alaback, an ecologist with the U.S. Forest Service in Juneau. Alaback published his work in a Chilean journal.[5]

Based on Alaback's definitions, the atlas depicted a narrow rainforest arcing 2,500 miles from the Northern California redwoods up the coast to Southeast Alaska's Tongass National Forest, and then west around the Gulf of Alaska to Kodiak Island—about the distance from New York to Las Vegas. It charted trends in biodiversity, tracking the severe decline of salmon runs. And it mapped the historic distribution of sixty-eight distinct, disappearing languages spoken by Indigenous people up and down the coast, including the common language shared by the Haisla and the Xenaksiala.

Beebe's team determined that the most intact and healthiest watersheds along the entire coast were all located in British Columbia. After surveying the province's 354 coastal watersheds, they could find only eighty-five that were still intact. Only twenty-five of those watersheds exceeded 100,000 hectares, and the Kitlope was the largest by far. "This was news to everyone," Beebe told us. As he wrote in his memoir:

> Virtually no one ever heard of the Kitlope. The environmental community was focused on one small watershed on the west coast of Vancouver Island, the Carmanah Valley. It had magnificent large trees but was on an island, insular, therefore less rich biologically than the continental mainland Kitlope. The minister of forests was perplexed. He said he had been trying to get the ministry to do an analysis like ours for years at great expense. It took CI six months and $40,000.[6]

Beebe's group produced the first maps of the Pacific coastal temperate rainforest in just six months.

In its twenty-five-year contract with the provincial government to log the mountains of coastal British Columbia, West Fraser, targeted four million acres in the broader Kitlope ecosystem. The company planned to clear-cut the entire Kitlope watershed, and then some, from headwaters to sea.

West Fraser's corporate executives thought the contract superseded any Indigenous claims, but Haisla elders disagreed. The Haisla demanded the company honor their ancient rights to their ancestral homelands. On a trip to Victoria, Cecil Paul informed the provincial minister of forestry that he would "be on the beach with a gun" if West Fraser ever tried to log the Kitlope.

Beebe believed the Haisla could chart their own future without resorting to violence. In 1991, he founded Ecotrust, a non-profit based in Portland, and invited Gerald Amos, the elected Haisla chief, to join its board. A year later they launched the Nanakila Institute an Ecotrust offshoot providing Indigenous people with training on conservation-based projects like ecotourism.

Logging had yet to begin in 1994 when Ecotrust and Nanakila organized a community meeting at a hot springs resort in Kitimaat Village at the head of nearby Douglas Channel. Contingents from local, provincial, and Canadian governments, the timber company, and the Haisla Nation met to air differences and find common ground. At the meeting, a West Fraser representative offered to set aside 25 percent of the Kitlope as a park, mainly bogs and bare cliffs largely devoid of any commercially valuable timber. The company promised to hire Haisla First Nation members to build logging roads, cut down the trees and float them down the river—essentially asking them to decimate their own ancestral lands and way of life in exchange for money. People in the room were not impressed by the offer. No one wanted to be bought off.

"My stomach dropped at the boldness of the offer, and at its strong temptation to a community plagued by unemployment and a lack of opportunity to work," Ken Margolis, then director of Nanakila Institute, told us. He later wrote about the meeting in an essay in *Cascadia Times*, the environmental journal edited by the authors of this book.[7] Margolis was a trusted ally of the Haisla nation. Later, the Haisla adopted Margolis as a member of their Eagle Clan, a high honor rarely bestowed on an outsider.

The following account of the meeting, a pivotal event in the conservation history of the temperate rainforest, is based on Margolis' essay as well as several interviews with him over coffee in Portland.

At one point in the meeting, Morris Amos, a younger brother of the chief, rose to speak. "You don't understand," Margolis heard Morris say. "This is not about jobs. This is about our heritage." One by one, Haisla people talked about the importance of the Kitlope to them and their culture. Thinking he heard enough, the West Fraser representative started to leave. But then, Amalaxa Louisa Smith, an Xenaksiala elder and Cecil Paul's younger sister, stood and pointed a steady finger at him. A silence filled the room as she began to speak: "You stay here! For years we've listened to the company telling us what we were going to do. Now you are going to listen to us." The company representative sat back down.

Margolis told us that by the end of the day, the Kitlope was saved. "The Haisla had taken an ethical stand. In absolute unity, they had demonstrated their willingness to sacrifice in order to protect the Kitlope."

Within a few months, West Fraser Timber Co. formally withdrew its plan to log the Kitlope, and did not seek any compensation from the B.C. government. In 1996, the province permanently protected the watershed under the Parks Act. Today, the area falls under the purview of the Kitlope Heritage Conservancy, and is collaboratively managed by the Haisla First Nation and the province.

In 2016, the province expanded the Kitlope conservancy eight-fold, creating a new 6.4-million-hectare (15.8-million-acre) conservation area called the Great Bear Rainforest. The B.C. Ministry of Forestry wanted to name the area the Central and North Coast and South Central Coast, but environmentalists argued for something more inspiring. Fortunately, they prevailed. The Great Bear has received international acclaim for protecting a wide swath of coastal British Columbia from Vancouver to the British Columbia-Alaska border, spanning some 700 miles. At the border, the Great Bear abuts the equally massive Tongass National Forest in Alaska.

An agreement to protect the Great Bear was engineered by twenty-six First Nations in collaboration with a coalition of environmental groups, including the Sierra Club, Rainforest Action Network, the Natural Resources Defense Council, and ForestEthics. ForestEthics led a campaign targeting businesses purchasing timber from the rainforest, shaming them with highly visible advertising. The campaign forced businesses to "bear responsibility for what their buying habits were doing to rainforests," Todd Paglia, executive director of ForestEthics, told the online news site Mongabay.org.[8]

The agreement provided a $120-million fund to support conservation management and sustainable economic development in First Nations' communities, financed by public and private sources. It also established a collaborative governing structure involving First Nations.

The rainforest contains one hundred large watersheds, hundreds of smaller ones, and Haida Gwaii, the offshore archipelago known until 2010 as the Queen Charlotte Islands. The agreement creating the Great Bear Rainforest recognized the rights to ancestral homelands for the twenty-six First Nations, just as the Kitlope agreement did for the Haisla. In the Great Bear and the Kitlope Watershed, a combination of the legal duty to consult and highly effective Indigenous and environmental publicity campaigns were able to conserve old-growth areas, according to Richard Overstall, an attorney from Smithers, B.C., who often represents First Nations.

The courts played a decisive role, particularly a 1997 Supreme Court of Canada ruling known as *Delgamuukw*. The court told the B.C. government that, "Aboriginal title does in fact exist, and has to be dealt with," Tara Marsden, an independent forestry consultant for First Nations, told us. Marsden, a member of the Gitanyow First Nation, holds the traditional name "Naxginkw."

The Great Bear Rainforest's conservation plan bans logging in 85 percent of the area and protects 70 percent of old growth. The province argues that these provisions provide a "high level" of ecological protection. However, today more than a dozen years after it was established, ecologists are realizing that the rainforest is in trouble. Logging is allowed in only

7 percent of the Great Bear, but this 7 percent is where the forests are most productive and contain the most biodiversity and carbon, as Karen Price, a forest ecologist in Smithers, told us. The province claims that by limiting logging to just this one area, it is promoting conservation, but this policy simply gives the timber industry permission to extract only the biggest trees, she said.

Price argues that the government is allowing logging to wipe out a lot more of the Great Bear Rainforest than it has acknowledged. She would know. She conducted a complete inventory of all British Columbia's old-growth forests for the government. After completing the inventory, the government refused to publish her findings, so she published them herself, as we will see in the next chapter. One of her findings revealed that most of the southern rainforest has virtually no high productivity old growth left, she told us.

# Chapter 14

# Up on Fairy Creek

In April 2020, we scheduled a trip to Vancouver Island, British Columbia, to check out the condition of its old-growth cedar and Douglas-fir forests. Reliable sources told us timber companies were liquidating the last of the old-growth at an alarming rate. We knew logging these forests would seriously damage a vital carbon sink.

Vancouver Island is home to some of the most majestic ancient forests still standing in the Pacific coastal temperate rainforest. But we couldn't get into Canada to check on their status. Covid-19 shut everything down. All flights from the United States were canceled. Ferries to the island weren't running. Swimming the frigid thirty-eight miles across the Salish Sea wasn't even an option. The border was completely closed.

Later that summer, our anxiety over what was going on in British Columbia heightened when we were told about logging about to take place at Fairy Creek, a narrow valley of old-growth trees some fifty miles from Victoria on the island's west coast, and the last unprotected, intact watershed on the south end of the island. Majestic stands of Douglas-fir, Sitka spruce, hemlock, yellow and red cedar, along with complex communities of fungi and lichens, pack the watershed. At the time, the Teal-Jones Group, a timber company based in Surrey, B.C., in the outskirts of Vancouver, was logging old growth in

Granite Creek, the next watershed over. Fairy Creek was next. Teal-Jones had already built two logging roads into the Fairy Creek headwaters, potentially causing permanent damage. In an ancient forest, seemingly minor actions can have major consequences. Ecologists told us the construction of just one logging road can severely damage the natural ecosystem by opening it up to invasive species, increasing human access, and changing patterns of animal movement. Cumulative effects of road building are irreversible.

Teal-Jones planned to start logging in fall 2020. The logging license allows clear-cutting of about 20 percent of the 1,200-hectare (3,000-acre) Fairy Creek watershed, with the remainder protected as habitat for the endangered marbled murrelet or as an old-growth management area. Logging even a small portion of an intact watershed also causes permanent damage, reducing its ability to function normally, address climate change, confront the biodiversity crisis, and maintain water supplies.[1] The Fairy Creek watershed is "crown land," meaning it is managed by the Canadian government on behalf of the King of England. The wet coastal valleys in and around Fairy Creek are among the most carbon-dense forests in the world, storing up to 1,300 metric tons of carbon per hectare, according to Suzanne Simard, the forest ecologist at the University of British Columbia. That amount is on par with the carbon-dense forests in coastal Washington and Oregon, though only about half the amount in California's redwoods. A quick mathematical calculation shows Fairy Creek containing as much carbon as the annual $CO_2$ emissions of a quarter of all new internal combustion vehicles produced worldwide in one year.

By any measure, the climate threat posed by logging Fairy Creek would be substantial. Although the thousand-year-old trees in the watershed don't break any height records, some reach seventy-five meters (246 feet). But you can find much larger trees growing nearby. For example, a few miles south of Fairy Creek, there's Red Creek Fir, the largest Douglas-fir on Earth in terms of its sheer mass. Red Creek Fir stands between the San Juan River and the Pacific Ocean.

Red Creek Fir measures 242 feet tall, but in the past might have exceeded 300 feet. Over its thousand-year lifespan, multiple violent storms repeatedly snapped off its crown. But Red Creek Fir is celebrated most for its ultra-wide girth, measuring nearly 44 feet around at the base. Eight tall basketball players, grasping hand to hand, could barely wrap their long arms around it. San Juan Spruce, another massive arboreal landmark, stands a few miles further south, *San Juan Spruce* measures 38.3 feet in circumference. Among the world's spruce trees, only the Quinault Lake Spruce in Olympic National Park is more massive, so far as we know.

We never made it to Vancouver Island. We rationalized this failure by telling ourselves that the internet can help reduce the carbon footprint of publishing a book. During a pandemic, the virtual world might be the only point of access to remote parts of the real world. With a good wi-fi connection, you can download interviews, documents, videos, and even recordings of the romantic trills of song sparrows in the canopies.

But it's not ideal. You can't download the sacred solitude of hiking among the bearded lichens in these cathedral forests, or the pain you feel when confronted with a fresh clear-cut in an ancient stand of conifers. On August 9, 2020, as logging equipment began to arrive in the headwaters of Fairy Creek, so did the drones and other digital recording equipment brought in by forest activists. All of the inevitable confrontations, arrests, and demonstrations to come would be livestreamed on social media platforms for the whole world to see.

We first heard about Fairy Creek a couple of days later, when an urgent email arrived from a forest activist named Andrew Wilson. A couple dozen protesters set up a road blockade on the western ridge of the watershed, and Wilson wanted to spread word about it in the United States. As editors of *Cascadia Times*, we were on his contact list:

> I am writing to you about the imminent logging of Fairy Creek. Many people here are pissed off, with blockades and hunger strikes happening now. Please raise awareness to keep the Fairy Creek watershed pristine for future generations and to ensure the long-term health of our planet. Thanks.

Wilson took drone videos of the place, posted them to YouTube, and sent us the links. In the videos, Fairy Creek does not look like a particularly large watershed, but stands out in stark relief against a vast sea of clear-cuts. The watershed is situated in the coastal foothills, a good distance from a chain of jagged, snow-covered peaks at the center of the 285-mile-long island. Nearby, the fierce Pacific Ocean crashes against Vancouver Island's rocky shore.

At its mouth, the creek backs up into pretty Fairy Lake. At one end of the lake, a sunken nurse log peeks slyly out of the water, gently nurturing a Douglas-fir sapling on its back. Known as the "Bonsai Tree," tourists can easily photograph this stunning spectacle from the highway. The island is known for scenery just like this. Sadly, the logging companies are making sure Vancouver Island possesses less and less beautiful scenery with each passing day.

Not far from the lake, Fairy Creek merges with the San Juan River, one of the largest of two hundred rivers pulsing across the water-logged island. Near the town of Port Renfrew, a short distance downstream, the San Juan flows through a braided delta and into a bay known as Port San Juan. The local Chamber of Commerce promotes Port Renfrew as a center for sports fishing, old-growth hiking, and eco-tourism. Its website shows stunning vistas of forests and big, beautiful trees, not clear-cuts.

The Fairy Creek watershed is part of the unceded ancestral homelands of the Pacheedaht First Nation, which has its home base in Port Renfrew. The protesters, calling themselves "forest defenders," set up three blockades up on Fairy Creek, stalling logging and road-building operations. They also set up three more blockades in other nearby forests. On April 1, 2021, Teal-Jones obtained a legal injunction prohibiting the roadblocks, exposing protesters and journalists alike to arrest and forcible removal from a wide area. But as we will see, the protests went far beyond Fairy Creek.

Over the summer, the Royal Canadian Mounted Police enforced the injunction with vigilance, arresting some 1,100 activists, in some cases spraying people with pepper spray and breaking bones. It was the biggest confrontation between forest activists and the mounties since the "War in the Woods" of 1993, when 971 people were arrested at Clayoquot Sound one hundred miles up the coast. A mass trial, held on a single day in Victoria, created quite the spectacle.

Some activists were arrested at both Clayoquot and Fairy Creek, including a 92-year-old woman. A group calling itself the Rainforest Flying Squad organized the protests at Fairy Creek as well as several others across Canada in Vancouver, Castlegar, Davis Bay, Kelowna, Prince George, Revelstoke,

Toronto, and even in New York. The group sponsored a change.org petition calling for the end of old-growth logging throughout British Columbia.[2] Endorsed by actor Mark Ruffalo, the action star in the Avengers movies, the petition quickly collected 75,000 signatures. Almost every Canadian was on board. One poll commissioned by the Sierra Club BC showed that 92 percent of British Columbians supported protecting old growth.[3]

Fairy Creek became a symbol of a much larger campaign to block logging in all old-growth forests throughout British Columbia, Kathy Code, a spokesperson for the Rainforest Flying Squad, told us. The group set up another blockade in forests near Revelstoke on the slopes of the Rocky Mountains at the province's eastern border with Alberta, not far from Banff. There, they hoped to stop clear-cutting in a rare inland temperate rainforest characterized by the same species of conifers and lichens typically seen in forests at the coast. One hundred years ago, before the advent of dams, both the coastal and inland rainforests even had the same species of salmon.

The Rainforest Flying Squad directed much of its fury toward a government agency known as B.C. Timber Sales (BCTS), which builds logging roads into old-growth forests and auctions off the timber to the highest bidder. Over the past decade, loggers have been cutting down about 10,000 hectares (24,700 acres) of old growth on Vancouver Island every year, according to a review of government data and recent satellite images by the Sierra Club BC.[4] In recent years, the pace has been accelerating.

"These endangered old-growth stands are becoming as rare as white rhinos," Jens Wieting, the Sierra Club BC forest campaigner who spearheaded the review, told us. Wieting says the logging emits a significant amount of carbon, but the B.C. government does not count most forest carbon emissions as part of its overall carbon footprint. The government even misrepresents its own data, Wieting said. One government report shows the timber industry emits 237 million tons $CO_2$, more than three times the amount reported by the Canadian government to the Intergovernmental Panel on Climate Change. "These emissions tend to be ignored," Wieting told us.

In recent years, clear-cutting has taken down some of the few intact old-growth forests still standing on Vancouver Island. On the island's northeast corner near Schmidt Creek, loggers stripped old-growth Douglas-firs and western redcedars from steep slopes in valley after valley. Clear-cutting in Ma'amtagila First Nation territory sparked concern over the potential for landslides near Robson Bight Ecological Reserve, a globally unique orca rubbing beach in Johnstone Strait, threatening to deposit sediment on top of protected orca habitat.

Towering ancient trees have also fallen west of Port Alberni in the Nahmint Valley near the middle of the island, in Hupacasath and Tseshaht First Nation territory. People were furious in 2018 when loggers cut down an 800-year-old Douglas-fir known as the Alberni Giant. Listed on a Big Tree Registry managed by the University of British Columbia, Alberni Giant was supposed to have legal protection under the province's "big tree policy." Apparently, the policy can be ignored whenever a timber company feels like it.

West of Port Alberni, on Edinburgh Mountain in Ditidaht First Nation territory, Teal-Jones has been logging old growth since 2016. Standing alone in a vast sea of stumps is a towering Douglas-fir known as Big Lonely Doug, the second-tallest

Douglas-fir in Canada. The image of this solitary tree offended Canadians so much that a book about it, *Big Lonely Doug: The Story of One of Canada's Last Great Trees*, became a national bestseller. In the book, author Harley Rustad offers this description of what this sea of stumps looked like hundreds of years ago:[5]

> The words "old-growth forest" evoke a Tolkienesque grove of trunk-to-trunk behemoths separated by flat patches of mossy ground. But in Pacific temperate rainforests, like those found on Vancouver Island, the reality is much more complex. There is no order in these forests: trees of every size grow here, and windfall litters the ground in various stages of decomposition. Under a canopy of dark green foliage, thick salal bushes make one section impenetrable to pedestrians, next to another that opens a small clearing. Some trees appear painted in moss, while grey lichen known colloquially as "old man's beard" droops from branches of older trees like tinsel left long after Christmas. The largest trees pierce the canopy, allowing long beams of light to penetrate the forest floor.

Nearby in the Caycuse watershed, also in Ditidaht First Nation territory, Teal-Jones has scraped every tree from several hillsides, leaving an ugly apocalyptic scene. The Ancient Forest Alliance posted grim photographs taken by a local activist, T.J. Watt, showing the bare Caycuse landscape, some taken from the ground,[6] some from the air.[7] In 2020, Watt photographed the intact forest before it was clear-cut. When he returned to the same spot later that year, all of the trees were gone. As he wrote on Instagram:

Gone were the vibrant flourishes of red, green, and gold. Instead, a bleak gray landscape lay before, utterly unrecognizable from what I remembered. Heart wrenching as they are, I hope these images stand as stark examples of what is still happening everyday across BC and what needs to end now.

A little further to the west in the Central Walbran Valley, Teal-Jones chainsaws have been clear-cutting old-growth in the spectacular Castle Grove. Castle Grove is home to colossal western redcedars with names like Karst Giant, Tolkien Giant, Castle Giant, Emerald Giant and Leaning Tower. The Walbran is in unceded Pacheedaht territory.

The valley, with its emerald lake, silvery waterfalls, giant cedars, and big Sitka spruce, is "the most beautiful ancient forest I've ever seen," Ken Wu, a longtime forest activist in British Columbia, told us.

Other old-growth forests along lower Walbran Creek all the way to the ocean are protected by Carmanah-Walbran Provincial Park. Fairy Creek is located just south of there.

Some old-growth forests in and around Fairy Creek are temporarily protected by the B.C. government as "old-growth management areas." The Ancient Forest Alliance regards old-growth management areas as offering no more than a "soft" level of protection that could easily be wiped away by the administrative actions. The alliance is calling for legislation requiring a much "harder" level of protection for the old growth, such as a conservancy, park, or ecological reserve, encompassing a much larger buffer area.

Avatar Grove, a beloved old-growth forest near the Walbran Valley, the namesake of the hit movie by director James Cameron, is located within one such old-growth management area. Each of the enormous cedars in Avatar Grove is adorned with gnomish knots and burls. The gnarliest, a cedar known as "The Gnarly Tree," is the main attraction in this Museum of the Misshapen. The Gnarly Tree is so unusual, Harley Rustad writes, that it appears to have been "squashed by some unseen force from above that was pushing bulbous lumps out from its base."

But we wondered: Exactly how much old-growth forest remains in British Columbia, and how quickly is it coming down? Will it be gone in just seven years, as Kathy Code and forest activists predict? Is the province even protecting its old-growth forests, as the forest ministry would have us believe? Given the scale of industrial logging elsewhere in the Pacific coastal rainforest, especially in Oregon, the concerns voiced by Kathy Code and others sound plausible. But, we wondered, is there any data to confirm the status of British Columbia's remaining old-growth forests?

We turned to a report released in 2020 by the British Columbia Ministry of Forests, Lands, Natural Resource Operations, and Rural Development.[8] This report said the province has about 13.2 million hectares (32.6 million acres) of old-growth forests left, equal to about 25 percent of all forests in the province.

Of the 13.2 million hectares, the province says it protects 10 million hectares from logging. Each year, about 50,000 hectares of old growth are logged. But a newer government analysis shows there's now actually only 11.1 million hectares of old growth left.

But hold on. The B.C. government's numbers are simply false, according to Karen Price, the independent ecologist. She says the province protects only 3.2 million hectares of old-growth, not 10 million hectares. What's more, most of these forests are nothing like the lush, wet coastal rainforests on the west coast of Vancouver Island, Price says. Instead, most consist of tiny trees growing at high elevations or in bogs.

The small trees, Price told us, provide valuable habitat, but aren't biodiversity hubs like the more productive forests, and don't store much carbon. They are so small, the timber industry isn't even interested in logging them. And most people wouldn't even see them as old growth anyway. "Not all old-growth forests are the same," Price told us. That's an important point the provincial government simply glosses over.

The British Columbia government hired Price to conduct an inventory of old-growth forests in the province, but the government refused to publish her data. Price felt so frustrated she decided to release the data herself, in collaboration with ecologist Rachel Holt and forest analyst Dave Daust.[9] Their self-funded report, which cost $150,000 to produce, is available from Sierra Club BC.[10] Her surprising results captured the attention of the news media in both the United States and Canada.

The key finding, Price told us, is that less than 1 percent of British Columbia's old-growth trees are left and protected, dismally less than the 25 percent claimed by the British Columbia Ministry of Forests, Lands, Natural Resource Operations, and Rural Development. At the current rate of logging, almost all the remaining forest could be gone in ten years, Price told us.

Losing any old-growth forests is bad news, and not just for the people who love them, or for the species that live among them. Clear-cutting old-growth forests will interfere with the planet's desperate search for a place to sequester carbon. We can't afford to lose any more of them.

In response to a public uproar over the old-growth logging, the B.C. government, in consultation with First Nations, has decided to defer logging in eleven areas throughout the province, including five areas on Vancouver Island: Fairy Creek, the Walbran Valley, Clayoquot Sound, McElvie Creek and H'Kusam Mountain.[11]

"On Vancouver Island, we have already acted to protect thousands of additional hectares of old growth, on top of the hundreds of thousands of hectares already protected," Tyler Hooper, a spokesperson for the ministry of forests, told us. But Hooper didn't deny that the province plans to continue clear-cutting old-growth forests. The deferrals, to stay in effect for just two years, temporarily protect 353,000 hectares of forest that supposedly is old growth, though Price's report raises doubts about what exactly is growing on that land. And anyway, none of it is permanently protected.

Price added that the provincial government's deception doesn't end there. She said a close reading of its forestry regulations shows that it places logging ahead of conservation as its highest priority. What's more, the regulations say protecting biodiversity cannot "unduly" reduce the commercial timber supply. Plants and animals are protected so long as they don't live where timber companies want to log. The world may be spinning out of control, but in the temperate rainforest, it's still business as usual.

The Pacheedaht name for the Fairy Creek watershed is Ada'itsx. In 2021, as Teal-Jones was building the logging roads leading into Ada'itsx, the Pacheedaht leaders negotiated a treaty with the B.C. government they hoped would acknowledge, for the first time, Indigenous title and governance over their homelands.

First Nations have been resisting colonization since their first contact with Europeans, as Tara Marsden of Smithers, B.C., the aforementioned member of the Gitanyow First Nation, told us. The government has been negotiating settlements with most First Nations individually, as opposed to as a group:

> Each nation is distinct unto themselves, and while alliances are often formed, there are also disputes amongst nations on how to deal with the land issue and colonization – for example whether to litigate, negotiate a treaty, direct action, or buy into a major pipeline as owners to have more control over how it is operated. I would say there has not been a period of time where some level of resistance was not happening, including today.

In June 2021, after 176 years of trying to colonize the Pacheedaht's land—and insisting Indigenous rights and title did not exist—the province seemed prepared to finally honor its Indigenous title. During negotiations, the Pacheedaht nation, along with two other First Nations, the Ditidaht and the Huu-ay-aht, demanded that Teal-Jones defer logging in the Fairy Creek watershed and in the nearby Walbran Valleys for two years.

Though the treaty was not yet final, the B.C. government readily agreed to defer logging. Loggers working for Teal-Jones turned off their chainsaws and went home. But dozens of protesters, forced to retreat to a perimeter decreed by the courts, remained in the woods. This battle is not over.

# PART FIVE

## ALASKA

*We must live according to the principle of a land ethic.*
*The alternative is that we shall not live at all.*
                                        —*Kathleen Dean Moore*

# Chapter 15

# Trump's Great Alaska Forest Liquidation Sale

On a crisp morning in October 2018, the Kennicott Ferry motored down Alaska's Marine Highway on its run from Juneau to Sitka, a nine-hour trip deep into the Tongass National Forest. As the Kennicott turned down the long and narrow Peril Strait, a pod of white-sided dolphins broke the water's surface. On Chichagof Island to our immediate right, an enormous Sitka brown bear, the doppelganger of the grizzly, played on the beach.[1]

Believe it or not, there is much more to see in the Tongass than just charismatic megafauna. We came here to check out the Tongass, a forest many call America's last great wilderness. Suddenly, an unnatural scarring on the heavily forested mountainside beyond the bear came into view. We were expecting to see a forest covered with deep green canopies, but instead here we were looking at a wide swath of dead Alaska yellow cedars.

While the sight of so many dead trees may disappoint tourists who came all the way to the Tongass to visit one of the most pristine and intact ecosystems on the planet, scientists have a different reason to worry. They say the die-off of yellow cedars is an indication that climate change could eventually lead to their extinction. To paraphrase Darwin, species that can't adapt to the new climate will be doomed.

The science of climate change is complicated by many conundrums, including something called "feedback loops," which are changes in the climate that trigger other changes.

Yellow cedars are an example. The warming that is killing the yellow cedars is releasing carbon back into the atmosphere, leading to even more warming.

Sadly, the 16.7-million-acre Tongass, by far the nation's largest national forest, faces a more immediate threat. At that moment, the U.S. Forest Service, which manages the forest, was preparing plans to build roads into untouched areas, possibly leading to the liquidation of one million acres of old-growth trees. Logging was banned within the roadless areas twenty years ago during the last year of the Clinton administration, and despite several court challenges brought by timber companies, was still not allowed in most cases. But in 2018, the Trump administration was going through the legal process for getting rid of the old rule.

Indeed, if Trump had an environmental policy, it was to ignore and deny the existence of the climate crisis. Repealing the roadless rule aligned perfectly with Trump's previous actions like withdrawing from the landmark Paris climate agreement, accelerating oil and gas extraction on public lands, and allowing offshore oil drilling in virtually all U.S. waters. His Department of Energy was running interference for the dying coal industry wherever it could.

"The Trump administration knows the planet is going to boil," Bill McKibben, the climate activist and author, once wrote. "It doesn't care."[2] Throughout its term in office, the Trump administration accelerated logging on federal lands all across the country. At the beginning of 2020, Trump signed an executive order calling for a harvest of four billion board feet of timber from all national forests, up from 3.8 billion in 2019 and 3.1 billion in 2018.

In January 2021, as it headed out the door, the administration launched a final assault on old-growth forests by announcing a plan to clear-cut another 3.5 million acres of old-growth forests in Oregon, Washington, and Northern California, including two million acres once owned by the Oregon and California Railroad—the so-called O&C lands that we wrote about in Chapter Six.

"Trump appears to be ordering the Forest Service to put an end to multiple-use management in favor of getting the cut out," said Steve Holmer, vice president of policy for the American Bird Conservancy. The term "multiple-use management" means the forest should be used for many activities, such as hiking, fishing, and protecting the climate and biodiversity—not just logging.

If voters had re-elected Trump in November 2020, giving him a second four-year term, there's no telling how far he would have gone to eviscerate this forest. He was also looking for roadless areas in other national forests elsewhere in the country to cut.

"If they can strip roadless protection from the Tongass, no National Forest is safe," said Buck Lindekugel, a retired grassroots attorney for the Southeast Alaska Conservation Council (SEACC), an environmental advocacy group based in Juneau.

The Biden administration took office just in time to block Trump's efforts to liquidate old growth nationally. But Trump was not the first president to liquidate old-growth forests, and probably won't be the last. As we've seen, the federal government began liquidating old growth long before Trump arrived. Whoever resides in the White House in the future might try it again.

The roadless rule, known formally as the National Forest Roadless Area Conservation Policy, bans road building and logging in designated wild, intact federal forests and is one of the most important conservation measures in U.S. history, alongside the creation of national parks and wilderness. The Clinton administration held more than 600 public hearings around the nation before adopting the rule. More than 1.6 million people made comments, more than any other rule in the nation's history. Most favored enacting the roadless rule.

Some 9.2 million acres of the Tongass lie within its roadless areas, but about 4.2 million acres are unforested, made up mostly of swamps and bogs known as muskegs, alpine lakes, steep-walled fjords, majestic mountains, and tidewater glaciers. The remaining five million forested acres contain about one million acres of old-growth Alaska yellow cedar, western redcedar, mountain hemlock and Sitka spruce, some 1,000 years old. These are just the remnants of what at one time was a massive, intact ancient forest. Many of the biggest and most easily accessible trees on the Tongass have already been logged. By restraining logging, the roadless rule protected habitat for a wide variety of forest creatures, such as the big brown bear we saw on the beach on Chichagof Island. The rule also bolstered the ability of Alaska Natives to practice subsistence lifestyles, as well as Southeast Alaska's booming recreation and tourism economies.

Nevertheless, every Alaska governor since 2000 has fought to repeal the roadless rule. In 2018, Alaska's then-governor, Bill Walker, an independent, formally petitioned Trump to repeal it. Without citing any evidence, Walker claimed the rule was killing Southeast Alaska's timber economy. "The extensive damage resulting from the application of the roadless rule to the social and economic fabric of Southeast Alaska is as real today as it was fifteen years ago," Heidi Hanson, deputy commissioner of Alaska state lands, explained to us in an interview.

But Evan Hjerpe, a resource economist from Boise and author of a report on Tongass economics, told us there is "zero evidence" the roadless rule damaged Alaska's economy at all. Walker's eight-page petition focused exclusively on the economic benefits of cutting down trees, but said nothing about the more sweeping benefits of leaving trees standing.

The consequences of climate change are apparent everywhere you look in Southeast Alaska. Its glaciers are disappearing faster than elsewhere on Earth. Its winter snows are becoming winter rains. Increased temperatures are warming streams to levels deadly to salmon. The rising temperatures are also warming the soils, the main cause of death for the yellow cedar.

We heard many scientists say getting rid of the roadless rule would accelerate global warming by removing large old trees capable of capturing far more carbon pollution than the young forests that will replace them.

An intact Tongass is on the planet's first line of defense against climate change, Dominick DellaSala, chief scientist with Wild Heritage, a project of Earth Island Institute, told us. But we are crippling the Tongass instead. "The Tongass stores substantially more carbon than any other national forest in the U.S. and is irreplaceable as a carbon sink," he told us, citing U.S. Forest Service data.[3]

DellaSala opposes logging all mature forests on publicly owned timberlands in the United States, not just the Tongass. "The 200-foot trees, the deep soils—it's just layers and layers of life," Brian Buma, a professor of integrated biology at University of Colorado Denver.[4]

The old forests protected by the roadless rule provide better habitat for biodiversity than young forests. The old forest is prime habitat for the rare Alexander Archipelago wolf and its prey, the Sitka black-tailed deer, as well as five species of salmon. It is also home to a vulnerable population of the Queen Charlotte goshawk, a raptor the province of British Columbia classifies as threatened under its Species at Risk Act. Many of these species are far less abundant in young forests.

The yellow cedar's die-off is a consequence of climate change, which triggered a reduction in snowfall and warmer temperatures. Without an insulating layer of snow, the tree's fragile roots are exposed to colder temperatures, causing them to freeze, eventually killing them. Despite the yellow cedar's decline, loggers still target it for the wood's high quality and market value. The durable Alaskan yellow cedar is often used in boats, bridges and landscaping.

In 2014, the Center for Biological Diversity, an advocacy group, petitioned the U.S. Fish and Wildlife Service to protect the Alaska yellow cedar under the Endangered Species Act because of threats from climate change and logging. In 2019, the agency rejected the petition, projecting it to persist across a wide variety of ecological niches extending as far south as Northern California. Southeast Alaska represents only 6 percent of its range. The denial came on the heels of other sweeping changes to the Endangered Species Act adopted by the Trump administration, Brett Hartl of the Center for Biological Diversity told us. These changes made it harder to win protection for an imperiled species, weakened habitat protections for protected species, and largely disregarded climate change.

One afternoon at Pioneer Bar, a popular hangout on the Sitka waterfront, we met with a half dozen local fishermen gathering to discuss the climate and how it is impacting their livelihoods. Over the course of several rounds of beer, the conversation turned to the shrinking size of fish netted in nearby marine waters and how fishing is likely to get worse. To them, the repeal of the roadless rule would further the decline. There's a lot of science to back them up. A graybeard named Cheston Clark, a commercial fisherman most of his life, succinctly sized up the situation. "You can't be a fisherman and not believe in climate change," he said.

Anyone traveling down a logging road in search of a hiking trailhead knows how public lands are carved up with roads. Today, more than 5,000 miles of logging roads crisscross the Tongass National Forest, fragmenting valuable wildlife habitat, threatening salmon by blocking fish passage, and mucking up streams with sediment. Roads enable the poaching of game, trigger landslides, and provide a pathway for exotic species and diseases to launch an invasion.

"Roads devastate salmon," says Dr. John Schoen, a retired wildlife ecologist and co-author of a conservation assessment of Southeast Alaska ecology published by the Nature Conservancy and Audubon Alaska.[5] Schoen also co-authored Audubon Alaska's Ecological Atlas of Southeast Alaska (Schoen is board chairman of the organization).

Schoen led a team of scientists who identified seventy-seven watersheds in Southeast Alaska needing permanent protection from logging. More than eight out of ten of these areas are fully within roadless areas that could be logged under the Trump rule. Nevertheless, the Forest Service classifies these watersheds as "unsuitable" for logging, Schoen told us:

The best way to ensure the highest level of salmon conservation is to minimize road development. For the highest priority salmon watersheds, there is little doubt that maintaining a roadless policy will maximize conservation of salmon.

Owen Graham, executive director of the Alaska Forest Association, an industry group, claims fish populations on the Tongass are about double what they were in 1954. Graham includes salmon raised in hatcheries in his calculation, ignoring the wild salmon born in forest streams. The timber industry would prefer not to deal with wild salmon because they interfere with logging operations.

In 2018, Alaska voters rejected a ballot measure known as "Yes for Salmon" that would have, for the first time in state history, protected forest streams from logging. Co-sponsored by SalmonState, an advocacy group based in Juneau, the measure would have made it tougher for industries like timber, mining, and oil and gas to disturb salmon habitat. Campaign Director Ryan Schryver says opponents spent $12.5 million to kill the measure, far more than the $2 million spent by supporters. "The opposition spent a lot of money making people nervous wondering what the unintended consequences might be," he said.

Each summer, many of the 1.2 million visitors who seek adventure in the Tongass National Forest visit Sitka, a city of 8,000 nestled next to the Pacific Ocean at the forest's western edge. Many who live in Sitka, located in the heart of a vibrant $2-billion-a-year tourism, hunting, and fishing economy, expect the loss of the roadless rule to wipe out 10,000 jobs in tourism and outdoor recreation industries for the sake of a handful of timber jobs.

The roadless rule may reduce timber jobs, but many of those jobs are in foreign countries. Forest Service rules allow companies to export 100 percent of logs cut from the Tongass. In Asian markets, for example, these logs fetch prices that are several times higher than domestic mills are willing to pay, according to Sealaska Corp., the region's major log exporter. Sealaska and Alcan Forest Products, a log export business based in Vancouver, B.C. are leading log exporters in Southeast Alaska.

At one time, timber was a leading employer in the state, but no more. For many years now, the timber industry has employed less than 1 percent of the workforce in Southeast Alaska.[6] In 2017, for example, the timber industry employed just 220 people, way down from levels as high as 1,800 in the 1990s, according to Dan Robinson of the state Department of Labor and Workforce Development. Timber, he says, "has been more of a niche industry for quite a while now."

"The economy of Southeast Alaska has moved on," says Hunter McIntosh, a vocal critic of the plan to roll back the roadless rule. He is president of The Boat Company, a non-profit educational organization that has been offering eco-cruises throughout Southeast Alaska since 1979.

> I believe the intent all along is to try to bring back clear cuts of old. Tongass timber is not financially feasible in today's market, yet tourism is consistently growing, and travelers want to see wilderness, wild places, old-growth forests, not clear cuts.

Davey Lubin, who runs Esther G Sea Tours and Taxi, a small eco-tour business based in Sitka, notes that Alaska's tourism economy needs no public subsidies, unlike its timber industry.

"Nature is the most incredible bank," he says. "You just leave it alone and the interest compounds naturally."

In 2018 the Forest Service aired its proposal to repeal the roadless rule at twelve public hearings from Sitka to Washington, D.C. More than 33,000 people submitted written comments, the vast majority in favor of retaining the rule as is. But the Forest Service produced no audio or video recordings of any hearing. "It is appalling that there is no official record of what was said at those meetings," says Larry Edwards of Alaska Rainforest Defenders, an advocacy group based in Sitka. He said the Trump proposal was met with a "strong, angry, near universal backlash."

Although Sealaska Corp., a corporation owned by Alaska Natives, supported logging in the roadless areas, many Alaska Natives themselves were staunchly opposed, such as Wanda Culp, a Tlingit artist and activist who lives in Hoonah, a small village west of Juneau. As Culp told us:

> If you can't relate to what you are destroying, then you are doing a thoughtless thing with no heart, and that's what we are doing now. The message we have to get out is, the Earth is in peril. It's been manipulated, mishandled, and abused by people who don't care. We need to protect it.

Even some timber companies opposed Trump's clear-cutting plans, including Tenakee Logging, a small family-owned business in Tenakee Springs, located about seventy miles northeast of Sitka. Owner Gordon Chew told us he prefers a selective approach to logging that leaves a viable stand of timber in every one of our small cutting units:

Clear-cutting is a process of deforestation and although it is still allowed and practiced in our old-growth forests of Alaska, it should not be. Roads could help small-scale family logger companies, but we are not willing to open that door, as who knows what it will bring.

In the eyes of many Alaska Natives we talked to, foreign powers located thousands of miles away have controlled Southeast Alaska for more than two centuries. The foreign occupation began in the 1790s when Russians in search of otter fur first settled here. From the start, relations between the Russians and the Tlingit, Haida, and Tsimshian—the three major Indian tribes with homelands in Southeast Alaska—were tense, and in 1802, escalated into armed conflict. The Tlingit and the Tsimshian tribes each have about 10,000 members, while the Haida have about 1,000 members.

Tlingit warriors drove the Russians out of Sheet'ká X'áat'i, a native village now known as Sitka. Two years later the Russian imperial navy returned, driving the Tlingits deep into the surrounding woods and separating them from their ancient homelands and from their salmon and venison. The Russians renamed the settlement Novoarkhangelsk and established it as the capital of what we now call Alaska. On October 18, 1867, with Alaska's population of sea otters nearly wiped out, Russia sold Alaska to the United States for a mere $7.2 million. (At the time, Western Canada was still a colony of Great Britain, and there's speculation that Russia didn't want to sell Alaska to England, its chief rival at the time.) Every October 18, Alaskans celebrate the transfer as "Alaska Day,"

but many Tlingits view it sadly as the day they lost their homeland, a sentiment echoed today in Ukraine.

Starting in 1902, the United States government under
President Teddy Roosevelt began conserving Southeast
Alaska as a forest reserve, beginning with the heavily forested
5,000-island Alexander Archipelago. At the time, Sitka was
still Alaska's capital. The capital was relocated to Juneau in
1906. In 1907 Roosevelt established the Tongass National
Forest by proclamation. In the early 1920s, President Calvin
Coolidge added 1.1 million additional acres to the Tongass.
The Tongass now covers 16.7 million acres, about 80 percent
of the Southeast Alaska Panhandle. Starting with Dwoght
Eisenhower in the 1950s, later presidents did not share
Roosevelt's environmental ethos, viewing the Tongass as little
more than an inventory of uncut logs rather than one of the
planet's greatest ecosystems.

"These unspoiled places must be managed through science,
not politics," President Clinton said when he signed the roadless rule in 2000. But in America, one president's priorities
are easily reversed by the next. And so, in 2020, when Trump
threw out the roadless rule, he signaled that in his America, science was not a priority. To him, conservation was just another
game. In turn, Joe Biden, the next president, reversed Trump.
The old-growth forests in the Tongass, and the Roadless Rule
that protects them, are still alive—for now.

# Chapter 16

# Coming Back for the Rest

In August 2019, as rain clouds cleared over Prince of Wales Island in Southeast Alaska, we hopped on a bush plane to check out the condition of its lush forests from the sky. But from an altitude of hundreds of feet, we were surprised to see a landscape plastered with brown patches of treeless ground. Clearcuts, as they say. Thin dark green swaths of unlogged trees separated the clear-cuts, providing only minimal habitat for the island's dwindling population of bears, wolves and deer.[1] The landscape resembled the checkerboard pattern typical of industrial forestry seen throughout the North American West.[2]

As we looked across the horizon, other parts of the forest displayed a lighter shade of green. These areas were clear-cut many years ago, we were told, but were now nursing young, second-growth stands. Prince of Wales Island sits at the extreme southwest corner of the Tongass National Forest, the most remote island in a 5,000-island seascape known as the Alexander Archipelago. Prince of Wales is the second-largest island in the Pacific coastal temperate rainforest, after Vancouver Island, and the fourth-largest in the United States.

At one time, deep green forests of spruce, hemlock, and cedar blanketed the entire island, but loggers came in and cut almost everything down. No other part of the Tongass has been logged as heavily—or "hammered," as forest activists say—as the northern half of Prince of Wales Island. Outside of Alaska, state laws are in place requiring loggers to replant their clear-cuts, but no one needs to replant a single tree on the Tongass. Forests here grow back quickly from seeds cast to the wind by other trees. Many of these second-growth forests are now approaching seventy years old—big enough to log commercially, some say, but not big enough to satisfy timber companies preferring to cut only the massive old-growth trees. In all, there are about 250,000 acres of old growth left on Prince of Wales Island, perhaps a little more. The timber industry may act like it owns the Tongass, but it does not. The Tongass belongs to the American people.

At the beginning of the Trump administration, the Forest Service was unsure what to do with the old-growth forests on the island. Should it liquidate them all, or cut down the second-growth instead? The final decision rested with Earl Stewart, supervisor of the Tongass National Forest. By the time our flight took off from the tiny Klawock airfield on the west side of the island, Stewart had already made up his mind. The old growth on Prince of Wales Island will be logged.

Stewart directed his staff to draw up two separate plans to log the island's old-growth forests. One plan called for cutting 225,000 acres of intact forest within roadless areas. But logging the roadless areas violated the roadless rule, which remained in effect for another year. As we saw in the previous chapter, President Trump rescinded the rule, but in the end, lost his presidency. Joe Biden, the next president, reinstated the roadless rule.

The other plan called for logging an additional 23,000 acres of old growth outside the roadless areas. This plan attracted much less public scrutiny than the effort to repeal the roadless rule. Logging these forests was legal and could be done almost immediately, so long as the logging complied with all environmental laws. Stewart's office named the plan the "Prince of Wales Island Landscape Level Analysis," a word salad masking the enormity of its devastating environmental impacts, no doubt intentionally. It was the largest timber sale in federal forests anywhere in the United States in three decades.

Holly Harris, an attorney with Earthjustice, the environmental law firm, thought the logging violated a series of environmental laws. She encouraged her clients to gear up for a fight to stop it:

> The timber industry already logged the very best habitat on Prince of Wales Island, and now the Trump administration is going to let the timber industry wipe out what little remains – all in the interest of corporate greed.[3]

After our bush flight returned to the Klawock Airport, we learned the logging was scheduled to begin in just a few weeks. Lawsuits were coming. Game on.

Second-growth trees on the Tongass were always considered too small to be of much commercial value, as Tongass Supervisor Forrest Cole, Stewart's predecessor in the job, explained in an op-ed published in January 2013 in the *Juneau Empire* newspaper:

> Most young growth is simply too young for commercial timber harvest – biologically, it is too small for an operator to make a profit. Further, young growth that is large enough for commercial harvest is scattered across the forest, making harvest prohibitively expensive and

logistically problematic. There is simply not enough young growth available today to support a viable timber industry.[4]

That was what the timber industry wanted to hear, but soon Cole was hearing a different message from the White House. The Obama administration's policy was to protect old forests, not cut them down. Six months later, Obama's secretary of agriculture, Tom Vilsack, ordered Cole to stop logging the old growth. "I am asking the Forest Service to immediately begin planning for the transition to harvesting second-growth timber while reducing old-growth harvesting over time," Vilsack announced. Cole quickly fell in line.

Several environmental groups were already pushing hard for the Tongass to stop logging old growth. Two groups, the Alaska office of the Natural Resource Defense Council and the Geos Institute, a scientific organization based in Oregon, hired Catherine Mater, a forestry engineer from Corvallis, Oregon, to research the economic feasibility of a transition to second growth. They asked Mater to answer a simple question: Can logging second growth become profitable?

Mater identified 140,000 acres of second-growth trees between fifty-five and seventy years old that were already big enough to harvest. All were within 800 feet of Forest Service roads, a factor in keeping down costs, and located far from steep slopes and other environmentally sensitive areas.[5]

Mater, who along with DellaSala guided us on our reporting trip to Prince of Wales Island, has the analytical mind of an engineer and the heart of an environmentalist. As owner of Mater Ltd., a forest products engineering and market research firm, she has clients in government, the timber industry, and the environmental advocacy community.

For a time, Mater also chaired a state task force in Oregon on forests and climate.

In her report, Mater said an acre of second growth trees in Southeast Alaska can produce as much or more timber than an acre of old growth. Though the trees in second-growth stands are smaller, they are more densely packed together than an old-growth stand. She also discovered that the second-growth trees can grow more rapidly than she expected. The bottom line: you *can* make money logging second growth.

Logging on Prince of Wales Island is more damaging to the climate than almost anywhere else. Timber companies toss out about 70 percent of all the old growth they cut down. The carbon in their wood will return to the atmosphere before long. Mater showed us a hillside northeast of Klawock covered with hundreds of discarded old-growth yellow cedar logs that had been rejected because they were somehow defective. Tons and tons of beautiful yellow cedar heartwood was rotting in the sun and rain. We saw similar carnage throughout the island.

In Southeast Alaska, it takes more effort to find a merchantable old-growth tree, adding to the economic advantage of logging the second-growth stands. In her research, Mater found a potentially strong market for the second-growth logs. Several companies in Alaska, Washington, and Idaho told her they were willing to invest in the specialized machinery necessary for processing the smaller logs growing on the Tongass. She introduced us to executives from a small company in Washington state who were eager to get started.

These second-growth forests, Mater told us, gave the Forest Service a rare opportunity to "reinvent" a forest products industry previously dependent on logging old growth. But as she soon discovered to her dismay, the Forest Service was not really ready to change. Mater released her report at the end of 2016, just as Obama was leaving office. When Trump took over, the Forest Service's interest in creating a second-growth timber economy in Southeast Alaska suddenly vanished.

By November 30, 2016, just three weeks after Trump's election, Stewart decided to move ahead with the Prince of Wales Landscape Level Analysis old-growth logging plan. On that date the Forest Service published a notice announcing the decision in the Federal Register.[6] This new logging plan contradicted the existing management plan for the Tongass, which was still legally in effect. The existing plan called for a phase-out of old-growth logging in sixteen years. But with Trump in office, the Forest Service went ahead with its new plan to liquidate the old growth.[7] Reinventing the timber economy would have to wait. "Since then all focus within the Forest Service to transition out of old growth came to a hard pause," Mater told us. Looking back, she says, "the incredible depth and breadth of intentional deception" exercised by the Tongass National Forest with industry leaders, environmental groups, policy makers, and members of the public during the last decade in particular "deserves to be fully exposed."[8]

The plan to transition to second growth also faced resistance from the timber industry. The biggest sawmill operation in Southeast Alaska, Viking Lumber Company on Prince of Wales Island, had no use for second growth, as Bryce Dahlstrom, a Viking vice president, told a State of Alaska legislative panel in 2015. Viking was not willing to invest in machinery for processing smaller-dimension logs, he said. It buys only old-growth logs.

Viking Lumber makes specialty wood products out of old-growth yellow cedar, Dahlstrom explained. Its product line, including soundboards for pianos, "demands the tight-grain characteristic of old growth and cannot be made from the low-quality lumber produced from second growth."[9] But Viking's reliance on old growth cannot continue indefinitely. At some point, Tom Waldo, another Earthjustice lawyer, told us, Viking will eventually have to transition to second-growth trees or "shut down altogether."[10]

Very little lumber is produced these days in timber-rich Southeast Alaska. No large sawmills are still operating. Viking, with just thirty-five employees, is now the largest sawmill in the region. In 1990, the timber industry in Southeast Alaska employed 4,200 workers, according to an economic report. By 2019, timber employment declined to less than 400, less than 1 percent of the region's total workforce of 46,000.[11]

However, you can find several small boutique mills scattered around Southeast Alaska. Some make cedar shakes and shingles. Others, like Viking, make musical instruments. One boutique sawmill, Alaska Specialty Woods in Craig, produces guitars, violins, mountain dulcimers, Native American flutes, Swedish nyckelharpas, European lutes, Greek bouzoukis, and pianos, according to an article in *Alaska Business*.[12] The magazine reported that Alaska Specialty Woods buys salvaged, dead, downed, and previously used wood from the Tongass National Forest, much like the rotting yellow cedar logs we saw lying on hillsides around Prince of Wales Island. Other boutique mills have popped up in Sitka, Ketchikan, Hoonah, Wrangell, and Petersburg.

The economics of industrial-scale logging in the Tongass has always been terrible. It's not profitable without hefty government subsidies and lax environmental regulations. Logging costs are driven up by the remote location, great distance to markets, and high labor costs. Loggers must also deal with the steep terrain, tall mountain ridges, and deep canyons in the Tongass.

From 1998 to 2018, the Tongass National Forest spent about $632 million preparing timber sales, mostly for the construction of logging roads. Over that same time period, revenues barely reached $34 million, for a total loss of almost $600 million, according to a study by Taxpayers for Common Sense, an advocacy group.[13] Most of the logs cut from the Tongass are exported to foreign countries, where they fetch higher prices. A Forest Service rule says no more than half of each harvest can be exported, but in practice, sometimes all of the logs are exported.[14] Local buyers can be hard to find. For example, in 2019 the Forest Service couldn't find anyone to buy timber logged on Kuiu Island east of Sitka, so each log was exported. The Forest Service collects a premium for each log sent overseas.

Industrial-scale logging didn't begin on the Tongass until the 1950s, when the Eisenhower administration signed fifty-year contracts with two large paper mills—one in Sitka and one in Ketchikan. Soon the old-growth forests on Prince of Wales Island, located roughly midway between the two paper mills, started vanishing.

The mills received heavy subsidies right from the start. At first, the Forest Service paid for roads, enabling cheap access to the timber. However, it's not clear these subsidies were legal. Congress didn't authorize subsidies until 1980, when it approved annual $40-million payments to the mills via the Alaska National Interest Lands Conservation Act (ANILCA).

However, in 1990, the Tongass Timber Reform Act repealed the subsidies over stiff objections from the entire Alaska congressional delegation. And yet, the subsidies continued to be paid through a loophole Taxpayers for

Common Sense described as "creative bookmaking." The Forest Service doesn't worry at all about losing money. When it does, taxpayers always foot the bill, as Jeff Ruch, executive director of Public Employees for Environmental Ethics, an advocacy group based in Washington, D.C., told us. "This national forest runs major commercial timber sales like a cookie jar without a lid," he said.[15]

Taxpayers are not the only ones to take a hit. Subsidized logging impacts birds, bears, wolves, and deer, who rely on the uncut forests for habitat, and the communities of Alaska Natives who rely on the wildlife for their subsistence diets, as Evan Hjerpe, the resource economist from Boise, told us. "We are talking about multiple billions of taxpayer dollars to clear-cut old-growth forests and cause major environmental degradation," Hjerpe said.

David Albert, a landscape ecologist with the Nature Conservancy in Alaska, told us that Prince of Wales Island's forested ecosystems are still recovering from seventy years of clear-cutting. But Albert fears the recovery process will have to start all over again if the Forest Service implements the Prince of Wales Island Landscape Level Analysis logging plan. "People on the island are increasingly concerned," Albert says.

Perhaps no one is as concerned as the 2,000 Alaska Natives who live on Prince of Wales Island. Many rely on subsistence foods. They cannot afford groceries flown in from Ketchikan on the mainland, fifty miles away, as Clinton Cook, president and member of the Craig Tribal Association, told us. His people rely on foods sourced locally from the wild, especially venison from deer. "We don't go to the store and buy meat."

Most of the 400 members of the Craig tribe live in Craig and Klawock, two adjacent towns on the island's western flank. The Craig Tribal Association, the largest federally recognized tribe on the island, is based in Craig. Klawock is also home of Viking Lumber as well as an international log export dock operated by Sealaska, an Alaska Native corporation. Cook is one of Sealaska's shareholders. Cook says the Forest Service has been logging the island at an unsustainable rate since the 1950s:

> Plain and simple we can't do that anymore. We get along well with the land. It feeds you, takes care of you. We get all our fish, all our meat, all our wood products from the land.

Old-growth forests, he told us, "not only provide our Alaska Native people with food, they essentially define who we are and where we come from." The Craig tribe relies on a healthy deer population, which thrived when the island was covered by old-growth trees, Cook said. As old-growth forests vanished, deer populations declined. The northern part of the island, where most tribal members live, has the most degraded deer habitat of anywhere in the Tongass National Forest. Cook believes liquidating the old growth will wipe out the remaining deer population.

If deer disappear from this landscape, other species that depend on them could also lose out, including the Alexander Archipelago wolf, a rare species found only on Prince of Wales and a few other nearby islands. The U.S. Fish and Wildlife Service found the wolf suffered a 75 percent population decline in recent decades and predicted "further declines" will occur over the next thirty years, Mike Douville, a member of the Craig tribal council, told us.

You need old growth for deer winter habitat. A lot of what was logged in the '50s is still not suitable habitat for deer, which is one of the things that we really have to have.

Douville compared tree plantations to "biological deserts," but as DellaSala told us, that's an insult to deserts. DellaSala consulted for the Forest Service in Southeast Alaska from 1990 to 1993.

DellaSala explained that deer can survive the island's cold winters only under the protection of an old-growth forest. Old-growth canopies spreading across the landscape catch the snow before it hits the ground, so deer can still eat the undergrowth. The spindly young forests replacing them are not exactly hospitable.

DellaSala says the young trees are packed together so densely they create an impenetrable "wall of wood." Deer pass through the trees only with great difficulty. Mostly, they stay away. The wall blocks almost all sunlight from passing through to the understory, an effect also known as "stem exclusion." Not much vegetation can grow in this dark space, Douville told us. He welcomes any plan to log the second-growth forest:

It's not even deer habitat anymore, because when the second growth closes in, it goes sterile underneath. Not only that, you can't even crawl through it.[16]

As the remaining amount of old-growth forest shrank over the years, the deer have been getting smaller, he added. Many deer retreat to the beaches to die. In many parts of the forest, all that's left of the old growth are the narrow wildlife corridors we spotted from the sky. The Prince of Wales Landscape Level Analysis timber sale could eliminate those corridors. "We need undisturbed land for us to do what we do to maintain our life-style," Douville said. "It's very upsetting. It's way wrong."

Cook urged the Forest Service to refocus their logging operations on second-growth forests, and leave the old growth alone. But Earl Stewart, the forest supervisor, claimed in a statement to the news media that logging old growth harms neither the deer populations nor the subsistence needs of Alaska Natives in any significant way. But Cook shook his head when asked about this statement. He claims Stewart never talked to him.

> They need to start doing a better job of government-to-government consultation. We're a government. We've been here for 10,000 years. This is our land. We are stewards of the land. The government has never listened to us.[17]

These failures, he noted, violate the Alaska National Interest Lands Conservation Act (ANILCA) requiring tribal consultation whenever federal actions affect traditional uses.

In May 2019, Holly Harris, the Earthjustice lawyer, filed an appeal of the Prince of Wales Landscape Level Analysis logging plan on behalf of eight environmental groups: the Southeast Alaska Conservation Council, Alaska Rainforest Defenders, Center for Biological Diversity, Sierra Club, Defenders of Wildlife, Alaska Wilderness League, National Audubon Society, and Natural Resources Defense Council.

Tom Waldo, an Earthjustice lawyer who also worked on the appeal, told us the logging plan violated the National Environmental Policy Act (NEPA) and ANILCA, among other laws. Like many lawsuits filed by environmental groups, this case leaned largely on NEPA, one of the nation's bedrock environmental laws. NEPA requires federal agencies to assess all the impacts of planned actions, like logging a federal forest. ANILCA requires the agency to also take the needs of Indigenous people into account. But Waldo said the Forest Service disclosed almost nothing about the logging's likely impacts. The Forest Service didn't even disclose which old-growth trees it was targeting for logging. Nor did it identify which wildlife species would be disturbed. What's more, the agency revealed nothing about impacts on Alaska Natives who rely on the forests for sustenance. Nor did it disclose anything about the potentially heavy impact of logging the carbon-rich Tongass on the climate. The Tongass sequesters more carbon than any other forest in the United States, DellaSala told us.

The first day of logging was scheduled in September 2019, a few weeks after our flight over the island. But before logging could begin, a federal court blocked it with a temporary injunction, putting to rest at least for now the largest logging operation proposed by the U.S. Forest Service in decades.[18] None of this means the big, old, carbon-rich trees on the Tongass are finally safe. As Dave Albert, the landscape ecologist, told us, once the old-growth ecosystems on the Tongass are gone, "they are gone forever."

# Chapter 17

# Greenwashing the Climate Apocalypse

Amid a heavy afternoon downpour on Prince of Wales Island in August 2019, a fully loaded log truck barreled toward the native village of Klawock, where the idled Viking sawmill awaited its next delivery. A log shortage had thrown the mill's employees out of work, but the truck had nothing for Viking. It ripped right past the front gate and turned down a dirt road leading to a log export dock on the waterfront behind the mill. When we flew over the dock the day before, Jessica photographed workers loading round spruce and cedar logs onto a cargo vessel named *Global Striker*.

That same day, in a court proceeding 100 miles north in Juneau, Kirk Dahlstrom, Viking's co-owner and general manager, testified the mill couldn't get ahold of enough old-growth logs to stay open. He spoke in favor of the U.S. Forest Service logging plan known as the Prince of Wales Landscape Level Analysis that would clear-cut 23,000 acres of old-growth trees on the island. The logging was delayed while Earthjustice, the environmental law firm, sued the Forest Service over concerns about its heavy environmental impacts.[1]

"If we had sufficient supply, we could run two shifts per day," Dahlstrom groused. "We need spruce and cedar logs to run our operations but have none." The next day, a fully loaded *Global Striker* departed for Lanshan, China, with the very logs that Dahlstrom wanted for his mill. A month later,

Earthjustice won a preliminary ruling in its lawsuit, putting a halt to logging old-growth forests on Prince of Wales Island. And a year later, the American public voted out Dahlstrom's ally in the White House, President Trump.

Viking was not a victim of a log shortage. It was battered by economic and environmental forces far beyond its control. And it was caught in the middle of an epic global battle over climate change that was playing out in the remote forests of Prince of Wales Island. Sealaska, an Alaska Native corporation and a player in the global log trade, owns the export dock and 362,000 acres of timberland in Southeast Alaska, mostly on Prince of Wales Island. Sealaska exports between fifty-five and sixty-five million board feet of timber annually, about twice the amount Viking needs to remain open, as Jaeleen Kookesh, Sealaska's vice president of policy and legal affairs, told the Alaska Legislature earlier in 2019.

She said log importers in China, Japan, Korea, and Canada are willing to pay four times as much as Viking for logs. If there was a log shortage on the island, it was a shortage of logs at prices Viking was willing to pay. "Sealaska does nothing but harvest for export," Catherine Mater, the former forestry consultant for Sealaska, told us.

Then, Mater corrected herself. Log exporters were not the only ones willing to pay top dollar for Sealaska's trees, she told us. Another player with even deeper pockets lurked in the shadows. That player, we learned later, was BP, the London-based oil company formerly known as British Petroleum. BP Alaska, its American subsidiary, paid $100 million for nearly half of Sealaska's entire forest. But BP had no use for logs. It was after the carbon. Sealaska's forests sequester an enormous amount of carbon.

The transaction between BP and Sealaska, known formally as the Sealaska Native Alaskan Forestry Project, was authorized in 2017 by the California Air Resources Board (CARB), under the state's cap-and-trade law. The law allows polluters to offset some of their carbon emissions by purchasing carbon offset credits from the owners of timberland, such as Sealaska. The complicated deal worked this way: Sealaska obtained 11.4 million offset credits from CARB by promising to refrain from commercially logging 162,000 acres of forest for the next one hundred years. Sealaska could then sell the offset credits to BP, which used them to cancel out carbon pollution emitted by cars running on BP gasoline in California. Logging the forest would have released 11.4 million tons of carbon over the 100 years, equal to the amount of carbon emitted by 2.36 million cars over the same 100 years. At least, that's how it penciled out on paper.

We wondered about the broader, global climate implications of carbon-offset deals of this size. So, we decided to take a closer look. We discovered this wasn't the largest carbon offset transaction ever completed in North America, but it was close. The largest involved BP and 500,000 acres of forest in the southcentral interior of Alaska owned by Ahtna, Inc., another Alaska Native corporation, just like Sealaska. The Sealaska Native Alaskan Forestry Project was the second largest.

We sifted through thousands of documents related to both transactions obtained from the California Air Resources Board (CARB) via the state's Public Records Act, and then looked for an expert to help us understand what they meant. We tracked down Danny Cullenward, a lecturer at Stanford Law School and a member of CARB's Independent Emissions Market Advisory Committee, which monitors California's cap-and-trade program. Cullenward agreed to talk to us on the record so long as we made clear he was expressing his personal views and not speaking for the committee.

Cullenward explained to us that players in California's carbon offset program can easily game the system to make it seem like they are doing something about the climate crisis when they are not. The BP-Sealaska transaction seemed to fit this pattern, he said. The documents showed Sealaska had been mulling the offsets market since around 2010, but things actually got rolling on June 6, 2016, when the company filed a formal application to participate in California's forest offset program.

Both Sealaska and Ahtna hired Finite Carbon, a Pennsylvania consulting firm, to help guide them through CARB's application process in exchange for a small share of the revenue. Finite Carbon is the second largest player in California's forest carbon offsets program. Interestingly, since December 2020, Finite Carbon has been a subsidiary of BP.

Finite Carbon says it is in the business of helping land-owners like Sealaska and Ahtna generate revenue by selling carbon offsets stemming from the "protection, restoration, and sustainable management of forests." Sealaska's application described the project area as several large blocks of contiguous old-growth forests on Prince of Wales Island, along with other forests on nearby Chichagof, Kupreanof, Kuiu, and Dall islands. The application said no "management activities" were scheduled within the project area, meaning there were no current plans to log it. That fact alone raised a red flag in Cullenward's mind.

CARB, the California Air Resources Board, issues carbon offsets to timberland owners like Sealaska if they agree to cancel all planned logging operations on specific parcels of land. But if Sealaska had no plans to log the forest, there would be no logging to cancel. This is key, because if no logging plan existed, then none of BP's carbon emissions can be offset, under CARB's rules.

In this scenario, BP is dumping additional carbon pollution into the atmosphere, increasing the climate threat, with nothing to offset it. And yet the state of California issued millions of offset credits to Sealaska. In order for the project to qualify for the offset credits under California law, Sealaska somehow needed to create a logging plan. And so, as the documents show, this is exactly what Sealaska did.

In 2018, two years after Sealaska filed its initial application, the company finally filed a logging plan with CARB. But the logging plan contained some puzzling information. For example, it stated that Sealaska logged sixty-three million board feet of timber in 2016, even though Sealaska previously reported no logging was planned for that or any other year. Was Sealaska backdating its books? Did Sealaska magically concoct a logging plan in order to qualify for the $100-million? We asked Cullenward what he thought:

> There's something strange about a project that says it has no land management plans, but in the course of applying for offset credits develops a management plan. That's what makes accurate carbon offsets accounting so difficult.

Moreover, the new logging plan called for cutting down a total of 4.2 billion board feet over one hundred years, a figure roughly equal to the maximum amount of timber Sealaska could get paid for under the offset program. To Cullenward, this seemed like too much of a coincidence.

> You might step back and call this the most sophisticated system for managing forest carbon offsets in the

world. You might also call it an invitation for fraud. It could easily be both. We'll never be able to monitor program outcomes to determine the objective truth of the matter and can only argue about what seems most likely given the context. That's what's so frustrating about carbon offsets.

We asked Catherine Mater, the forest engineer from Oregon, what she thought. In addition to working for Sealaska, Mater had consulted for the U.S. Forest Service, timber companies, and environmental advocacy organizations. She was also a past chair of a state of Oregon task force studying forests and carbon. It's doubtful anyone knows more about the timber industry and carbon offsets on the West Coast than her.

> Technically, the trees could have been harvested by Sealaska, but that would likely not have happened due to historic native cultural aspects of the acres. I know this because I was under contract with Sealaska at the time and worked directly with their then-tribal forester.

Mater says she was surprised CARB approved the deal. "The acres in all likelihood were protected from harvest anyway," she says. "If those lands got accepted for offsets by California that's a problem." We also contacted William Moomaw, the emeritus professor at Tufts University, to hear his thoughts:

> This sounds like business as usual in the carbon offsets game. I suppose it is one way to repay native people for ripping them off in the past. Unfortunately, gaming the carbon offset system is what it has been about since the beginning.

Carbon offsets work by "asking someone else, at some other time, at some other place, to remove carbon from the air so I can emit more," Moomaw told us. "It's no way to save the climate." The Sealaska Forestry Project seems to fit a troubling pattern first identified by Barbara Haya, a University of California, Berkeley research fellow. Haya, who leads the Berkeley Carbon Trading Project, examined the outcomes of California's carbon offset program and found 82 percent of offset transactions failed to help the climate. She published a paper saying so in 2019. Most transactions reduced logging at one location, Haya found, but led to logging increases elsewhere to meet timber demand—a phenomenon she calls "leakage."[2]

Haya's results align with the findings of CarbonPlan, a group Cullenward and colleagues launched to analyze California's forest carbon offsets program—the largest such program in existence, worth more than $2 billion. In 2021, the group published a report co-authored by Cullenward showing that "the vast majority" of projects failed to offset emissions with a comparable amount of pollution reductions, a phenomenon it called "over-crediting."[3]

"Our analysis of crediting errors demonstrates that a large fraction of the credits in the program do not reflect real climate benefits," the report said.

In 2018, when BP and Sealaska finalized the forest carbon offsets deal, the BP brand was in deep trouble. BP, the company responsible for the massive Deepwater Horizon oil spill in the Gulf of Mexico in 2010 had become one of the world's most notorious polluters, taking a spot in an environmental rogue's gallery alongside the Exxon Valdez oil spill, Bhopal, and Love Canal, no small feat.

BP leveraged the $100 million paid to Sealaska to tout—or, as some say, greenwash—the oil company's purportedly good corporate behavior. The company portrayed itself as a protector of forests, the climate, and Indigenous people, and shifted focus away from atrocities on its environmental record and its heavy greenhouse gas emissions.

"We will use offsets as one of the tools to underpin our low-carbon ambitions," BP executive Janet Weiss said in a speech at an industry conference in Anchorage in January 2019, according to a report by KTOO, an independent radio station in Juneau. "These credits will amount to significant revenue for Sealaska and it will benefit their region and its communities for a very long time."[4]

At the time, BP owned a 25 percent stake in the oil field at Prudhoe Bay on Alaska's North Slope, the largest in North America, as well as interests in the nearby Point Thompson, Milne Point and Liberty oil fields, the TransAlaska Oil Pipeline, and oil leases in the Arctic National Wildlife Refuge. It also owned an oil platform in the Gulf of Mexico known as Deepwater Horizon.

On April 23, 2010, Deepwater Horizon exploded, triggering the worst environmental disaster in U.S. history. Some 210 million gallons of oil spilled into the Gulf of Mexico, nineteen times greater than the infamous Exxon Valdez spill in 1989. For eighty-seven days, oil flowed unchecked into the gulf, destroying hundreds of miles of coastal habitats, including salt marshes, wetlands, sandy beaches, and mangroves, and killing at least 100 endangered sperm whales and more than 150 dolphins.[5] Previously, in 2006, a BP oil platform in Prudhoe Bay spilled 267,000 gallons of crude oil onto the Arctic tundra, a leak that went undetected for up to five days.[6]

Comically, BP had tried its hand at greenwashing once before. In 2002, Lord John Browne, BP's chief executive, declared the company would "reinvent the energy business," according to *Forbes* magazine. "We need to go beyond petroleum."[7] BP, then known as British Petroleum, announced it was rebranding itself as "Beyond Petroleum." It even introduced a snazzy new green-and-yellow logo. But no amount of greenwashing could paint over the fact that BP was still neck-deep in thick, black crude and an environmental record to match.

Today, the company just goes by its initials, BP, and no longer calls itself "beyond petroleum." Paul Erwood, a media spokesperson at BP's corporate headquarters in London, explained what Janet Weiss meant by "low-carbon ambitions." She meant the company will have "net zero" emissions by 2050, as though this somehow represents progress toward taming the climate. As Erwood told us:

> Investing in low and no carbon businesses, and implementing technology such as CCUS (a technology known as carbon capture, utilization, and storage) at scale are some of the things that will help us get to net zero.

As we reported in the Prologue, only twenty-six carbon capture plants are in operation today, removing a paltry 0.1 percent of annual carbon emissions. The technology has a long way to go before it begins to make a difference.

The term "net zero" is a common element in corporate climate strategies, but many people misunderstand the term. If you think "net zero" means zero emissions, think again. Net zero means overall carbon emissions will stay the same, as if keeping things the same will somehow solve the problem. But when corporations rely on carbon offsets as part of their climate strategies, as the University of California's Barbara Haya found, carbon emissions often increase. Simply put, "net zero" strategies enable polluters to continue polluting.

Moreover, net zero strategies paralyze the urgent work of removing excess carbon dumped into the atmosphere over the last three hundred years. And yet, in a news release, BP said, confusingly, that it intends to achieve "absolute reductions, to net zero, which is what the world needs most of all." This is an obvious example of corporate doublespeak. What the world needs most is a reduction to zero emissions, or "real zero," not "net zero."

The list of pollutants associated with oil drilling goes far beyond carbon. Oil refineries and cars release toxic fumes like benzene that cause cancers and other health problems, disproportionately impacting low-income communities and communities of color. The BP-Sealaska deal won't offset those impacts, either. The Sealaska Native Alaskan Forestry Project may not benefit the climate, but it did appear to provide BP a tax break worth nearly $100 million.

BP is one of at least 1,500 corporations worldwide with "net zero" plans, according to a 2021 report by the Global Forest Coalition and Friends of the Earth.[8] Other names on its list are Shell, Microsoft, Apple, Amazon, Walmart, HSBC, Bank of America, BlackRock, United Airlines, and Delta. Two of these companies, BP and Microsoft, found that the forests cannot reliably provide carbon offsets because they can vanish in a fire, as the *Financial Times* reported.[9] One such fire swept through the Colville Indian Reservation in Washington, damaging forests set aside to offset Microsoft's emissions. The 500,000-acre Bootleg Fire in Southern Oregon reduced the value of offsets purchased by BP.

The Global Forest Coalition report says these schemes are being used to mask inaction, foist the burden of emissions cuts and pollution avoidance on historically exploited communities, and "bet our collective future" by ensuring long-term, destructive impacts on lands, forests, and oceans, and through advancing geoengineering technologies.

> Emissions are nothing more than a math equation in these plans. They can be added in one place and subtracted from another place. This equation is simple in theory but deeply flawed in reality.

Are "net zero" emissions really something to be celebrated? Can we trust the net zero strategies of polluters like BP? Will net zero strategies enable polluters to exceed mandatory legal limits on carbon emissions established by international climate treaties?

We asked Gary Hughes, a California-based climate activist with the international organization biofuelwatch, what he thought. His blunt response:

> Net zero is bullshit. Once one unpeels the onion of these declarations about "net zero" you can usually find some pretty smelly accounting. All claims to "net zero" upon closer examination are usually a collection of contradictions, fictions, and misrepresentations.

BP is only one of many polluters weaponizing net zero in their messaging, as Amy Moas, a climate scientist with Greenpeace, told us. BP appears to rely on offsets and potentially even controversial geoengineering technology to maintain oil and gas extraction "while having enough 'green' projects with fuzzy numbers to allow it to advertise progress toward a 'net zero' future." This scheme is so disingenuous it needs a name. We call it "greenwashing the climate apocalypse."

Alaska's conservationists and Native Alaskans have applauded the idea of protecting 162,000 acres of forest owned by Sealaska. These natural forests are of high importance to Southeast Alaska's ecology. An example is a place known as Nutkwa Inlet on Prince of Wales Island, near Hydaburg on the island's south side.

The thirteen streams entering Nutkwa Inlet support subsistence harvests of salmon, bottom fish, shrimp, abalone, and crab, according to the Alaska Department of Fish and Game. More than 350,000 pink salmon spawn annually in one of those streams, Nutkwa Creek, one of the most important salmon streams in the state, according to a report by the Alaska chapter of the Audubon Society.[10]

Sealaska's website notes that it "takes great pride in responsible forest management" and is committed to finding the best methods to responsibly manage its forest, fish, and wildlife habitats "to ensure future generations the benefit of a productive timber environment." And yet, Sealaska supported Trump's repeal of the roadless rule, which could have resulted in logging hundreds of thousands of acres of old growth on Prince of Wales Island. The Sealaska Native corporation also supported the Prince of Wales Landscape Level Analysis, which would have logged another 23,000 acres of the island's old growth and impacted a subsistence culture.

Clinton Cook, a Sealaska shareholder and president of the Craig Tribal Association, told us cutover forests owned by Sealaska are in poor shape. From the air, we could see a dense network of logging roads connecting Sealaska's clear-cuts, many of which appeared to slump under the weight of landslides. "It looks like a moonscape. Nothing left," he told us.

Sealaska did not respond to our numerous requests for comment. As Nico van Aelstyn, a Sealaska attorney, told a CARB public hearing in 2016, the carbon offset project was designed to generate income for Alaska's rural villages which are some of the most economically depressed in the country.[11]

> Sealaska's forest project will bring economic developments to the native peoples of Southeast Alaska. The project also will preserve and protect large forests, including some that were selected because they border sensitive marine habitats and thus will help to protect those as well.

Sealaska's shareholders consist of some 23,000 Native Alaskans from the Haida, Tlingit, and Tsimshian tribes. Sealaska was one of thirteen for-profit corporations formed in 1971 under the Alaska Native Claims Act that sought to resolve century-old land-claim disputes between Alaska Natives and the state and federal governments. (Native leaders say the act helped them "retain" only a portion of their ancestral lands that were stolen by European settlers.)

Sealaska has a $700-million business portfolio that includes seafood processing, natural resources, land management, and logging. The corporation's subsidiary, Sealaska Timber Company (STC), exports western hemlock, Sitka spruce, western redcedar, and Alaska yellow cedar logs. The log exports were not expected to be affected by the carbon-offset program.

The forest offset project could also benefit Sealaska's share-holders, beyond the $100-million check from BP. Revenue from oil extracted from the Alaska National Wildlife Refuge would flow to the corporation, thanks to a law passed in Congress in 2018 granting all Alaska Native corporations a share of royalties from drilling on the wildlife refuge. Sealaska had lobbied Congress since the early 1980s to pass the legislation.

The Arctic refuge is the ancestral homeland of Gwich'in Indigenous people, who fear oil operations will decimate a large herd of caribou and threaten their ancient culture. Other species likely to be impacted include polar bears, ringed seals, wolves, musk-ox and 135 species of migratory birds. There was nothing in the forest offset project to offset any damage caused by oil drilling to the Arctic environment, its unique biodiversity, or the local Indigenous community.

In 2019, BP sold its oil assets in the Alaska Arctic to Hilcorp Energy, a Houston-based conglomerate, for $5.6 billion. Founded in 1989, Hilcorp is the largest privately held oil and gas production and exploration company in the United States, but may be best known for its fracking operations. Hilcorp has fracking operations in Ohio and Pennsylvania linked to dozens of earthquakes, which are otherwise rare in that part of the country.[12] The company also runs fracking operations in several other states, including New Mexico, where in 2019 it was cited for methane pollution violations.[13] Hilcorp also operates 146 oil wells in Alaska's Cook Inlet and North Slope. In 2022, the EPA fined Hilcorp $180,000 for taking too long to inspect and repair dozens of leaks at these sites.[14]

As part of the deal, Hilcorp acquired BP's forest carbon offset credits, taking BP's place in the Sealaska Native Alaskan

Forestry Project. It's not clear, however, whether Hilcorp also absorbed what BP executive Janet Weiss described as her company's "low-carbon ambitions." And anyway, Hilcorp might not be able to reconcile low-carbon ambitions with its shoddy environmental record.

As an investigation in 2017 by *Inside Climate News* revealed, a string of incidents at Hilcorp oil drilling sites suggested the company put profits ahead of environmental protection.[15] "They were just going to drive forward and continue production, and continue reaping profits, rather than shut down," Bob Shavelson, the longtime head of Cook Inletkeeper, told the Pulitzer Prize-winning news outlet. "It was a reflection of their corporate philosophy."

The Alaska Oil and Gas Commission, another of Hilcorp's critics, fined the company $200,000 (reduced from $720,000) for a 2015 incident on the North Slope that nearly killed three workers. "The disregard for regulatory compliance is endemic to Hilcorp's approach to its Alaska operations and virtually assured the occurrence of incident," the chair of the commission wrote to the company in 2015. "Hilcorp's conduct is inexcusable."[16]

"Hilcorp has one of the worst safety and environmental records of any oil company operating in Alaska," said the Alaska Public Interest Research Group, an environmental advocacy organization. A commentary in a Cordova, Alaska, newspaper, referred to the company as "Spillcorp," citing the company's dozens of environmental violations, including a 10,000-gallon spill in 2015. The author wondered "if the BP-Hilcorp deal is setting Alaska up for the next Exxon Valdez oil spill."[17] Hilcorp did not respond to our emailed questions and phone calls.

*A version of this chapter was published in the December 2020 issue of* Earth Island Journal, *the environmental magazine based in Berkeley, California. A month later, without giving any advance warning, Sealaska suddenly quit the logging business altogether. In a statement, Anthony Mallott, the Sealaska CEO, hailed the decision as a step toward a more sustainable business model. But Mallott did not indicate whether some other entity might log Sealaska's forests instead. Mallott did not respond to our numerous efforts to find out.*

# PART SIX

## AFTERMATH

*You've got to be a thermostat rather than a thermometer. A thermostat shapes the climate of opinion; a thermometer just reflects it.*

— Cornel West

# Chapter 18

# The Run-up to Glasgow

Entering the austral summer of 2021, the climate chaos seemed to pause for a moment. After a horrifying 2020, Australia had its calmest fire season and coolest summer in years. In Antarctica, a below-average amount of ice melted. Huge lakes that in recent summers formed on ice shelves failed to appear.

Less heat, less fire, more ice. Just what our burning wreck of a planet needed. But as summer approached in the northern hemisphere, the climate resumed its relentless march, sending a vicious heat wave over Portland, Oregon, our home. In June, the temperature in parts of the city hit 124° F, far across the bright red line between a hot day and an unbearable one.[1] In Portland's moderate, moist, maritime climate, temperatures rarely exceed 100° F. But we should not have been surprised. The new climate will not resemble the old climate. Sooner or later, all the old weather records will get smashed.

Under the old climate, the odds of experiencing 124° F in Portland were infinitesimally small, or as a *New York Times* podcaster put it, "the statistical equivalent of never."[2,3] What does 124° F feel like? For many, it was deadly. And Portland wasn't the only place to cook. In Lytton, British Columbia, some four hundred miles to the north, temperatures burned so hot, the entire town burst into flames. That summer alone, more than fourteen hundred people, from Northern California to Alaska, died from the heat.

Within a few days, Portland's runaway heat wave eased, clouds reappeared, and it rained. Back to normal. But the new climate is a repeat offender. It will hit and run. It will send superhot air, torrential rains, and vicious wildfires to different parts of the globe, all at once. Then it will vanish while its victims try to recover. And then it will come back to hit you again and again.

As Portland recuperated from its heat stroke, a few hundred miles to the south in Southern Oregon, the massive Bootleg Fire triggered giant pyrocumulus "fire clouds," scorching a half million acres of forest with flames, dry lightning, and treacherously hot winds. Across the border in Northern California, the Dixie Fire torched twice as much forest while demolishing two small towns. On the other side of the planet, massive forest fires torched forty million acres in Siberia[4] and seven hundred thousand acres across southern Europe from Portugal to Turkey.[5] At about the same time, some of the worst flooding in recorded history killed two hundred forty people in northern Europe from London to Moscow,[6] and another three hundred people in China.[7] Massive flooding also deluged Nigeria, Uganda, and India.

The new climate is reworking more than just the weather forecasts. It is reshaping the entire Earth. Some glaciers have melted entirely, ice shelves have fallen into the sea, oceans are more acidic, coral reefs are bleaching, and sea levels are rising. The melting Arctic regions have warmed more than any other part of the planet. Unless the Arctic refreezes, island nations like the Maldives, Kiribati, and Tuvalo will be wiped off the map by rising sea levels. That could happen this century. Miami, Shanghai, and Alexandria could be next. And on and on.

The human toll, felt most acutely by the billions of people who live in developing nations, could exceed a quarter million deaths every year by 2030 from things like malnutrition, malaria, diarrhea, heat stress, and pandemics, many or all related to the changing climate.[8]

The trend is toward more and greater calamities. That much is obvious, but if you need data, here is some: climate-related disasters have surged five-fold over the last fifty years, leading to two million deaths and more than three trillion dollars in damages, the World Meteorological Organization has reported.[9] Almost every day on, the new climate triggers another unprecedented weather disaster somewhere on Earth. Through it all, the world breathlessly awaits a solution to the crisis. Perhaps one would be found at the global climate summit scheduled for November 2021 in Glasgow, Scotland. Would this be the summit that fixed everything?

Three months before the summit was set to begin, the Intergovernmental Panel on Climate Change, the world's leading scientific authority on the climate, laid out several horrifying future scenarios facing the planet.[10] Without strong and sustained reductions in greenhouse gas emissions, it's a future to avoid at all costs.

But 2021 gave us reasons to hope. The four-year presidency of Donald Trump, the reckless climate denier, was over. The new president, Joseph Biden, fashioned a fresh new plan to address the climate emergency. The chronic failure to fix the climate was the manifestation of dysfunctional politics, personified by Trump himself. The mendacious Republican was known for tweeting fantasies such as "The concept of global warming was created by and for the Chinese in order to make U.S. manufacturing non-competitive."[11]

With Biden now in office, climate denial and inaction disappeared from the White House agenda. Biden recommitted the United States to the 2015 Paris climate agreement, canceled the Keystone XL pipeline, and reinstated regulations on greenhouse gas emissions. But curiously, Biden also confounded his supporters by doing Trumpish things like approving a mammoth oil lease in the Gulf of Mexico. Biden claimed he had no choice. He was simply responding to a court order, which he was appealing, but the timing clearly stepped on his climate messaging. Biden also refused to block two pipelines to transport oil from North Dakota's Bakken shale formation, the Line 3 project, and the Dakota Access pipeline. One wondered: Is Biden really committed to solving this crisis?

Nevertheless, Biden pledged to reduce greenhouse gas emissions in the United States by half before the end of the decade, and to end the use of fossil fuels by 2050. Biden was upping our game. His commitments went much further than President Barack Obama's promises in Paris.

But Biden went beyond emission cuts, which will never be sufficient to solve the crisis, no matter how deep. The American president proposed a second plan to deal with the legacy carbon already in the atmosphere, the carbon that has been the driving force behind all our current climate troubles: heat waves, flooding, and other disasters.

The amount of carbon in the air is always in flux. Carbon emissions push it up, carbon sequestration brings it down. Since 2016, the trend has been up: we have steadily added a net fourteen gigatons of carbon to the atmosphere yearly, a number calculated after weighing both additions and subtractions. As we've seen, the atmosphere contains about three hundred gigatons of carbon that shouldn't be there. Until we remove this excess carbon from the air, we can expect more and more climate calamities to head our way, each potentially deadlier than the last. Turning off the oil spigot won't do it. This is where forests are needed. .

At the end of his first week in office, Biden unveiled a plan that purportedly dealt with this excess carbon. He called this initiative "Conserving and Restoring America the Beautiful," or the "30 by 30 plan." This plan would conserve 30 percent of all lands and waters in U.S. territory by 2030, according to a White House synopsis. It supplements the plan to phase-out fossil fuels. The White House synopsis of the 30 by 30 plan cited "the need to fight climate change with the natural solutions that our forests, agricultural lands, and the ocean provide." The plan has been touted as a significant step forward by some leaders of the conservation community.

"This is the very first national conservation goal that we've ever had as a country," said Sean DeWitt, director of the Global Restoration Initiative at the World Resources Institute, an environmental think tank based in Washington, D.C. The Natural Resources Defense Council said the plan "opens the door to a new, more inclusive model for science-based, locally driven conservation of lands, inland waters, and ocean areas." *National Geographic* gushed that the 30 by 30 plan would conserve more than four hundred million acres, an area twice the size of Texas, within the next eight years.[12]

Sounds great. Who wouldn't want to add a pair of Texases to the nation's existing network of national parks, wilderness lands, and marine sanctuaries? But that is *not* what Biden's plan proposes to do. His plan would expand no existing protected areas or add new ones. Instead, it calls on farmers, ranchers, forest owners, tribal leaders, and outdoor recreationists to voluntarily "safeguard the lands and waters they know and love."

Voluntary efforts may help, but the track record of voluntarism to save the environment in this country is not great. The EPA and NOAA have been suing the state of Oregon for years for refusing to require mandatory compliance with water quality regulations and for asking for no more than voluntary compliance.

The 30 by 30 plan is also fraught with some troubling contradictions. The plan proposes a dramatic shift in how the United States defines conservation. Traditionally, the nation conserved lands by protecting them as parks, monuments, and wilderness areas in public ownership. This protection was always enshrined into law. But under the Biden plan, natural areas would remain in private ownership wherever possible. And consider how the Biden plan uses the term "conservation." Conservation is typically defined as the act of protecting nature resources for current and future generations. But under the Biden plan, conservation can involve exploiting natural resources. The plan would allow property owners to drill for oil, log forests, and mine for gold on the newly "conserved" lands.

Andy Kerr, the Oregon conservationist, told us that if the Biden plan had been in effect since 1868, Yellowstone National Park would never have been created. Nor would the United States have any of its treasured national parks, national monuments, national forests, and wildernesses. The Biden plan suggests it is rooted in science:

> The goal of conserving 30 percent of lands and waters by 2030 echoes the recommendations of scientists who encourage world leaders to work together to conserve or restore a substantial portion of our planet.

Biden's plan does not see the value of conserving broad areas, and is modest in comparison to other models. For example, the late Harvard ecologist E. O. Wilson, author of the 2016 book *Half-Earth: Our Planet's Fight for Life*, [13] argues that half the planet must get ironclad protection as nature reserves if we hope to save it. The key point, Wilson wrote, is that these nature reserves must be "inviolable." Not open for logging or mining. Wilson had no interest in the soft conservation measures offered by Biden. "I am convinced that only by setting aside half the planet in reserve, or more, can we save the living part of the environment and achieve the stabilization required for our own survival," he wrote.

The Biden plan claims to rely on "natural solutions" provided by ecosystems like forests and agricultural lands. These words echo an acclaimed 2017 paper, "Natural Climate Solutions," written by a team of thirty-two ecologists led by Bronson Griscom, then with the Nature Conservancy.[14]

But the Biden plan has little in common with what Griscom's paper proposed. The Griscom paper laid out twenty specific actions to increase the amount of carbon stored in ecosystems, but the vague Biden plan proposed no specific actions, just the voluntary measures. Griscom found that forests can provide two-thirds of the natural climate mitigation necessary to keep global temperatures low. The Biden plan did not call for protecting forests, though in 2022 he signed an executive order envisioning the eventual protection of old-growth and mature forests, which are relatively rare. But the order provides no current protection for mature forests that are likely to become old growth in the near future.

The Griscom paper calculated that half the actions proposed on its list can be done relatively cheaply, especially when compared to the cost of doing nothing. The Biden plan offered no cost estimates. In an interview, Griscom projected that the twenty actions he proposed could remove carbon from the air at a rate of five gigatons per year, or enough to remove it all within sixty years. If we started today, we could finish the job by around 2080. Until Biden supplies more details about his plan, it will be impossible to project its potential impact on the climate.

We asked William Moomaw, a noted climate scientist, what he thought of the Biden plan. Moomaw, the proponent of the "proforestation" strategy of protecting existing forests as carbon sinks, found little to like. "It has already been captured by the forestry industry and others to allow extractive practices and logging," he told us. The Oregon ecologist Dominick DellaSala was even more blunt. "It's a big fat nothing-burger," he told us.

The road to Glasgow began in 1992 in Rio de Janeiro, Brazil, at a gathering of 179 world leaders known as the "Earth Summit." The Earth Summit gave us the highly acclaimed Rio Declaration, the statement that gave birth to the Precautionary Principle[15]—the idea that when a proposed activity threatens the environment or human health, precautionary measures must be taken before it can proceed.

The Earth Summit also produced two powerful international treaties to protect the environment: the United Nations Framework Convention on Climate Change (UNFCCC), the first treaty to protect the climate; and the Convention on Biological Diversity (CBD), the first treaty to protect biodiversity. The United States Senate ratified the climate treaty a few months after it was signed, but never ratified the biodiversity treaty.

The climate treaty called for a reduction in greenhouse gas emissions, but didn't specify how this should happen.

The details would be ironed out at future climate summits, known as the annual Conference of the Parties (COP). COP1, the first Conference of the Parties, was held in Berlin in 1995. The summit in Glasgow would be the 26th such meeting, COP26. Over the decades, the COPs enacted several legally binding agreements to implement the climate treaty, though none offered much improvement over the previous one. The most significant agreements were the Kyoto Protocol, approved at COP3 in 1997; the Copenhagen Accord at COP15 in 2009; and the Paris agreement at COP21 in 2015.

The agreements were weak. The Kyoto Protocol required small reductions in the emissions of industrialized countries, but had no discernible effect on the climate.[16] The Copenhagen accord was equally disappointing, lacking firm targets for reductions of greenhouse gas emissions, as the *New York Times* reported.[15] The Paris agreement was stronger, but was still insufficient to meet the goal of keeping the global temperature increase below 2° C. The purpose of the Glasgow summit was to strengthen the Paris agreement.

The Rio summit in 1992 also produced a set of non-legally binding agreements, including something it called the "Forest Principles," a set of recommendations for the management, conservation, and sustainable development of all forest types: austral, boreal, sub-temperate, temperate, subtropical, and tropical, in every geographical region and climatic zone. The forest principles were so weak they did not require anyone to do anything, such as sustainably manage them. That would come later.

In the ensuing years, efforts to protect forests were bogged down under disputes between developed and developing countries. In Paris, developed nations agreed to pay undeveloped countries money to halt deforestation under a new policy known as "Reducing Emissions from Deforestation and Degradation," or REDD.

REDD applied only to tropical forests. The Conference of the Parties has yet to approve any mechanism to protect forests outside the tropics, such as those in temperate zones like the Pacific coastal temperate rainforest. Politics always stand in the way. Proforesation could sequester some 120 gigatons of carbon by the end of the 21st century, or about 40 percent of the atmosphere's excess carbon, Moomaw, a co-author of five major IPCC reports, has found.[18]

At the COP25 in Madrid in 2019, the delegates expanded the REDD program to encourage the sustainable management of forests, renaming it "REDD Plus." Moomaw lobbied delegates to include "proforestation" within the program, but got nowhere, as he told us in an interview during a break in the summit:

> At Madrid, I was trying to get decision-makers to realize the potential that proforestation has for removing carbon dioxide from the atmosphere in the near term, and to store it for the long term.

But delegates to the Madrid COP were not interested in proforestation. Proforestation would reduce the timber harvest and interfere with the profits for timber companies operating in Europe, the United States, and the west coast of North America, where the massive Pacific coastal temperate rainforest had been a cash cow for decades. The companies wanted the summit to stay focused on protecting rainforests only in the tropics. "The forestry industry was too powerful," Moomaw told us. "This is why they focused on tropical forests."

# Chapter 19

# The Procrastination Summit

Delegates to COP26, the 2021 global climate summit, began arriving in Glasgow, Scotland, on Halloween. No one was quite sure whether to be excited or very afraid. But by the end of the thirteen-day affair, the entire world was spooked. On the streets of Glasgow, a hundred thousand angry protestors chanted "no more blah, blah, blah," led by Greta Thurnberg, the young Swedish activist. The crowd demanded action, not more words.

But words—occasionally powerful, desperate, words—were all they got. Delegates from 200 nations filled Glasgow's SEC Centre, the summit venue, with passionate speeches about the doom their countries will surely face if the family of nations fails to act. Prime Minister Mia Mottley of Barbados, the Caribbean island nation threatened by hurricanes and rising seas, made an elegant case for action:

> Can there be peace and prosperity if one-third of the world literally prospers and the other two-thirds of the world lives under siege and faces calamitous threats to our well-being?[1]

Inside the plenary hall, herds of corporate lobbyists rubbed elbows with the delegates, tipping the scales in their favor. An analysis by the London-based environmental group Global Witness counted more than 500 lobbyists in attendance representing fossil-fuel companies like ExxonMobil, Shell, Gazprom, and BP. No single nation had as many delegates. In all, more than 100 fossil fuel companies were represented, along with thirty industry trade associations. The delegations of twenty-seven nations included registered fossil fuel lobbyists.[2]

It's not clear what they talked about, but we have a clue. These companies, with long histories of denying climate science, most likely asked world leaders to invest large sums of money on expensive, unproven "carbon capture" technologies they hope will protect their core businesses without reducing their greenhouse gas emissions. Is it a gamble worth taking? If it works, it might help solve the crisis. But there's a good chance it won't. Clearly, there is not enough money to finance many worthy projects, let alone the potentially sketchy ones. In one example, ExxonMobil called for help in raising $100 billion to capture carbon from heavy industrial plants along the fifty-mile-long Houston Ship Channel in Southeast Texas. The project would inject the carbon deep under the Gulf of Mexico.[3] As of this writing, no cost-effective technology exists that can remove carbon from the air at even this scale, and there is no guarantee it ever will.

We think the Glasgow conference should be remembered as "the procrastination summit." Throughout the history of global climate diplomacy, starting with the first Earth Summit in 1992, procrastination has always been a key part of the playbook. On every issue discussed at the Glasgow summit, procrastination took center stage:

**TEMPERATURE REDUCTION:** Before the Glasgow summit began, the nations of the world submitted national climate action plans, or nationally determined contributions (NDCs) specifying how they will limit global warming to 1.5°C by the end of the century. But the pledges were too anemic. At best, they would allow the planet to heat by a disastrous 2.7°C. During the summit, the nations promised to take actions lowering the temperature to a still far-too-high 2.5°C.[4] The nations now have until COP27 in 2022 to get it down below 2.0°C, their stated goal. The dream of 1.5°C might still be alive, but barely. But everything depends on everyone keeping their promises. Doing nothing, also known as business as usual, is the worst-case scenario.[5] This path leads to a temperature increase of 4.3°C, damn close to the end of the road for civilization.

**COAL:** Burning coal is responsible for about 40 percent of global greenhouse gas emissions from fossil fuel use. Many delegates, including John Kerry of the United States, expected the final agreement at Glasgow to call for a phase-out of coal over twenty years.[6] Instead, after some watering down by China, India, and other coal-rich nations, the agreement called for only a "phase-down" of coal, with no definitive timelines. No one is quite sure what a phase-down will actually look like or when it will happen, a big win for the procrastinators.

**EQUITY:** In 2009, rich nations promised to put up one hundred billion dollars a year, starting in 2020, to help poor countries convert their economies to renewable energy and increase their resilience to climate change. The idea is that poor nations, who disproportionately suffer the deadly impacts of climate change, will need help cutting their emissions and surviving the onslaught caused by the richer nations. However, as *Nature Magazine* points out, one hundred billion dollars is miniscule.[7] Trillions will be needed each year to reduce temperatures to 1.5° C. And yet, the rich nations have failed to pay much of the modest amounts they have pledged in the past for this purpose, and some of the money they have paid has been misspent.[8] The Glasgow agreement called on them to "significantly" increase these payments, but didn't specify by how much.

**DAMAGES:** Nations hard hit by the impacts of climate change, such as those likely to be submerged under the rising seas, want to be compensated for those damages. Eventually, that might happen. But not now. Instead, the summit promised only to begin talking about the issue. The damages would be paid by the mostly rich nations whose heavy use of fossil fuels caused the climate crisis.

**DEFORESTATION:** A group of 141 countries – collectively containing 90 percent of the world's forests – pledged "to halt and reverse forest loss and land degradation by 2030," another victory for the procrastinators.[9] Why end deforestation today when you can end it eight years from now?

The world's disappearing rainforests don't have eight years to spare. Deforestation in the Amazon Basin, the world's largest rainforest, has destroyed 17 percent of the rainforest in the last fifty years.[10] The deforestation rate in 2020 was the greatest in a decade. If the tree mortality continues at

that pace for another ten to fifteen years, the entire southern Amazon could turn into a giant savannah. Gigatons of
carbon would be emitted into the atmosphere as trees die
and vegetation burns.[11] The world's second largest rainforest, located in Africa's Congo Basin and home to forest ele-
phants, chimpanzees, bonobos, and gorillas, could be gone
by the end of the century if deforestation continues at the
current rate.[12]

The picture is also bleak in temperate rainforests. On
British Columbia's Vancouver Island, ecologists project all
old-growth forests outside a few protected areas could be
gone within ten years.[13] The *New York Times*, nevertheless,
cheered the deforestation agreement, calling the voluntary initiative a "sweeping accord aimed at protecting some
85 percent of the world's forests." Boris Johnson, the former
UK prime minister, put it this way: "Let's end this great
chainsaw massacre."[14]

But William Moomaw put Boris Johnson's statement in
perspective. The UK, he told us, is spending $2 billion per
year to clear-cut forests in the Southeastern United States
"for fuel wood to replace coal in its power plants and claim
they emit zero carbon." What's more, Moomaw noted,
the UK is the second most deforested country in Europe.
"The deforestation declaration was not about ending deforestation at all," Moomaw said. "It was about suggesting rules for
commercial harvests."

Nevertheless, many environmentalists were buoyed by the
summit. "COP26 was very much the Nature COP," the
Wetlands Conservancy, an environmental group, declared in
a post to its blog.[15] As the conservancy points out, some 92

percent of all nations pledged to "tackle the loss" of natural ecosystems, a sign that countries are listening to the science and recognizing the crucial role nature must play as a solution to the crisis. It is unclear, however, what is meant by "tackle the loss." Collectively, the nations pledged to spend $8 billion annually for forests and other nature-based solutions. It is unclear how much of this money will be spent on planting trees, and how much will be spent on protecting forests. Not all proposed solutions are equal.

Many were heartened by the fact that delegates to Glasgow discussed "natural climate solutions," the first COP summit to do so. Delegates even inserted the phrase into an early draft of the final agreement, though the final agreement did not include those words. Somewhat vaguely, the final agreement called for:

> protecting, conserving and restoring nature and ecosystems to achieve the Paris Agreement temperature goal, including through forests and other terrestrial and marine ecosystems acting as sinks and reservoirs of greenhouse gasses and by protecting biodiversity, while ensuring social and environmental safeguards.[16]

The agreement did not make clear how any of this should be accomplished. Nor did the final agreement call for proforestation, the climate strategy William Moomaw considers essential to any climate mitigation plan. "Glasgow was an extreme disappointment in many ways, but especially for forests," as Moomaw told us:

> There was lots of talk about reaching net zero by 2050, without any realization that requires more forests, more wetlands, and more grasslands. It will also require

restoring mangroves, coastal marshes, estuaries, and kelp forests in the oceans.[17]

The Glasgow deforestation agreement was not the first initiative to attempt to halt deforestation. The most prominent of these initiatives was the New York Declaration on Forests (NYFD) of 2014, a voluntary and non-binding international promise to halt global deforestation. The NYDF was signed by forty national governments and was adopted by the UN Secretary General's Climate Summit. The agreement called for cutting the rate of deforestation in half by 2020, and ending it entirely by 2030, but these goals are not being met, a fact that suggests the deforestation promises made at Glasgow won't be met, either. As the NYDF said in its 2019 annual report:

> Instead of slowing down, tropical deforestation has continued at an unsustainable pace since the adoption of the NYDF. Since 2014, the world has lost an area of tree cover the size of the United Kingdom every year.[18]

Part of the problem is a lack of money. The international community has pledged to spend only about 5 percent of the amount needed to save and restore forests worldwide, the NYDF said in the report.

Days after the Glasgow summit concluded, eighteen-year-old Greta Thunberg, a powerful voice for the climate concerns of young people, denounced the summit as a failure in an interview with the Washington *Post*:

> We won't be able to solve the climate crisis unless there is massive pressure from the outside. Nothing will come

out of these conferences unless there is a huge increase in the level of awareness and unless people actually go out on the streets and demand change.[19]

Boris Johnson famously billed COP26 as a "last chance" to end the climate emergency. No one knows how many more last chances we will get.

# Epilogue

# The Solution Grows on Trees

Despite what you may have heard, climate change will not destroy the planet. A million years from now, this round orb will still be hurtling across the universe, still attached to its star, still covered with mountains and oceans and deserts. Damaged ecosystems will regenerate. Burnt forests will regrow. Melted glaciers will refreeze. The only thing missing from this picture is people. Climate change will be hell on human civilization. The year 2021 could be known as the year of procrastination, except every other year is vying for the same title. An old Meat Puppets song sums it all up: *Who needs action when you got words?*

During the months following the Glasgow summit, the procrastination continued. The United States Congress put off action on a bill to deal with the climate. The bill, known as "Build Back Better," was the centerpiece of President Biden's climate plan. Congress dithered on the bill before Glasgow, and dithered afterwards. A year later, Congress passed a modest version of the bill.

Meanwhile, in April 2022, Biden issued an executive order that appeared to endorse proforestation, though he did not use the term. He directed the government to conduct an inventory of mature and old-growth forests on federal lands within one year so that policies can be adopted to protect them. The administration framed the move as key to storing carbon and addressing climate change. The executive order recognized the logic behind proforestation: an effective use of forests as a climate-mitigation strategy must go far beyond saving just old-growth forests, though it must do that. It also means protecting mature forests that will become old-growth in the foreseeable future. And it means protecting carbon-rich forest ecosystems like the Pacific coastal temperate rainforest. If adopted globally, proforestation could steer the entire planet toward victory in this epic battle for the future. So, let's take the win. "Protecting America's old-growth forests, and letting new giants grow, is one of the biggest single steps we can take to combat climate change," said Steve Pedery of Oregon Wild.

It is clear that the fossil fuel industry is not solely responsible for the climate calamity, and we cannot expect it to shoulder the entire burden of addressing itself. Timber companies must also be part of the solution. They know what to do. Hesitant world leaders, and there are many, must commit to protecting their carbon-rich forests. Timber companies must avoid logging them. As Andy Kerr suggested to us in an interview, they should take a hard look at alternative sources of raw material like hemp. And we all should think about the impact of our actions on future generations, as ancient Indigenous wisdom urged us to do:

> *Treat the Earth well. It was not given to you by your parents, it was loaned to you by your children. We do not inherit the Earth from our ancestors, we borrow it from our children.*

# Acknowledgements

We acknowledge the scientists and other experts who gave valuable time to help us understand the complex concepts described in this book: Paul Alaback, Dave Albert, Marina Anderson, Lisa Arkin, Inka Bajandas, Bill Bakke, Steven Dow Beckham, Spencer Beebe, Nina Bell, Robert Beschta, Ralph Bloemers, Michael Blumm, Laura Brophy, Tim Bristol, Susan Jane Brown, Torrance Coste, Danny Cullenward, Dominick DellaSala, Lawrence Dill, Angus Duncan, Francis Eatherington, Larry Edwards, Paul Engelmeyer, Harry Esteve, Suzanne Fouty, Jerry Franklin, Jim Furnish, Nick Gayeski, Bronson Griscom, Mark Haggerty, Chad Hanson, Mark Harmon, Holly Harris, Nick Heinemann, Doug Heiken, Jim Helfield, Greg Hood, Gary Hughes, Chris Jordan, Tommy Joseph, James Carr, J. Boone Kauffman, Heather Keith, Andy Kerr, Martha Ketelle, Celeste Kieran, Mollie Kile, Russell Kramer, Robert Lackey, Beverly Law, Haley Leslie-Bole, David G. Lewis, Jim Lichatowich, Buck Lindekugel, Misty MacDuffee, Ken Margolis, Tara Marsden, Mary Catherine Martin, Catherine Mater, David McCloskey, Bruce McIntosh, Hunter McIntosh, Chad Meengs, Rebecca Miller, Amy Moas, William Moomaw, Alexandra Morton, Dave Moskowitz, Jim Myron, Robert Naiman, Rich Nawa, Kim Nelson, Ernie Niemi, Reed Noss, Richard Overstall, Steve Pedery, Dan Pennington, Sharalyn Peterson, Erik Piikkila, Karen Price, John Reynolds, William Riggle, Katie Riley, William Robbins, Mike Roselle, Jeff Ruch, Bob Sallinger, John Schoen, Gabe Scott, Wayne Shammel, Erika Smithwick, Randi Spivak, Sean

Stevens, Esther Stutzman, John Talberth, Meredith Trainor, Bob Van Dyk, Carol Van Strum, Robert Van Pelt, Tom Waldo, Wayne Walker, Chuck Willer, Jens Wieting, Andrew Wilson, Ken Wu, and Lionel Youst. Special thanks also go to Catherine Mater and Dominick DellaSala for guiding our exploration of the ancient forests on Prince of Wales Island in Alaska's Tongass National Forest.

Originally, *Canopy of Titans* was to be published as a special issue of *Cascadia Times* (www.times.org), an environmental journal based in Portland edited by the book's two authors, Jessica Applegate and Paul Koberstein. We are grateful for the fundraising support provided by the Cascadia Media Lab, *Cascadia Times*' non-profit partner. The media lab's past and present board of directors, Ken Margolis, Joel Koberstein, John Haines, Andrea Carlos, Katharine Salzmann, Jennifer Jones, Mary Scurlock, and Rowan Baker all deserve our deepest gratitude. We also want to thank Terri Crawford Hansen, author of Chapter 12: A Resilient Community, as well as Deb Lowenthal, Jo Ostgarden, Miranda Hansen, the late Sarah Clark, and Steve Law for their support as we formulated our vision. We also give a shout out to the staff at Dan & Louie's Oyster Bar in Portland, where the Cascadia Media Lab board met with us regularly.

We are also grateful to Maureen Nandini Mitra and Zoe Loftus-Farren at Earth Island Journal, Morgan Erickson-Davis at Mongabay, Jason Mark at Sierra Magazine, and Maya Schenwar at Truthout for their editorial feedback; Meagan Jeanette and the Society of Environmental Journalists for their grant support; the San Francisco Press Club and the Society of Professional Journalists, Northern California Chapter, for honoring "Carbon Conundrum," a version of Chapter 17: Greenwashing the Climate Apocalypse published in *Earth*

# ACKNOWLEDGEMENTS

*Island Journal*, with awards for excellence in investigative and environmental journalism; and Bill McKibben and Elizabeth Kolbert for endorsing our book.

Finally, we'd like to thank John Oakes and OR Books for believing in our project and giving us a long leash.

# Endnotes

## Prologue

1. Gatti, L.V., Basso, L.S., Miller, J.B. et al. Amazonia as a carbon source linked to deforestation and climate change. *Nature* 595, 388–393 (2021). https://doi.org/10.1038/s41586-021-03629-6.
2. Ben Ehrenreich, "Climate Change Is Here – and It Looks Like Starvation," *The Nation*, March 1, 2019, online at https://www. thenation.com/article/archive/climate-change-media-humanitarian-crises/.
3. Al Jazeera, "'Nothing left': A catastrophe in Madagascar's famine-hit south," July 23, 2021, online at https://www.aljazeera. com/news/2021/7/23/nothing-left-catastrophe-madagascar-famine-hit-south.
4. USGCRP, 2017: Climate Science Special Report: Fourth National Climate Assessment, Volume I [Wuebbles, D.J., D.W. Fahey, K.A. Hibbard, D.J. Dokken, B.C. Stewart, and T.K. Maycock (eds.)]. U.S. Global Change Research Program, Washington, D.C., USA, 470 pp, doi:10.7930/J0J964J6.
5. A gigaton is 1 billion metric tonnes, or 2.2046 trillion pounds.
6. As of May 2022, the concentration of CO2 in the atmosphere was about 421 parts per million, equal to about 300 gigatons of carbon. Personal communication, Wayne Walker, Carbon Program Director, Woodwell Climate Research Center.
7. Garcia Freites, S., and Jones, C. (2021), "A Review of the Role of Fossil Fuel-Based Carbon Capture and Storage in the Energy System," Tyndall Centre, online at https://www.research. manchester.ac.uk/portal/files/184755890/CCS_REPORT_FINAL_ v2_UPLOAD.pdf.
8. Robert Van Pelt, Stephen C. Sillett, William A. Kruse, James A. Freund, Russell D. Kramer, "Emergent crowns and light-use complementarity lead to global maximum biomass and leaf area in Sequoia sempervirens forests," *Forest Ecology and Management*, Volume 375, 2016, Pages 279-308, ISSN 0378-1127, https://doi. org/10.1016/j.foreco.2016.05.018.
9. David Wallace-Wells, *The Uninhabitable Earth: Life After Warming* (New York: Penguin Random House, 2017), 5.
10. Michael E Mann, *The New Climate War: The Fight to Take Back Our Planet* (New York: PublicAffairs, 2021), 81.

11. Working Group I, Sixth Assessment Report, Intergovernmental Panel on Climate Change, August 2021, online at https://www. ipcc.ch/assessment-report/ar6.

## Chapter 1

1. A version of Chapter 1, "Where the forest has no name," was first published by *Mongabay*, May 24, 2019, online at https://news. mongabay.com/2019/05/where-the-forest-has-no-name.
2. Allan, Stuart; Buckley, Aileen R.; Meacham, James E. (2001) [1976]. Loy, William G. (ed.). *Atlas of Oregon, 2nd ed.* (Eugene: University of Oregon Press, 2001.)
3. Kathie Durbin and Paul Koberstein, "Northwest Forests: Day of Reckoning," *The Oregonian*, October 15, 1990.
4. Carl Segerstrom, "Timber is Oregon's biggest carbon polluter," *High Country News*, May 16, 2018, online at https://www.hcn.org.
5. *Seattle Times*, "Giant logged long ago but not forgotten," September 4, 2011, online at https://www.seattletimes.com/life/giant-loggedlong-ago-but-not-forgotten.
6. Al Carder, *Giant Trees of Western America and the World* (Madeira Park, B.C.: Harbour, 2005), 14.
7. Suzanne Simard, *Finding the Mother Tree: Discovering the Wisdom of the Forest* (New York: Alfred A. Knopf, 2021).
8. Suzanne Simard, "The Disappearing Mother Trees," talk in Victoria, Canada, September 22, 2021, archived at https://www.facebook. com/streamocon/videos/2894007690929567.
9. Paul Alaback, "Comparative ecology of temperate rainforests of the Americas along analogous climatic gradients," *Revista Chilena de Historia Natural*, 1991, online at https://link.springer.com/chapter/10.1007/978-1-4612-3970-3_7.
10. Dominick DellaSala is chief scientist at Wild Heritage, a project of Earth Island Institute.
11. A hectare is a square kilometer, or 2.47 acres. Eighty million hectares equals 192 million acres.
12. Dominick A. DellaSala, *Temperate and Boreal Rainforests of the World* (Washington, D.C.: Island Press, 2011), 16-17.
13. Ecotrust, Pacific GIS, and Conservation International, *The Rain Forests of Home: An Atlas of People and Place*, Portland, Oregon, 1995.
14. Peter Schoonmaker, Bettina von Hagen, and Edward C. Wolf, *The Rain Forests of Home: Profile of a North American Bioregion* (Washington, D.C.: Island Press, 1997), 1.

# ENDNOTES

15. Rainforest Foundation Norway, "State of the Tropical Rainforest: The Complete Overview of the Tropical Rainforest, Past and Present," 2021, online at https://d5i6is0eze552.cloudfront.net/ documents/ Publikasjoner/Andre-rapporter/RF_StateOfTheRainforest_2020.pdf.

16. Constance Best, "Concepts in Action: The Pacific Forests Trusts," in *The Rain Forests of Home: Profile of a North American Bioregion*, 200.

17. Mark E. Harmon, William K. Ferrell, Jerry F. Franklin, "Effects on Carbon Storage of Conversion of Old-Growth Forests to Young Forests," *Science*, February 9, 1990, online at https://www.science.org/ doi/10.1126/science.247.4943.699.

18. *Glaucomys oregonensis.*

19. *Brachyramphus marmoratus.*

20. Reed Noss ed., *The Redwood Forest: History, Ecology, and Conservation of the Coast Redwoods* (Washington, D.C.: Island Press, 2000), xxi.

21. E. O., Wilson, *Half-Earth: Our Planet's Fight for Life* (New York: WW Norton, 2016), 136-137.

22. *Strix occidentalis caurina.*

23. Famous Redwoods website, online at http://famousredwoods.com/strat-osphere_giant/.

24. *Pseudotsuga menziesii.*

25. *Picea sitchensis.*

26. Robert Van Pelt, *Forest Giants of the Pacific Coast* (Vancouver, San Francisco, Seattle: Global Forest Society in association with University of Washington Press, 2001), xxii.

27. *Sequoiadendron giganteum.*

28. *Shorea faguetiana.*

29. *Eucalyptus globulus.*

30. *Eucalyptus regnans.*

31. Robert Van Pelt, Stephen C. Sillett, William A. Kruse, James A. Freund, Russell D. Kramer, "Emergent crowns and light-use complementarity lead to global maximum biomass and leaf area in Sequoia sempervirens forests," *Forest Ecology and Management*, Volume 375, 2016, 279-308.

32. *Tsuga heterophylla.*

33. *Chamaecyparis lawsoniana.*

34. *Thuja plicata.*

35. *Abies procera.*

36. *Abies alba.*

37. *Tsuga mertensiana.*

38. *Cupressus nootkatensis.*

39. *Calocedrus decurrens.*

40. *Umbellularia californica.*

41. *Taxus brevifolia.*
42. George Bundy Wasson Jr., "The Coquille Indians and the Cultural 'Black Hole' of the Southwest Oregon Coast," (master's thesis, University of Oregon, 1994), 15.
43. Russell Kramer, "Sitka Spruce Grow Fast and Die Young," canopywatch. com, Jan. 20, 2019, online at https://www.canopywatch.com/sitka-spruce-grow-fast-and-die-young-2/.
44. Victoria *Times-Colonist*, "Rainforest name has more complex origin," February 23, 2018, online at https://www.timescolonist. com.
45. Ian and Karen McAllister, *The Great Bear Rainforest: Canada's Forgotten Coast* (San Francisco: Sierra Club Books, 1997), 7.
46. Jill Eilperin, "Trump to strip protections from Tongass National Forest, one of the biggest intact temperate rainforests," *Washington Post*, October 28, 2020, online at https://www.washingtonpost. com/climate-environment/2020/10/28/trump-tongass-national-forest-alaska/.

## Chapter 2

1. Beverly Law and William Moomaw, "The best carbon capture technology? Leaving forests alone," Green Biz, March 21, 2021. Online at https://www.greenbiz.com/article/best-carbon-capture-technology-leaving-forests-alone.
2. Crowther, Timothy et. al., Mapping tree density at a global scale, *Nature*, September 2, 2015. Online at https://www.nature.com/ articles/nature14967.
3. Griscom, B. W., et al., "Natural climate solutions," *Proceedings of the National Academy of Sciences*, October 27, 2017, online at https:// www.pnas.org/content/114/44/11645.
4. Jean-Francois Bastin, Yelena Finegold, Claude Garcia, Danilo Mollicone, Marcelo Rezende, Devin Routh, Constantin M. Zohner, Thomas W. Crowther, "The global tree restoration potential," *Science*, July 5, 2019, online at https://www.science.org/doi/ abs/10.1126/science.aax0848.
5. Carrington, Damien, "Tree planting 'has mind-blowing potential' to tackle climate crisis," *The Guardian*, July 4, 2019, online at https:// www.theguardian.com/environment/2019/jul/04/planting-billions-trees-best-tackle-climate-crisis-scientists-canopy-emissions.
6. Whitton, Mark, "The most effective way to tackle climate change? Plant 1 trillion trees," CNN, April 17. 2019, online at https://www. cnn.com/2019/04/17/world/trillion-trees-climate-change-intl-scn/ index.html.

7.  Steve Hanley, "Got An Overheating Planet? Plant 1 Trillion Trees. Problem Solved," *CleanTechnica*, July 5, 2019, online at https:// clean-technica.com/2019/07/05/got-an-overheating-planet-plant-1 trillion-trees-problem-solved/.

8.  Leahy, Stephen, "How to erase 100 years of carbon emissions? Plant trees—lots of them," *National Geographic*, July 4, 2019, online at https://www.nationalgeographic.com/environment/ article/how-to-erase-100-years-carbon-emissions-plant-trees.

9.  Rahmstorf, Stefan, "Can planting trees save our climate?" *Realclimate. org*, July 16, 2019, https://www.realclimate.org/index.php/ archives/2019/07/can-planting-trees-save-our-climate.

10. Pierre Friedlingstein, "Comment on "The global tree restoration potential," *Science*, October 18, 2019, online at https://www. science.org/ doi/10.1126/science.aay8060.

11. Science Media Center, "Expert Reaction to Study Looking at Trees, Carbon Storage and Climate Change, online at https://www. science-mediacentre.org/expert-reaction-to-study-looking-at-treescarbon-storage-and-climate-change/.

12. Jean-Francois Bastin, Yelena Finegold, Claude Garcia, Danilo Mollicone, Marcelo Rezende, Devin Routh, Constantin M. Zohner, Thomas W. Crowther, "Erratum for the Report: The global tree restoration potential," *Science*, May 29, 2020, online at https:// www.science.org/ doi/10.1126/science.abc8905.

13. Alan Grainger, Louis R. Iverson, Gregg H. Marland, Anantha Prasad, "Comment on "The global tree restoration potential," *Science*, Oct 18, 2019, online at https://www.science.org/doi/ full/10.1126/science. aay8334.

14. Paget, Sharif, "Ethiopia plants more than 350 million trees in 12 hours," CNN, July 30, 2019.

15. Carley Petesch, "Africa's 'Great Green Wall' shifts focus to hold off desert," Associated Press, November 12, 2021, online at https:// apnews.com.

16. Jim Morrison, "The 'Great Green Wall' Didn't Stop Desertification, but it Evolved Into Something That Might," *Smithsonian Magazine*, August 23, 2016, online at https://www.smithsonianmag. com/science-nature/great-green-wall-stop-desertification-not-somuch-180960171.

17. Zastrow, Mark, "China's tree-planting drive could falter in a warming world," *Nature*, September 23, 2019.

18. Raul Roman, Lauren Kelly, Rafe H. Andrews and Nick Parisse, "Can We Turn a Desert Into a Forest?", *New York Times*, January. 23, 2022 online

at https://www.nytimes.com/2022/01/23/opinion/ great-green-wall-niger.html.

19. World Economic Forum, "A platform for the trillion tree community," online at https://www.1t.org.
20. Stephanie Ebbs, "Trump Virginia golf course cited for illegally cutting down trees from protected area," ABC News, March 7, 2019, online at https://abcnews.go.com/Politics/trump- virginia-golf-cited-illegally-cutting-trees-protected/ story?id=61531413 &sa=D&source=docs&ust=1644762726093532& usg=AOvVaw0QkOM-Kp5XYD2kIE1blTPRQ.
21. https://www1.plant-for-the-planet.org/.
22. Fischer, Tin, "Do you know how many trees there are?," *Die Zeit*, March 6, 2019.
23. *Science Daily*, "Restore natural forests to meet global climate goals," April 2, 2019, online at https://www.sciencedaily.com/ releases/2019/04/190402081533.htm.
24. Simon L. Lewis, Charlotte E. Wheeler, Edward T. A. Mitchard and Alexander Koch, "Restoring natural forests is the best way to remove atmospheric carbon," *Nature*, April 2, 2019, online at https://www. nature.com/articles/d41586-019-01026-8.

## Chapter 3

1. Ann Sullivan, "Dethroned Washington Tree Contains More Wood in Trunk Than Oregon Fir," *The Oregonian*, August 28, 1962.
2. https://en.wikipedia.org/wiki/Queets_Fir.
3. https://www.monumentaltrees.com/en/can/britishcolumbia/portrenfrew/2491_sanjuanriver/4972/.
4. Suzanne Simard, *Finding the Mother Tree: Discovering the Wisdom of the Forest* (New York: Alfred A. Knopf), 225.
5. JM Kimble, R Lal, R Birdsey, LS Heath, *The potential of US forest soils to sequester carbon and mitigate the greenhouse effect*, CRC Press, 2002.
6. Hannah Connuck, A. Peyton Smith, Keylor Munoz Elizondo, James K Brumbelow, and Georgianne W Moore, "Soils In Old-Growth Treetops Can Store More Carbon Than Soils Under Our Feet," American Geophysical Union, December 14, 2021, online at https://phys.org/ news/2021-12-soils-old-growth-treetops-carbonfeet.html.
7. James R. Strittholt, Dominick A. DellaSala and Hong Jiang, "Status of Mature and Old-Growth Forests in the Pacific Northwest," *Conservation Biology*, April 2006, online at https://www.jstor.org/ stable/3591344.

8. N. L. Stephenson et. al., "Rate of tree carbon accumulation increases continuously with tree size," *Nature*, March 6, 2014, online at https://www.nature.com/articles/nature12914.

9. Western Ecological Research Center, US Geological Survey, "Trees do not slow in their growth rate as they get older and larger," Jan. 15, 2014, online at https://www.usgs.gov/news/large-old-trees-grow-fastest-storing-more-carbon.

10. William R. Moomaw, Susan A. Masino, Edward K. Faison, "Intact Forests in the United States: Proforestation Mitigates Climate Change and Serves the Greatest Good," *Frontiers in Forests and Global Change*, 2019, online at https://www.frontiersin.org/articles/10.3389/ffgc.2019.00027/full.

11. Smithwick, E. A., Harmon, M. E., Remillard, S. M., Acker, S. A., and Franklin, J. F. (2002). Potential upper bounds of carbon stores in forests of the Pacific Northwest. *Ecological Applications*, 12(5), 1303–1317. Online at https://www.researchgate.net/publication/228684067_Potential_Upper_Bounds_of_Carbon_Stores_in_ Forests_of_the_Pacific_Northwest.

12. Heather Keith, Brendan G. Mackey, David B. Lindenmayer, "Re-evaluation of forest biomass carbon stocks and lessons from the world's most carbon-dense forests," *Proceedings of the National Academy of Sciences*, July 14, 2009, online at https://www.pnas.org/ content/106/28/11635.

13. Aly Lawson, "World's Tallest Eucalyptus Tree Found with Lidar and GIS," *ESRI*, February 2010, online at https://www.esri.com/news/arcwatch/0210/the-centurion.html.

14. World Wildlife Fund, "3 billion animals harmed by Australia's fires," July 28, 2020, online at https://www.worldwildlife.org/stories/3billion-animals-harmed-by-australia-s-fires.

15. Robert Preston, *The Wild Trees: A Story of Passion and Daring* (New York: Random House, 2007).

16. Robert Van Pelt, *Forest giants of the Pacific Coast* (Vancouver, San Francisco, Seattle: Global Forest Society in association with University of Washington Press, 2001).

17. Robert Van Pelt, Stephen C. Sillett, William A. Kruse. James A. Freund, Russell D. Kramer, "Emergent crowns and light-use complementarity lead to global maximum biomass and leaf area in Sequoia sempervirens forests," *Forest Ecology and Management*, September 2016, online at https://www.sciencedirect.com/science/ article/pii/S0378112716302584.

18. Preston, 203.

19. Suzanne Simard, "Next for Fairy Creek? Science Must Trump Politics," *The Tyee*, October 21, online at https://thetyee.ca/Opinion/2021/10/01/Next-Fairy-Creek-Science-Must-Trump-Politics/.

20. Organized Village Of Kasaan, Organized Village Of Kake, Klawock Cooperative Association, Hoonah Indian Association, Ketchikan Indian Community, Skagway Traditional Council, Organized Village Of Saxman, Yakutat Tlingit Tribe, Central Council Tlingit And Haida Indian Tribes Of Alaska, "Petition For Usda Rulemaking," June 22, 2021, online at https://www.laststands.org/blog/2020/8/21/justice-alert-stand-with-the-tribes-ofthe-tongass.

21. Oregon Department of State Lands, "Elliott State Research Forest Habitat Conservation Plan. Working Draft," May 2021, online at https://www.oregon.gov/dsl/Land/Documents/WorkingDRAFT_ElliottStateResearchForestHCP_May2021.pdf.

22. Thomas A. Spies, David E. Hibbs, Janet L. Ohmann, Gordon H. Reeves, Robert J. Pabst, Frederick J. Swanson, Cathy Whitlock, Julia A. Jones, Beverly C. Wemple, Laurie A.Parendes, and Barbara A. Schrader, "The Ecological Basis of Forest Ecosystem Management in the Oregon Coast Range." Oregon State University Forestry Research Laboratory, 2003. Online at https://www.academia.edu/28490616/The_ecological_basis_of_forest_ecosystem_management_in_the_Oregon_Coast_Range.

23. Brent Davies, Steve Dettman, Matthew Goslin, Mike Mertens, and Howard Silverman, "Carbon Analysis of Proposed Forest Management Regimes on the Elliott State Forest," Ecotrust, 2011.

24. Oregon State University College of Forestry, "Proposal: Elliott State Research Forest," April 2021, online at https://www.forestry.oregon-state.edu/elliott-state-forest.

25. Public Hearing, Oregon State Land Board, December 8, 2020, written testimony online at https://www.oregon.gov/dsl/Board/Documents/Written_Testimony_December2020_LandBoard2.pdf.

26. List of donors to the Oregon State University Forest Science Complex, online at https://www.forestry.oregonstate.edu/ofsc.

27. Public Hearing, Oregon State Land Board, December 8, 2020, written testimony online at https://www.oregon.gov/dsl/Board/Documents/Written_Testimony_December2020_LandBoard2.pdf.

28. Washington State Legislature, HB 2528, 2020 Regular Session, online at https://app.leg.wa.gov/billsummary?BillNumber=2528&Year=2019.

29. Video of Washington State Legislature hearing before the House Rural Development, Agriculture, & Natural Resources Committee, Jan 28, 2020, online at https://www.tvw.org/video/watch/?eventID=2020011324.

## Chapter 4

1. Telephone interview with Beverly Law, October 22, 2019.
2. Beverly E. Law, Tara W. Hudiburg, Logan T. Berner, Jeffrey J. Kent, Polly C. Buotte, and Mark Harmon, "Land use strategies to mitigate climate change in carbon dense temperate forests," *Proceedings of the National Academy of Sciences*, April 3, 2018, online at https:// www.pnas.org/ content/115/14/3663.
3. Don Grant et al. "Reducing $CO_2$ emissions by targeting the world's hyper-polluting power plants," *Environmental Research Letters*, 2021, online at https://iopscience.iop.org/article/10.1088/1748-9326/acl3fl.
4. Mark E. Harmon, William K. Ferrell, Jerry F. Franklin, "Effects on Carbon Storage of Conversion of Old-Growth Forests to Young Forests," *Science*, February 9, 1990, online at https://www.science.org/ doi/10.1126/science.247.4943.699.
5. John Talberth, " Oregon Forest Carbon Policy: Scientific and technical brief to guide legislative intervention," Center for Sustainable Economy, Dec. 12, 2017, online at https://sustainable-economy.org/wp-content/ uploads/2017/12/Oregon-Forest-Carbon-Policy-Technical-Brief-1.pdf.
6. Personal communication, Dominick DellaSala.
7. Telephone interview with Beverly Law, October 22, 2019.
8. Tara W Hudiburg, Beverly E Law, William R Moomaw, Mark E Harmon and Jeffrey E Stenzel, "Meeting GHG reduction targets requires accounting for all forest sector emissions," 2019 *Environ. Res. Lett.*
9. The Oregon Forest and Industries Council, "Forest Products: Part of the Solution to Climate Change," online at https://ofic.com/forestproducts-part-of-a-solution-to-climate-change/.
10. Nate Stevenson, Western Ecological Research Center, USGS, "Rate of tree carbon accumulation increases continuously with tree size," *Nature*, January 15, 2014, online at https://www.nature.com/articles/ nature12914.
11. Simon L. Lewis, Charlotte E. Wheeler, Edward T. A. Mitchard and Alexander Koch, "Restoring natural forests is the best way to remove atmospheric carbon," *Nature*, April 2, 2019, online at https://www. nature.com/articles/d41586-019-01026-8.
12. Mark E. Harmon, William K. Ferrell, Jerry F. Franklin, "Effects on Carbon Storage of Conversion of Old-Growth Forests to Young Forests," *Science*, February 9, 1990, online at https://www.science. org/ doi/10.1126/science.247.4943.699.

13. Oregon Forest and Industries Council, "Forest Products: Part of the Solution to Climate Change," online at https://ofic.com/forestproducts-part-of-a-solution-to-climate-change/.

14. William R. Moomaw, Susan A. Masino, Edward K. Faison, "Intact Forests in the United States: Proforestation Mitigates Climate Change and Serves the Greatest Good," Frontiers in Forests and Global Change, 2019, online at https://www.frontiersin.org/articles/10.3389/ffgc.2019.00027/full.

15. Oregon Global Warming Commission, "Forest Carbon Accounting Project Report," 2018, online at https://www.keeporegoncool.org/forest-carbon.

16. Atkins, David, "In zeal to restrict logging, advocacy groups exploit dubious research," Treesource, June 13, 2018.

17. Nabuurs, Gert-January, "By 2050 the Mitigation Effects of EU Forests Could Nearly Double through Climate Smart Forestry," Forests, December 5, 2017.

18. Telephone interview with Beverly Law, October 22, 2019.

19. Donato, D.C., et. al., "Post-wildfire logging hinders regeneration and increases fire risk," Science, January. 20, 2006.

20. M. Newton, S. Fitzgerald, R. Rose, P. W. Adams, S. D. Tesch, J Sessions, T. Atzet, R. F. Powers, C. Skinner, "Comment on 'Post-Wildfire Logging Hinders Regeneration and Increases Fire Risk,'" Science, August 4, 2006, online at https://pubmed.ncbi.nlm.nih.gov/16888122/.

21. Blaine Harden, "In Fire's Wake, Logging Study Inflames Debate University Study Challenges Cutting Of Burnt Timber," Washington Post, February 27, 2006, online at https:// www.washingtonpost.com/archive/politics/2006/02/27/ in-fires-wake-logging-study-inflames-debate-span-classbankheaduniversity-study-challenges-cutting-of-burnt-timberspan/937f23c9-8047-4ff2-a7de-628a16ef98d8/.

22. Telephone interview with Beverly Law, October 22, 2019.

23. Peterson, Jim, "The Donato-Law Fiasco Mixing Politics and Science: Alchemy at OSU," Evergreen Magazine, Winter 2006.

24. Chuck Willer, "Challenging Wall Street Forestry," Coast Range Association, 2020, online at https://coastrange.org/challenging-wall-street-forestry/ownership/.

25. Tony Schick, Rob Davis, Lylla Younes, "Big money bought the forests. Small timber communities are paying the price," The Oregonian and ProPublica, June 11, 2020, online at https://projects.oregonlive.com/timber.

26. Oreskes, Naomi and Conway, Erik, Merchants of Doubt (New York: Bloomsbury Publishing, 2010), 236.

27. Heartland Institute online at https://www.heartland.org/publications-resources/publications/the-global-warming-crisis-is-over.
28. oregonforests.org.

## Chapter 5

1. Mark E. Harmon, William K. Ferrell, Jerry F. Franklin, "Effects on Carbon Storage of Conversion of Old-Growth Forests to Young Forests," *Science*, February 9, 1990, online at https://www.science. org/doi/10.1126/science.247.4943.699.
2. Oregon Biodiversity Information Center, Institute for Natural Resources, Oregon State University, "Rare, Threatened and Endangered Species of Oregon," 2019, online at https://inr.oregonstate. edu/orbic.
3. Native Fish Society, Center for Biological Diversity, Umpqua Watersheds, "Petition to List the Oregon Coast ESU of Spring-Run Chinook Salmon (Oncorhynchus tshawytscha) under the Endangered Species Act," 2019, online at www.biologicaldiversity.org.
4. Elliott Norse, *Ancient Forests of the Pacific Northwest* (Washington, D.C.: Island Press, 1990), 6.
5. Strittholt JR, DellaSala DA, Jiang H. "Status of mature and old-growth forests in the Pacific Northwest." Conserv Biol. 2006 Apr;20(2):363-74. doi: 10.1111/j.1523-1739.2006.00384.x. PMID: 16903097.
6. Chris Maser, "Remembering the moral and spiritual dimensions of forests," in *clear-cut*, Bill Devall, ed. (San Francisco: Sierra Club Books and Earth Island Press), 1993, 17.
7. Telephone interview with Jim Furnish, February 19, 2020.
8. Jim Furnish, *Toward a Natural Forest* (Corvallis: OSU Press, 2015), 103.
9. Finn J.D. John, "Childhood tree-planting memories for thousands," *Offbeat Oregon History*, Aug. 10, 2014, online at http://offbeatoregon. com/1408b.schoolkids-replant-tillamook.html
10. Furnish, p 105.
11. United States Forest Service, "Forest Products Cut and Sold from the National Forests and Grasslands," online at https://www.fs.fed.us/forest-management/products/cut-sold/index.shtml.
12. Telephone interview with Paul Engelmayer, May 14, 2020.
13. Telephone interview with Martha Ketelle, March 13, 2020.
14. Telephone interview with Mike Roselle, June 3, 2020.
15. Kathie Durbin, *Tree Huggers: Victory, Defeat and Renewal in the Northwest Ancient Forest Campaign* (Seattle: The Mountaineers, 1996), 58.

16. Andy Stahl, executive director at Forest Service Employees for Environmental Ethics, told this to Paul Koberstein about ten years ago during a public meeting in Portland.

17. Seattle Audubon Soc. v. Evans, 771 F. Supp. 1081 (W.D. Wash. 1991).

18. Freudenburg WR, Wilson LJ, O'Leary DJ. Forty Years of Spotted Owls? A Longitudinal Analysis of Logging Industry Job Losses. *Sociological Perspectives*. 1998;41(1):1-26. doi:10.2307/1389351.

19. DellaSala, D.A., et al. 2015. "Building on two decades of ecosystem management and biodiversity conservation under the Northwest Forest Plan," *Forests*, September 2015, online at https://www.researchgate.net.

20. Dominick A. DellaSala, Robert G. Anthony, Monica L. Bond, Erik S. Fernandez, Chris A. Frissell, Chad T. Hanson, Randi Spivak, "Alternative Views of a Restoration Framework for Federal Forests in the Pacific Northwest," *Journal of Forestry*, Volume 111, Issue 6, November 2013, 420–429, https://doi.org/10.5849/jof.13-040.

21. Lisa Friedman and Catrin Einhorn, "Trump Opens Habitat of a Threatened Owl to Timber Harvesting," New York *Times*, January. 13, 2021, online at https://www.nytimes.com/2021/01/13/climate/ trump-spotted-owl.html.

22. Nate Mackay, "White House reverses Trump-era gut of spotted owl habitat," Missoula *Current*, November 11, 2021, online at https://missoulacurrent.com/outdoors/2021/11/spotted-owl-habitat.

## Chapter 6

1. Associated Press, "Remote, Ore.: Name of Town Says it All," *New York Times*, October 7, 1982, online at https://www.nytimes.com/1982/10/07/garden/remote-ore-name-of-town-says-it-all.html.

2. "Graft is Charged Against Governor: Chamberlain to be Defendant in Action to Secure Return of $10,000," The *Morning Oregonian*, June 27, 1908.

3. Michael C. Blumm and Tim Wigington, The Oregon & California Railroad Grant Lands' Sordid Past, Contentious Present, and Uncertain Future: A Century of Conflict, *Boston College Environmental Affairs Law Review* (2013), http://lawdigitalcommons.bc.edu/ealr/vol40/iss1/2.

4. Ibid.

5. S.A.D. Puter, *Looters of the Public Domain: Embracing a Complete Exposure of the Fraudulent System of Acquiring Titles to the Public Lands of the United States* (Portland: Portland Printing House, 1908.)

6. Thomas Tuchmann and Chad Davis, "O&C Lands Report," Prepared for Gov. John Kitzhaber, February 6, 2013, online at http://media.oregon-live.com/environment_impact/other/ OCLandsReport.pdf.

7. American Forest Resource Council v. Hammond, 422 F.Supp.3d 184 (2019).

8. Tim Freeman, Bob Main and Craig Pope. "Ruling ensures a sustained harvest on Oregon counties' timber land," *Portland Tribune*, December 17, 2019, online at https://pamplinmedia.com/ wbi/153-opinion/446088-361822-ruling-ensures-a-sustainedharvest-on-oregon-counties-timber-land.

## Chapter 7

1. VanStrum, Carol, *A Bitter Fog: Herbicides and Human Rights* (San Francisco: Sierra Club Books), 1983.

2. Carson, Rachel, *Silent Spring* (New York: Houghton Mifflin), 1962.

3. VanStrum, Carol, *A Bitter Fog: Herbicides and Human Rights* (San Francisco: Sierra Club Books), 2014.

4. Online at https://www.poisonpapers.org/the-poison-papers.

5. Kruger, Greg R.; Klein, Robert N.; Ogg, Clyde L. Ogg; Viera, Bruno C., "Spray Drift in Pesticides," University of Nebraska Extension, September 2019.

6. Lacoste, M., Ruiz, S. and Or, D. "Listening to earthworms burrowing and roots growing – acoustic signatures of soil biological activity," *Scientific Reports* July 6, 2018, online at https://doi. org/10.1038/s41598-018-28582-9.

7. K.E. Ukhurebor, U.O. Aigbe, A.S. Olayinka, W. Nwankwo. And J.O. Emegha, "Climatic Change and Pesticides Usage: A Brief Review of Their Implicative Relationship," *Assumption University-eJournal of Interdisciplinary Research*, 2020, online at http://www.assumptionjour-nal.au.edu/index.php/eJIR/article/view/4398/2619.

8. Laurie A. Clark, Gary J. Roloff, Vickie L. Tatum, Larry L. Irwin, "Forest Herbicide Effects on Pacific Northwest Ecosystems: A Literature Review," National Council for Air and Stream Improvement (NCASI), 2009, online at https://www.ncasi.org/wp-content/ uploads/2019/02/tb970.pdf.

9. Gratkowski, H., "Silvicultural Use of Herbicides in Pacific Northwest Forests," U.S. Department of Agriculture, 1975, online at https://www.fs.usda.gov/treesearch/pubs/25326.

10. Robert G. Wagner, Michael Newton, Elizabeth C. Cole, James H. Miller, Barry D. Shiver, "The role of herbicides for enhancing forest productivity and conserving land for biodiversity in North America," *Wildlife Society Bulletin*, December 2004, online at https://www.fs.usda.gov/treesearch/pubs/8975.

11. Environmental Protection Agency, "Prioritized Chronic Dose-Response Values for Screening Risk Assessments," September 21, online at https://www.epa.gov/system/files/documents/2021-09/chronicfinaloutput_9_29_2021-12-46-18-pm_0.pdf.

12. Gough, Michael, Doxin, *Agent Orange: The Facts*, Plenum Press, 1986.

13. Norris, L.A. "Chemical Brush Control and Herbicide Residues in the Forest Environment," in *Symposium proceedings: Herbicides and vegetation management in forests, ranges, and noncrop lands*," (Corvallis: Oregon State University, 1967), 104, online at https:// ir.library.oregonstate.edu/concern/technical_reports/kk91fr378?locale=en.

14. Whiteside, Thomas, "Defoliant," *The New Yorker*, February 6, 1970.

15. Martin, Douglas, "Thomas Whiteside, 79, Dies; Writer Exposed Agent Orange," *New York Times*, October 12, 1997.

16. Uhrhammer, Jerry, "Outlawed Chemical Used on Oregon Lands," Eugene *Register-Guard*, June 7, 1973.

17. Norris, L.A. *Symposium proceedings: Herbicides and vegetation management in forests, ranges, and noncrop lands* (Corvallis: Oregon State University, 1967), 111, online at https://ir.library.oregonstate.edu/concern/technical_reports/kk91fr378?locale=en.

18. Institute of Medicine (US) Committee to Review the Health Effects in Vietnam Veterans of Exposure to Herbicides, *Veterans and Agent Orange: Health Effects of Herbicides Used in Vietnam* (Washington, D.C.: National Academies Press (US); 1994, online at https://www.ncbi.nlm.nih.gov/books/NBK236351/.

19. Mike Newton, "Vegetation Management: One of the Most Important tools in Forestry," Western Forester, September/October 1999, online at https://vmrc.forestry.oregonstate.edu/system/files/publicfiles/27_Ketchum-etal_1999_Veg-Management_Tools.pdf.

20. Mike Newton, "Agent Orange Research Update," Oregon State University video, May 18, 2011, online at https://media.oregonstate.edu/media/agent_orange_research_update/0_ug5joe07.

21. Mike Newton, "I've Had More Exposure To Agent Orange Than Anyone: Here's What I Know," American Council on Science and Health blog, August 25, 2016, online at https://www.acsh.org/news/2016/08/25/ive-had-more-exposure-to-agent-orange-thananyone-heres-what-i-know.

22. August 31, 1983. memorandum by John L. Griffith, EPA senior researcher, online at https://www.documentcloud.org/documents/3440461-Poison-Papers-B-3121-Griffith-Letter.htm.

23. Griffith, Jack, Heath, Robert and Frankenberry, Mary, "Preliminary Assessment of a Field Investigation of Six-Year Spontaneous Abortion Rates in Three Oregon Areas in Relation to Forest 2,4,5-T Spray Practices," (the Alsea II Study), U.S. Environmental Protection Agency, February 27, 1979, online at https://nepis. epa.gov.

24. EPA, "Decision and Emergency Order Suspending Registrations for Certain Uses of 2-(2, 4, 5-trichlorophenxy) Propionic Acid (silvex)," February 28, 1979 online at https://nepis.epa.gov.

25. Griffith memorandum.

26. Sheldon Wagner, James Witt, Logan Norris, James Higgins, Alan Agresti, Melchoir Ortiz, "A Scientific Critique of the EPA Alsea II Study and Report," Environmental Health Center, Oregon State University, October 25, 1979, online at https://ir.library.oregonstate.edu/concern/technical_reports/tt44pn52k.

27. Dow Chemical Co. v. Blum, No. 79-10064 (469 F. Supp. 892, 13 ERC 1129) (E.D. Mich. April 12, 1979), online at https://www.elr.info/sites/default/files/litigation/9.20583.htm.

28. Norris, L.A. *Symposium proceedings: Herbicides and vegetation management in forests, ranges, and noncrop lands* (Corvallis: Oregon State University, 1967), 111, online at https://ir.library.oregonstate. edu/concern/technical_reports/kk91fr378?locale=en.

29. Anne B. Hairston-Strang, Paul W. Adams, and George G. Ice, "The Oregon Forest Practices Act and Forest Research," in *Hydrological and Biological Responses to Forest Practices: The Alsea Watershed Study* (ebook, Springer 2008), 97, online at https://link.springer. com/book/10.1007/978-0-387-69036-0.

30. National Academies of Sciences, Engineering, and Medicine, Veterans and Agent Orange: Update 11 (Washington, D.C.: The National Academies Press, 2018), 7-119, doi: https://doi. org/10.17226/25137.

31. Committee to Review the Health Effects in Vietnam Veterans of Exposure to Herbicides, *Veterans and Agent Orange: Health Effects of Herbicides Used in Vietnam.* (Washington, D.C.: The National Academies Press, 1994), 24, online at https://www.publichealth. va.gov/exposures/agentorange/publications/health-and-medicine-division.asp.

32. Hayes TB, et. al., "Demasculinization and feminization of male gonads by atrazine: consistent effects across vertebrate classes," *Journal of Steroid Biochemistry and Molecular Biology.* 2011 Oct;127(1-2):64-73.

33. USGS pesticide usage database online at https://water.usgs.gov/nawqa/pnsp/usage/maps/county-level/.
34. Newton, Michael, "Letter: Story on concern about forestry weed killers displays bias [letter to the editor]," *Corvallis Gazette-Times*, December 24, 2013.
35. Oregon Department of Forestry, "Forest Activity Electronic Reporting and Notification System," online at https://ferns.odf. oregon.gov/e-notification.
36. Campbell Global, Greenwood Resources, Hampton Lumber, Hancock NR Group, Lone Rock Resources, Oregon Small Woodlands Association, Pope Resources, Port Blakely, Roseburg Forest Products, Seneca Sawmill Co, Starker Forests, Stimson Lumber and Weyerhaeuser.
37. Audubon Society, Beyond Toxics, Cascadia Wildlands, Klamath Siskiyou Wildlands Center, Northwest Guides and Anglers, Oregon League of Conservation Voters, Oregon Stream Protection Coalition, Oregon Wild, Pacific Coast Federation of Fishermen's Association, Rogue Riverkeeper, Trout Unlimited (Oregon Council), Umpqua Watersheds, and Wild Salmon Center.

## Chapter 8

1. This chapter is based in part on a lengthy interview with Alexandra Morton, several of her research papers and three of her books: *Not on My Watch* (2021, Toronto: Penguin Random House Canada), *Beyond the Whales* (Victoria: Touchwood 2004), and *Listening to Whales* (New York: Ballantine Books, 2002).
2. *Not on My Watch*, 31.
3. *Listening to Whales*, 267, 268.
4. *Not on My Watch*, 46 6. *Not on My Watch*, xvii.
5. Morton, A. B., and Symonds, H. K., "Displacement of Orcinus orca (L.) by high amplitude sound in British Columbia, Canada," *ICES Journal of Marine Science*, January. 2002, online at https://academic.
6. oup.com/icesjms/article/59/1/71/650034.
7. Alexandra Morton and Richard Routledge, "Risk and precaution: Salmon farming," *Marine Policy*, December 2016, online at https://dx.doi.org/10.1016/j.marpol.2016.09.022.
8. Martin Krkošek, Jennifer S. Ford, Alexandra Morton, Subhash Lele, Ransom A. Myers, and Mark A. Lewis, "Declining Wild Salmon Populations in Relation to Parasites from Farm Salmon," *Science*, December 14, 2007, online at https://science.sciencemag.org/content/318/5857/1772.

# ENDNOTES

9.  Stephen Hume, Alexandra Morton, Betty Keller, Rosella M. Leslie, Otto Langer, Don Staniford, *A Stain on the Sea: West Coast Salmon Farming* (Madeira Park, B.C.: Harbour Publishing, 2004), 22.
10. Vancouver Island *Free Daily*, "Emaciated grizzlies photographed off north end of Vancouver Island," October 25, 2019, online at https://www.vancouverislandfreedaily.com/news/emaciated-grizzlies-photographed-off-north-end-of-vancouver-island.
11. Alexandra Morton and Richard Routledge, "Risk and precaution: Salmon farming," *Marine Policy* 74 (2016) 205–212, online at https://dx.doi.org/10.1016/j.marpol.2016.09.022.
12. Ted Gresh, Jim Lichatowich, and Peter Schoonmaker, "An estimation of historic and current levels of salmon production in the northeast Pacific ecosystem: evidence of a nutrient deficit in the freshwater systems of the Pacific Northwest," *Fisheries* 25:15–21, January 2000, online at https://www.tandfonline.com/doi/abs/ 10.1577/1548-8446%282000%29025%3C0015%3AAEOHAC%3E2.0.CO%3B2.
13. ibid.
14. Fisheries and Oceans Canada, "Minister Jordan announces longterm commercial closures and Licence Retirement Program in effort to save Pacific Salmon," News Release, June 29, 2021, online at https://www.canada.ca/en/fisheries-oceans/news/2021/06/minister-jordan-announces-long-term-commercial-closures-and-licencetetirement-program-in-effort-to-save-pacific-salmon.html.
15. Cohen Commission of Inquiry, "The Uncertain Future of Fraser River Sockeye," October 2012, online at https://sportfishing.bc.ca/ wp-content/uploads/2017/12/CohenCommissionFinalReport_ Vol01_Full.pdf.
16. Alexandra Morton, Richard D. Routledge, Rob Williams, "Temporal patterns of sea louse infestation on wild pacific salmon in relation to the fallowing of Atlantic salmon farms," *North American Journal of Fisheries Management*, 2005, online at https://www.tandfonline. com/doi/abs/10.1577/M04-149.1.
17. Eva B. Thorstad et. al., "Incidence and impacts of escaped farmed Atlantic salmon Salmo salar in nature," *World Wildlife Fund*, 2008.
18. Kent, M. 2011. Infectious diseases and potential impacts on survival of Fraser River sockeye salmon. Cohen Commission Tech. Rept. 1: 58p. Vancouver, B.C.
19. Margaret Munro, "Feds Silence Nanaimo Scientist Over Salmon Study," *Vancouver Sun*, July 17, 2011.
20. Ibid.
21. "Fabian Dawson, "Wild rhetoric about aquaculture does nothing to save wild salmon," *SeaWestNews*, Oct. 17, 2020.
22. Ibid.

23. Marie Fazio, "Northwest's Salmon Population May Be Running Out of Time," *New York Times*, Jan. 20, 2021.
24. James Helfield and Robert Naiman, "Effects of Salmon-Derived Nitrogen on Riparian Forest Growth and Implications for Stream Productivity," *Ecology*, Sept 21, 2001.

**Chapter 9**

1. Oregon Public Service Commission, Transcript of Testimony, June 24, 1924.
2. Jessica D. Phelps, "The Geomorphic Legacy of Splash Dams in the Southern Oregon Coast Range," master's thesis, University of Oregon, 2010. https://scholarsbank.uoregon.edu/xmlui/bitstream/ handle/1794/11292/Phelps_Jessica_D_ms2011wi.pdf.
3. James R. Sedell and Wayne S. Duval, "Water Transportation and Storage of Logs," in *Influences of Forest and Rangeland Management on Salmonid Fishes and Their Habitats*, American Fisheries Society Special Publication, 1991, 325.
4. Chris Lupoli and Tamara Quandt, "Mill Watershed Assessment," Yamhill Basin Council, December 1999, online at https://nrimp. dfw.state.or.us/nrimp.
5. Meengs, Chad C., and Robert T. Lackey. "Estimating the size of Historic Salmon Runs, Reviews in Fisheries Science," *Reviews in Fisheries Science*, 2005, online at http://osu-wams-blogs-uploads. s3.amazonaws.com/blogs.dir/2961/files/2017/07/9.-Estimating-the-Size-of-Historical-Oregon-Salmon-Runs.pdf.
6. Wendler, H.O., and G. Deschamps, "Logging dams on coastal Washington streams," Washington State Department of Forestry, 1955.
7. December 7, 1956 letter from M. C. Davis to Charles Heltzel
8. Jim Lichatowich, *Salmon Without Rivers: A History of the Pacific Salmon Crisis* (Washington, D.C.: Island Press, 1999), 62-64 9. Cederholm, C. J., D. H. Johnson, R. E. Bilby, L.G. Dominguez, A. M. Garrett, W. H. Graeber, E. L. Greda, M. D. Kunze, B.G. Marcot, J. F. Palmisano, R. W. Plotnikoff, W. G. Pearcy, C. A. Simenstad, and P. C. Trotter. 2000. Pacific Salmon and Wildlife – Ecological Contexts, Relationships, and Implications for Management. Special Edition Technical Report, Washington Department of Fish and Wildlife, Olympia, Washington, 2000.
9. Rebecca R. Miller, "Is the Past Present? Historical Splash-dam Mapping and Stream Disturbance Detection in the Oregon Coastal Province," master's thesis, Oregon State University, 2010.

# ENDNOTES

10. James R. Sedell and Wayne S. Duval, 328.
11. Lionel Youst, *Lost in Coos* (Alleghany, Oregon: Golden Falls Publishing, 2011), 28-29.
12. Dow Beckham, *Swift Flows the River* (Coos Bay, OR.: Arago Books, 1990), 113.
13. ibid., 113.
14. Rob Davis, "Polluted by Money," a four-part series in The *Oregonian/OregonLive*, February 22, 2019.
15. Rob Davis and Tony Schick, "A timber lobbyist called our investigation 'completely bogus.' We have the receipts to show it's not," The *Oregonian/OregonLive* and Oregon Public Broadcasting, March 8, 2021.
16. Ibid.

## Chapter 10

1. Heady, W.N., K. O'Connor, J. Kassakian, K. Doiron, C. Endris, D. Hudgens, R. P. Clark, J. Carter, and M. G. Gleason. An Inventory and Classification of U.S. West Coast Estuaries. The Nature Conservancy, 2014.
2. Brophy, L.S. Comparing historical losses of forested, scrub-shrub, and emergent tidal wetlands on the Oregon coast, USA: A paradigm shift for estuary restoration and conservation. 2019, Prepared for the Pacific States Marine Fisheries Commission and the Pacific Marine and Estuarine Fish Habitat Partnership. Estuary Technical Group, Institute for Applied Ecology.
3. Arni Magnusson and Ray Hilborn, "Estuarine Influence on Survival Rates of Coho (Oncorhynchus kisutch) and Chinook Salmon (Oncorhynchus tshawytscha) Released from Hatcheries on the U.S. Pacific Coast," *Estuaries*, Vol. 26, No. 4B, p. 1094–1103 August 2003.
4. Brophy is the director of the Estuary Technical Group at the Institute of Applied Ecology in Corvallis, Oregon.
5. Dalrymple, R.W. and Choi, K. (2007) Morphologic and facies trends through the fluvial–marine transition in tide-dominated depositional systems: A schematic framework for environmental and sequence-stratigraphic interpretation. *Earth-Science Reviews* 81: 135–174
6. *Picea sitchensis.*
7. Oregon Department of Land Conservation and Development, *The Oregon Estuary Plan Book*, 1987, online at Oregon Estuary Plan Book.
8. Andy Kerr, *Oregon Wild: Endangered Forest Wilderness* (Portland: Oregon Natural Resources Council, 2004.

9. Jerry F. Franklin and C. T. Dyrness, *Natural Vegetation of Oregon and Washington* (Corvallis: Oregon State University Press, 1988), 296, online at http://www.fsl.orst.edu/rna/Documents/publications/ Natural%20vegetation%20of%20Oregon%20and%20Washington%20 1988.pdf.

10. J. Boone Kauffman, Leila Giovanonni, James Kelly, Nicholas Dunstan, Amy Borde, Heida Diefenderfer, Craig Cornu, Christopher Januaryousek,Jude Apple, Laura Brophy. 2020. Total ecosystem carbon stocks at the marine–terrestrial interface: Blue carbon of the Pacific Northwest Coast, USA. *Global Change Biology* 26:5679–5692. doi:10.1111/gcb.15248.

11. ibid.

12. Hood, W.G. "Beaver in Tidal Marshes: Dam Effects on Low-Tide Channel Pools and Fish Use of Estuarine Habitat," *Wetlands*, online at https://doi.org/10.1007/s13157-012-0294-8.

13. *Oncorhynchus tshawytscha*

14. Thompson, S., Vehkaoja, M., Pellikka, J. and Nummi, P. (2021), Ecosystem services provided by beavers Castor spp. *Mam Rev*, 51: 25-39. https://doi.org/10.1111/mam.12220.

15. NMFS (National Marine Fisheries Service). 2016. Recovery Plan for Oregon Coast Coho Salmon Evolutionarily Significant Unit. National Marine Fisheries Service, West Coast Region, Portland, Oregon, online at https://repository.library.noaa.gov/view/noaa/15986.

16. Ben Goldfarb, *Eager: the Surprising, Secret Life of Beavers and Why They Matter* (White River Junction, Vt: Chelsea Green Publishing, 2018), 187-188.

## Chapter 11

1. "Palmer Treaties," Special Collection, University of Oregon Library.

2. ibid.

3. Fourth National Climate Assessment, U.S. Global Change Research Program, 2018.

4. Oregon Secretary of State, "Black in Oregon, 1840 to 1870," online at https://sos.oregon.gov/archives/exhibits/black-history/Pages/ context/ chronology.aspx.

5. S.A.D. Puter, *Looters of the Public Domain: Embracing a Complete Exposure of the Fraudulent System of Acquiring Titles to the Public Lands of the United States* (Portland: Portland Printing House, 1908), 469.

6. Stephen Dow Beckham, *The Indians of Western Oregon: This Land Was Theirs*, Arago Books, 1977.

# ENDNOTES

7. David G. Lewis and Thomas J. Connolly, "White American Violence on Tribal People on the Oregon Coast," *Oregon Historical Quarterly*, winter 2019.

8. George Bundy Wasson Jr., "Growing Up Indian: An Emic Perspective," doctoral dissertation, University of Oregon, 2001, 137.

9. ibid. 350

10. George Bundy Wasson Jr., "The Coquille Indians and the Cultural 'Black Hole' of The Southwest Oregon Coast," master's thesis, University of Oregon, 1994, 32.

11. Wasson 2001, 98

12. Don Whereat, Patty Whereat Phillips, Melody Caldera, Ron Thomas, Reg Pullan and Stephen Dow Beckham, *Our Culture and History* (self-published, 2010), 1, online at shichils.files.wordpress. com/2017/10/ our_culture_history.pdf.

13. Wayne Suttles, ed., *Handbook of North American Indians* (Washington, D.C.: Smithsonian Institution, 1990), 135.

14. Michael C. Blumm, "Indian Treaty Fishing Rights and the Environment: Affirming the Right to Habitat Protection and Restoration," *Wash. L. Rev.* 1, 2017. Online at https://digitalcommons.law.uw.edu/wlr/vol92/ iss1/2.

15. Wasson, 107.

16. Wasson, 127.

17. Confederated Tribes of Coos, Lower Umpqua, and Siuslaw, "A Brief History of the Coos, Lower Umpqua & Siuslaw Indians," online at https://ctclusi.org/history/.

18. Wasson, 13.

19. Wasson, 187.

20. Wasson, 353.

21. Wasson, 14.

22. ibid.

23. Where, 92.

24. ibid.

25. Coos (or Lowes) Bay, Lower Umpqua (or Kalawatset), and Siuslaw Indian Tribes vs. the United States of America, No. K-345, online at https://public.csusm.edu/nadp/d129.htm.

26. ibid.

27. Wasson, 18.

28. Stephen Dow Beckham, *The Indians of Western Oregon: This Land Was Their Land* (Coos Bay, OR: Arago Books, 1977), 182.

29. Alcea Band of Tillamook's v. United States (1945), 59 F. Supp. 934 (Fed. Cl. 1945).

30. Alysa Landry, "Dwight D. Eisenhower: Tried to Knock Out Jim Thorpe, and Assimilate Indians," Indian Country Today, September 13, 2018, online at https://indiancountrytoday.com/archive/ dwight-d-eisenhower-tried-to-knock-out-jim-thorpe-and-assimilate-indians.
31. Coquille Indian Tribe, "Our Lands Today," online at https://www.coquil-letribe.org/?page_id=37.
32. Telephone interview with Andy Kerr on December 11, 2019
33. The Sawmill Database, online at https://www.sawmilldatabase.com/productiontoplist.php.
34. Arthur V. Smythe, *Millicoma: Biography of a Pacific Northwest Forest* (Durham, North Carolina: Forest History Society, 2000), 7.
35. Email interview with David G. Lewis on February 22, 2021.
36. New York Declaration on Forests refresh launch webinar, October 13, 2021, online at https://www.youtube.com/watch?v=v7_ cW7F-ykE.

## Chapter 12

1. National Wildlife Federation, *Sea-level Rise and Coastal Habitats in the Pacific Northwest*, online at https://www.nwf.org/~/media/ PDFs/Water/200707_PacificNWSeaLevelRise_Report.ashx.
2. https://www.eopugetsound.org/magazine/clam-hunger.
3. https://toolkit.climate.gov/case-studies/quinault-indian-nation-plans-village-relocation.
4. U.S. Global Change Research Program, "Fourth National Climate Assessment," online at https://nca2018.globalchange.gov.
5. Swinomish Indian Tribal Community, "Swinomish Climate Change Initiative," online at https://www.swinomish-climate.com/swinomish-climate-change-initiative.
6. Sonia Waraich, "Yurok vice chairman touts tribal forestry practices at congressional hearing," Eureka *Times-Standard*, October 22, 2019, online at https://www.times-standard.com/2019/10/22/ yurok-vice-chairman-touts-tribal-forestry-practices-at-congressional-hearing.

## Chapter 13

1. The Sawmill Database, online at https://www.sawmilldatabase.com/.
2. Cecil Paul, as told to Brittany Penn, *Stories from the Magic Canoe of Wax Aid* (Calgary: Rocky Mountain Books, 2019), 29.
3. Spencer Beebe, *Cache* (Portland: Ecotrust, 2010), 133.
4. Allison L Bidlack, Sarah M Bisbing, Brian J Buma, Heida L Diefenderfer, Jason B Fellman, William C Floyd, Ian Giesbrecht,

Amritpal Lally, Ken P Lertzman, Steven S Perakis, "Climate-Mediated Changes to Linked Terrestrial and Marine Ecosystems across the Northeast Pacific coastal temperate rainforest Margin," *BioScience*, Volume 71, Issue 6, June 2021, Pages 581–595, online at https:// doi.org/10.1093/biosci/biaa171.

5.   Paul Alaback, "Comparative ecology of temperate rainforests of the Americas along analogous climatic gradients," *Revista Chilena de Historia Natural* 64: 399-412, 1991, online at https://link.springer.com/chapter/10.1007/978-1-4612-3970-3_7.

6.   *Cache*, 122.

7.   Ken Margolis, "Drawing the Line: How the Haisla Nation is Saving British Columbia's Largest Intact Coastal Rainforest," *Cascadia Times*, January 1997, online at https://www.times.org/archives-2back/2018/3/6/January-1997.

8.   Mike Gaworecki, "The inside story of how Great Bear Rainforest went from a 'War In The Woods' to an unprecedented environmental and human rights agreement," *Mongabay*, February 22, 2016, online at https://canopyplanet.org/the-inside-story-of-thegreat-bear-rainforest.

## Chapter 14

1.   James E. M. Watson, Tom Evans, et. al, "The Exceptional Value of Intact Ecosystems," *Nature*, April 2018, online at https://www. nature.com/articles/s41559-018-0490-x.

2.   Change.org, "End the logging of British Columbia's old-growth forests," online at https://www.change.org/p/john-horgan-end-thelogging-of-british-columbia-s-old-growth-forests.

3.   Sierra Club BC, "Poll Shows Nine in Ten British Columbians Support Action to Protect Endangered Old-Growth Forest," November 4, 2019, online at https://sierraclub.bc.ca/forestpoll/.

4.   Sierra Club BC, "Vancouver Island Old-Growth Logging Speeding Up," online at https://sierraclub.bc.ca/vancouver-island-old-growthlogging-speeding-up/.

5.   Harley Rustad, *Big Lonely Doug: The Story of One of Canada's Last Great Trees* (Toronto: House of Anansi Press, 2018), 17-18.

6.   Ancient Forest Alliance, "Before & After Logging – Caycuse Watershed," online at https://www.ancientforestalliance.org/photos/ before-after-logging-photos-caycuse.

7.   Ancient Forest Alliance, "Caycuse Logging From Above," online at https://www.ancientforestalliance.org/photos/caycuse-loggingfrom-above.

8.  Gorley, A., and Merkel, G. 2020. "A new future for old forests:
    A Strategic Review of How British Columbia Manages for Old Forests
    Within its Ancient Ecosystems," Prepared for the Minister, BC Ministry
    of Forests Lands Natural Resource Operations and Rural Development,
    online at https://engage.gov.bc.ca/app/ uploads/sites/563/2020/09/
    STRATEGIC-REVIEW-20200430.pdf.
9.  Karen Price, Rachel F. Holt, and Dave Daust, "Conflicting portrayals of
    remaining old growth: the British Columbia case," *Canadian Journal of
    Forest Research*, April 5, 2021, online at https://doi.org/10.1139/cjfr-
    2020-0453
10. Karen Price, Rachel F. Holt, and Dave Daust, "BC's old-growth Forest:
    A Last Stand for Biodiversity," April 2020, Sierra Club BC, online at
    https://sierraclub.bc.ca/laststand.
11. Justin Catanoso, "With British Columbia's last old-growth at risk,
    government falters: Critics," April 20, 2021, online at https://news.
    mongabay.com/2021/04/with-british-columbias-last-old-growthat-risk-
    government-falters-critics/ and https://vancouversun.com/ news/local-
    news/report-on-b-c-s-old-growth-forest.

## Chapter 15

1.  A version of this chapter was first published December 19, 2018, in
    *Sierra Magazine*, online at https://www.sierraclub.org/sierra/ forest-
    liquidators.
2.  Bill McKibben, "The Trump administration Knows the Planet is Going
    to Boil. It Doesn't Care," *The Guardian*, October 2, 2018, online at
    https://www.theguardian.com/commentisfree/2018/ oct/02/trump-
    administration-planet-boil-refugee-camps.
3.  John Kirkland and Tara Barrett, "Colossal carbon! Disturbance and
    biomass dynamics in Alaska's national forests," U.S. Forest Service, 2016,
    online at https://www.fs.usda.gov/treesearch/pubs/50263.
4.  Allison L. Bidlack, Sarah M Bisbing, Brian J. Buma, Heida L.
    Diefenderfer, Jason B. Fellman, William C. Floyd, Ian Giesbrecht,
    Amritpal Lally, Ken P. Lertzman, Steven S. Perakis, David E. Butman,
    David V. D'Amore, Sean W. Fleming, Eran W. Hood, Brian P. V.
    Hunt, Peter M. Kiffney, Gavin McNicol, Brian Menounos, Suzanne E.
    Tank, "Climate-Mediated Changes to Linked Terrestrial and Marine
    Ecosystems across the Northeast Pacific coastal temperate rainforest
    Margin," *BioScience*, 2021, online at https:// academic.oup.com/biosci-
    ence/article/71/6/581/6128397.

5. Albert, D., and J. Schoen, *A conservation assessment and resource synthesis for the coastal forests and mountains ecoregion in southeastern Alaska and the Tongass National Forest*. The Nature Conservancy and Audubon Alaska, 2007, online at http://www. conserveonline.org/workspaces/akcfm.

6. Southeast Conference, "Southeast Alaska by the Numbers 2021," September 2021, online at https://www.seconference.org/wp-content/uploads/2021/09/SE-by-the-numbers-2021-final.pdf?2070f3&2070f3.

## Chapter 16

1. A version of Chapter 15, "Trump Doubles Down on His Assault on Alaska's Old-Growth Forests, was first published in *Earth Island Journal* on October 7, 2019, online at https://www.earthisland.org/ journal/index.php/articles/entry/trump-doubles-down-on-his-assault-on-alaska's-old-growth-forests.

2. US Geological Survey, Earth Resources Observation and Science Center, "clear-cutting A Logging in Oregon, USA story," online at https://eros.usgs.gov/image-gallery/earthshot/clear-cutting.

3. Holly Harris, interview in her Juneau office in October 2018.

4. Cole's op-ed is cited in Catherine Mater, "Tongass Second-Growth Transition Project," National Resource Defense Council and GEOS Institute, November 2016.

5. Mater, ibid.

6. *Federal Register*, "Craig and Thorne Bay Ranger Districts, Tongass National Forest; Alaska; Prince of Wales Landscape Level Analysis Project Environmental Impact Statement, November 30, 2016, online at https://www.federalregister.gov/documents/2016/11/30/2016-28760/craig-and-thorne-bay-ranger-districts-tongass-national-forest-alaska-prince-of-wales-landscape-level. 7. U.S. Department of Agriculture, "Tongass Land and Resource Management Plan Record of Decision," December 2016, online at https://www.fs.usda.gov/Internet/FSE_DOCUMENTS/fseprd527420.pdf.

7. Telephone interview with Catherine Mater on July 21, 2021.

8. Bryce Dahlstrom, testimony before the Alaska House of Representatives, February 25, 2016.

9. Tom Waldo, telephone interview, August 29, 2019.

10. Southeast Conference, "Southeast Alaska by the Numbers," September 2020, online at www.seconference.org.

11. *Alaska Business*, "A Portrait of Southeast Alaska's Sawmills," November 30, 2017, online at https://www.akbizmag.com/ industry/ manufacturing/a-portrait-of-southeast-alaskan-sawmills/.

12. Taxpayers for Common Sense, "Cutting Our Losses: 20 Years of Money-Losing Timber Sales in the Tongass," October 2019, online at https:// www.taxpayer.net/wp-content/uploads/2019/09/ TCS-Cutting-Our-Losses-2019-.pdf.

13. Jean M. Daniels, "Timber harvest vs. log exports in Alaska: resolving the discrepancies," U.S. Forest Service Pacific Northwest Research Station, April 2016, online at http://www.timbermeasure.com/ CDA_2016/08-Daniels.pdf.

14. Quoted in SitNews, "Forest Service Loses On Tongass Timber Sales Costing Taxpayers & Alaska Schools Big Money," April 19, 2017, online at http://www.sitnews.us/0417News/041917/041917_ tongass.html.

15. In-person interview with Mike Douville and Cinton Cook on August 24, 2019, Craig Tribal Headquarters, Craig, Alaska.

16. In-person interview with Mike Douville and Cinton Cook on August 24, 2019, Craig Tribal Headquarters, Craig, Alaska.

17. Southeast Alaska Conservation Council et al.v. United States Forest Service et al. No. 1:2019 cv 00006 - Document 40 (D. Alaska 2020).

## Chapter 17

1. The eight plaintiffs were Southeast Alaska Conservation Council, Alaska Rainforest Defenders, Center for Biological Diversity, Sierra Club, Defenders of Wildlife, Alaska Wilderness League, National Audubon Society, and the Natural Resources Defense Council.

2. Barbara Haya, "The California Air Resources Board's U.S. Forest offset protocol underestimates-leaka.," Center for Environmental Public Policy, University of California, Berkeley, May 7, 2019, online at https:// gspp.berkeley.edu/faculty-and-impact/working-papers/policy-brief-arbas-us-forest-projects-offset-protocol-underestimates-leaka

3. Grayson Badgley, Jeremy Freeman, Joseph Hamman, Barbara Haya, Anna Trugman, William R L Anderegg, Danny Cullenward, "Systematic over-crediting of forest offsets," *CarbonPlan*, April 21, 2021, online at https://doi.org/10.1101/2021.04.28.441870.

4. Elizabeth Harball, "Native corporations maintaining Alaska forests find a carbon credit buyer: oil company BP," KTOO Public Radio, Juneau, January. 18, 2019, online at https://www.ktoo. org/2019/01/18/native-corporations-maintaining-alaska-forests-find-a-carbon-credit-buyer-oil-company-bp/.

5. Oceana, "Hindsight 2020: Lessons We Cannot Ignore from the BP Disaster," April 2020, online at https://usa.oceana.org/publications/reports/hindsight-2020-lessons-we-cannot-ignore-bp-disaster.

6. Felicity Barringer, "Large Oil Spill in Alaska Went Undetected for Days," New York *Times*, March 15, 2006, online at https://www. nytimes. com/2006/03/15/us/large-oil-spill-in-alaska-went-undetected-for-days. html.

7. Scott Carpenter, "After Abandoned 'Beyond Petroleum' Re-brand, BP's New Renewables Push Has Teeth," *Forbes*, August 4, 2020, online at https://www.forbes.com/sites/scottcarpenter/2020/08/04/ bps-new-renewables-push-redolent-of-abandoned-beyond-petroleum-rebrand/?sh=27b56d451ceb.

8. Global Forest Coalition, "The Big Con: How Big Polluters are advancing a 'net zero' climate agenda to delay, deceive, and deny," June 2021, online at https://www.corporateaccountability.org/ wp-content/uploads/2021/06/The-Big-Con_EN.pdf.

9. Camilla Hodgson, "US forest fires threaten carbon offsets as company-linked trees burn," *InsideClimate News*, August 2, 2021, online at https://www.ft.com/content/3f89c759-eb9a-4dfb-b768-d4af1ec5aa23.

10. Melanie Smith, "Tongass 77 Watersheds," *Ecological Atlas of Alaska*, April 2017, online at https://ak.audubon.org/conservation/ecological-atlas-southeast-alaska.

11. Joint meeting, Alaska House and Senate Resources Standing Committees, February 20, 2020, online http://www.akleg.gov/ basis/Meeting/Detail?Meeting=HRES%202020-02-26%20 17:00:00.

12. Becky Oskin, "Fracking Led to Ohio Earthquakes," *LiveScience*, January. 5, 2015, online at https://www.livescience.com/49326fracking-caused-ohio-earthquakes.html.

13. Alan Septoff, "New Mexico issues violations to Texas-based Hilcorp for operations in San Juan Basin," Earthworks, Math 19, 2019, online at https://earthworks.org/media-releases/new-mexico-issues-violations-to-texas-based-hilcorp-for-operations-in-san-juan-basin.

14. Sabine Poux, "Hilcorp fined for its response to Cook Inlet and North Slope leaks," Alaska Public Radio, March 9, 2022, online at https://www.alaskapublic.org/2022/03/09/hilcorp-fined-for-its-response-to-cook-inlet-and-north-slope-leaks.

15. Sabrina Shankman, "As Hilcorp Plans to Drill in Arctic Waters, a Troubling Trail of Violations Surfaces," *InsideClimate News*, August 10, 2017, online at https://insideclimatenews.org/news/10082017/ hilcorp-alaska-oil-gas-offshore-drilling-arctic-expansion-environment-violations.

16. Cathy Foester, letter to David Wilkins, senior vice president, Hilcorp, November 12, 2015, online at https://s3.documentcloud. org/documents/3921678/2015-11-12-AOGCC-Notice-of-Proposed-Enforcement.pdf.

17. Margi Dashevsky, "Commentary: Why has Hilcorp developed the nickname 'Spillcorp'?" *Cordova Times*, March 10, 2020, online at https://www.thecordovatimes.com/2020/03/10/commentary-whyhas-hilcorp-developed-the-nickname-spillcorp.

## Chapter 18

1. The official high temperature in Portland on June 28, 2021 was 115° F, but a survey by Vivek Shandas of Portland State University detected far higher temperatures in certain parts of the city, according to an article in *Willamette Week*. Online at https://www. wweek.com/news/city/2021/07/14/this-is-the-hottest-place-inportland/.

2. Sjoukje Y. Philip, Sarah F. Kew, Geert January van Oldenborgh, Faron S. Anslow, Sonia I. Seneviratne, Robert Vautard, Dim Coumou, Kristie L. Ebi, Julie Arrighi, Roop Singh, Maarten van Aalst, Carolina Pereira Marghidan, Michael Wehner, Wenchang Yang, Sihan Li, Dominik L. Schumacher, Mathias Hauser, Rémy Bonnet, Linh N. Luu, Flavio Lehner, Nathan Gillett, Jordis Tradowsky, Gabriel A. Vecchi, Chris Rodell, Roland B. Stull, Rosie Howard, and Friedere E. L. Otto, "Rapid attribution analysis of the extraordinary heatwave on the Pacific Coast of the US and Canada June 2021," European Geosciences Union, November 21, 2021, online at https://esd.copernicus.org/preprints/esd-202190/.

3. The Daily Podcast hosted by Astead W. Herndon, "The Heat Wave That Hit the Pacific Northwest," New York *Times*, July 14, 2021, online at https://www.nytimes.com/2021/07/14/podcasts/ the-daily/heat-wave-climate-change-pacific-northwest.html.

4. Andrew Roth, "Russia forest fire damage worst since records began, says Greenpeace," *The Guardian*, September 21, 2021, online at https://www.theguardian.com/world/2021/sep/22/russia-forestfire-damage-worst-since-records-began-says-greenpeace.

5. *Deutsche Welle*, "Europe is burning: Four explanations," June 8, 2021, online at https://www.dw.com/en/europe-is-burning-four-explanations/a-58771341.

6. *Topos Magazine*, "European Floods 2021 – An Overview," September 29, 2021, online at https://www.toposmagazine.com/ european-floods-2021/.

7.   Keith Bradsher and Steven Lee Myers, "How Record Rain and Officials' Mistakes Led to Drownings on a Subway," New York *Times*, October 12, 2021, online at https://www.nytimes.com/2021/09/25/world/asia/china-floods-subway-train.html.

8.   World Health Organization, "Climate change and health," Oct, 30, 2021, online at https://www.who.int/news-room/fact-sheets/detail/climate-change-and-health.

9.   World Meteorological Organization, "The Atlas of Mortality and Economic Losses from Weather, Climate and Water Extremes," 2021, online at https://library.wmo.int/index.php?lvl=notice_ dis-play&id=21930#.YZkh29DMI2y.

10.  IPCC, "Climate Change 2021: The Physical Science Basis. Contribution of Working Group I to the Sixth Assessment Report of the Intergovernmental Panel on Climate Change," Masson-Delmotte, V., P. Zhai, A. Pirani, S.L. Connors, C. Péan, S. Berger, N. Caud, Y. Chen, L. Goldfarb, M.I. Gomis, M. Huang, K. Leitzell, E. Lonnoy, J.B.R. Matthews, T.K. Maycock, T. Waterfield, O. Yelekçi, R. Yu, and B. Zhou (eds.)]. Cambridge University Press. In the press.

11.  Sarah Gibbens, "The U.S. commits to tripling its protected lands. Here's how it could be done," *National Geographic*, January. 27, 2021, online at https://www.nationalgeographic.com.

12.  E. O. Wilson, *Half-Earth: Our Planet's Fight for Life*, W.W. Norton, 2016. The works in the trilogy are *The Social Conquest of Earth* (2012) and *The Meaning of Human Existence* (2014).

13.  Bronson W. Griscom et. al., "Natural Climate Solutions," *Proceedings of the National Academy of Sciences*, October 31, 2017, online at https://www.pnas.org/content/114/44/11645.

14.  Rio Declaration, "Rio declaration on environment and development." Report of the United Nations conference on environment and development, Rio de Janeiro, pp. 3-14. 1992.

15.  Scott Barrett, "Climate treaties and the imperative of enforcement," *Oxford Review of Economic Policy*, 2008, online at https://ycsg.yale. edu/sites/default/files/files/barrett_OxREP.pdf.

16.  Andrew C. Revkin and John M. Broder, "A Grudging Accord in Climate Talks," New York *Times*, December 19, 2009, online at https://www.nytimes.com/2009/12/20/science/earth/20accord. html.

17.  William R. Moomaw, Susan A. Masino, Edward K. Faison, "Intact Forests in the United States: Proforestation Mitigates Climate Change and Serves the Greatest Good," *Frontiers in Forests and Global Change*, 2019, online at https://www.frontiersin.org/articles/10.3389/ffgc.2019.00027/full.

18. William R. Moomaw, Susan A. Masino, Edward K. Faison, "Intact Forests in the United States: Proforestation Mitigates Climate Change and Serves the Greatest Good," Frontiers in Forests and Global Change, 2019.

## Chapter 19

1. Randy Bennet, "Under siege," *Barbados Today*, November 2 2021, online at https://barbadostoday.bb/2021/11/02/under-siege/.
2. Global Witness, "Hundreds of fossil fuel lobbyists flooding COP26 climate talks," online at https://www.globalwitness.org/en/press-releases/hundreds-fossil-fuel-lobbyists-flooding-cop26-climate-talks/.
3. Cathy Bussewitz, "Exxon seeks $100 billion for Houston carbon capture plan," Associated Press, November, 2021, online at https:// apnews.com/article/climate-technology-business-paris-f76df7ee4e6a8a4b6bab96badb2eb41a.
4. United Nations, "Emissions Gap Report 2021: The Heat Is On," November 2021, online at https://wedocs.unep.org/bitstream/ handle/20.500.11822/36995/EGR21_CH4.pdf.
5. Christopher R. Schwalm, Spencer Glendon, and Philip B. Duffy, "RCP8.5 tracks cumulative CO2 emissions," *Proceedings of the National Academy of Sciences*, August 18, 2020, online at https:// www.pnas.org/content/117/33/19656.
6. Valerie Volcovici, "How a dispute over coal nearly sank the Glasgow Climate Pact," *Reuters*, November 14, 2021, online at https://www.reuters.com/business/cop/how-dispute-over-coalnearly-sank-glasgow-climate-pact-2021-11-14/.
7. Jocelyn Timperley, "The broken $100-billion promise of climate finance – and how to fix it," *Nature*, October 20, 2021, online at https://www.nature.com/articles/d41586-021-02846-3.
8. Fred Pearce, "In Glasgow, Experts Warn of Widespread Misspending of Climate Adaptation Funds," *Yale Environment 360*, November 5, 2021, online at https://e360.yale.edu/digest/in-glasgow-experts-warn-of-widespread-misspending-of-climate-adaptation-funds.
9. A common definition of deforestation is the complete removal of forest cover for any reason (such as for agriculture or oil extraction), although some trees may remain.
10. Celso H. L. Silva Junior, Ana C. M. Pessôa, Nathália S. Carvalho, João B. C. Reis, Liana O. Anderson, and Luiz E. O. C. Aragão, "The Brazilian Amazon deforestation rate in 2020 is the greatest of the decade,"

*Nature*, December 21, 2020, online at https://www. nature.com/articles/s41559-020-01368-x.

11. Ignacio Amigo, "When will the Amazon hit a tipping point?," *Nature*, February 25, 2020, online at https://www.nature.com/articles/d41586-020-00508-4.

12. Morgan Erickson-Davis, "Congo Basin rainforest may be gone by 2100, study finds," *Mongabay*, November 7, 2018, online at https:// news. mongabay.com/2018/11/congo-basin-rainforest-may-begone-by-2100-study-finds/.

13. Personal communication, Karen Price.

14. Jim Tankersley, Katie Rogers and Lisa Friedman, "With Methane and Forest Deals, Climate Summit Offers Hope After Gloomy Start," *New York Times*, November 4, 2021, online at https://www. nytimes. com/2021/11/02/world/europe/climate-summit-methane-forests.html.

15. Wetlands Conservancy, "Growing realization that without enabling nature to recover, including wetlands, there is no 1.5 C future," November 16, 2021, online at wetlands.org/blog/wetlands-and-nature-take-center-stage-at-glasgow-climate-talks/.

16. The Conference of the Parties, United Nations Framework on the Convention of Climate Change, "Glasgow Climate Pact," November 13, 2021, online at https://unfccc.int/sites/default/files/ resource/cop26_auv_2f_cover_decision.pdf.

17. Email interview with Moomaw, November 21, 2021.

18. New York Declaration on Forests, "Fifth edition of the NYDF Progress Assessment," November 2021, online at https://forestdeclaration.org/images/uploads/resource/2020NYDFReport.pdf.

19. K. K. Ottesen, "Greta Thunberg on the State of the Climate Movement," *Washington Post*, December 27, 2021, online at https://www.washingtonpost.com/magazine/2021/12/27/greta-thunbergstate-climate-movement-roots-her-power-an-activist/.

# Further Reading

Beckham, Dow, *Swift Flows the River* (Coos Bay: Arago Books, 1990).

Beckham, Stephen Dow, *The Indians of Western Oregon: This Land Was Theirs*, (Coos Bay: Arago Books, 1977).

Beebe, Spencer, *Cache: Creating Natural Economies* (Portland: Ecotrust, 2010).

Carson, Rachel, Silent Spring, (New York: Houghton Mifflin), 1962.

Carder, Al, *Giant Trees of Western America and the World* (Madeira Park, B.C.: Harbour, 2005).

DellaSala, Dominick A., ed. *Temperate and Boreal Rainforests of the World: Ecology and Conservation*, (Washington, D.C.: Island Press, 2011).

Devall, Bill, ed. *Clearcut: The Tragedy of Industrial Forestry*, (San Francisco: Sierra Club Books and Earth Island Press, 1993).

Durbin, Kathie, *Tree Huggers: Victory, Defeat & Renewal in the Northwest Ancient Forest Campaigns*, (Seattle: The Mountaineers, 1996).

Furnish, Jim, *Toward a Natural Forest: The Forest Service in Transition (A Memoir)* (Corvallis: OSU Press, 2015).

Goldfarb, Ben, *Eager: The Surprising, Secret Life of Beavers and Why They Matter* (White River Junction, Vt: Chelsea Green Publishing, 2018).

Kellogg, Erin L., ed. *The Rain Forests of Home: An Atlas of People and Place*, (Portland: Ecotrust, Pacific GIS, and Conservation International, 1995).

Kerr, Andy, *Oregon Wild: Endangered Forest Wilderness* (Portland: Oregon Natural Resources Council, 2004).

Kimmerer, Robin Wall, *Braiding Sweetgrass: Indigenous Wisdom, Scientific Knowledge, and the Teaching of Plants*, (Minneapolis: Milkweed Editions, 2013).

Lichatowich, Jim, *Salmon Without Rivers: A History of the Pacific Salmon Crisis* (Washington, D.C.: Island Press, 1999).

Mann, Michael E., *The New Climate War: The Fight to Take Back Our Planet* (New York: PublicAffairs, 2021).

McAllister, Ian and Karen, *The Great Bear Rainforest: Canada's Forgotten Coast* (San Francisco: Sierra Club Books, 1997).

McCloskey, Michael, *Conserving Oregon's Environment*, (Portland: Inkwater Press, 2013)

Morton, Alexandra, *Not on My Watch: How a renegade whale biologist took on governments and industry to save wild salmon* (Toronto: Penguin Random House Canada, 2021).

*Beyond the Whales: The Photographs and Passions of Alexandra Morton* (Victoria: Touchwood 2004).

*Listening to Whales: What the Orcas Have Taught Us* (New York: Ballantine Books, 2002).

Norse, Elliott A., *Ancient Forests of the Pacific Northwest*, (Washington, D.C.: Island Press, 1990).

Noss, Reed, *The Redwood Forest: History, Ecology, and Conservation of the Coastal Redwoods*, (Washington D.C.: Island Press, 2000).

Oreskes, Naomi and Conway, Erik, *Merchants of Doubt: How a Handful of Scientists Obscured the Truth on Issues from Tobacco Smoke to Climate Change* (New York: Bloomsbury Publishing, 2010).

Paul, Cecil, *Stories from the Magic Canoe of Wa'xaid*, (Calgary: Rocky Mountain Books, 2019).

Puter, S.A.D., *Looters of the Public Domain: Embracing a Complete Exposure of the Fraudulent System of Acquiring Titles to the Public Lands of the United States* (Portland: Portland Printing House, 1908).

Preston, Richard, *The Wild Trees*, (New York: Random House, 2007).

Rustad, Harley, *Big Lonely Doug: The Story of One of Canada's Last Great Trees* (Toronto: House of Anansi Press, 2018).

Schoonmaker, Peter K., von Hagen, Bettina, and Wolf, Edward C., *Rain Forests Of Home: Profile Of A North American Bioregion*, (*Washington, D.C.: Island Press,1997*).

Simard, Suzanne, *Finding the Mother Tree: Discovering the Wisdom of the Forest* (New York: Alfred A. Knopf, 2021).

Smyth Arthur V., *Millicoma*, (Durham, S.C., Forest History Society, 2000).

Suttles, Wayne, ed., *Handbook of North American Indians* (Washington, D.C.: Smithsonian Institution, 1990).

Van Pelt, Robert, *Forest giants of the Pacific Coast* (Vancouver, San Francisco, Seattle: Global Forest Society in association with University of Washington Press, 2001).

Van Strum, Carol, *A Bitter Fog: Herbicides and Human Rights* (San Francisco: Sierra Club Books), 1983).

Wallace-Wells, David, *The Uninhabitable Earth: Life After Warming* (New York: Penguin Random House, 2017).

Wilson, E.O., *Half-Earth: Our Planet's Fight for Life*, (New York: W.W. Norton, 2016). Youst, Lionel, *Lost in Coos* (Alleghany, Oregon: Golden Falls Publishing, 2011).

# About the Authors

**Paul Koberstein** is the editor of *Cascadia Times*, which he co-founded in 1995. He was previously a staff writer for *The Oregonian* and for *Willamette Week*. In 2016 he won the Bruce Baer Award given annually to an Oregon journalist for excellence in investigative journalism and, in 2004, the John B. Oakes Award for the most distinguished environmental journalism in the United States.

**Jessica Applegate** is managing editor and photographer for *Cascadia Times*. A lifelong environmental activist, she works with special needs young children and is a founding member of Eastside Portland Air Coalition, a grassroots group that spurred creation of statewide air toxics regulatory overhaul, Cleaner Air Oregon.